A Note Slipped Under the Door

A Note Slipped Under the Door

TEACHING FROM POEMS WE LOVE

Nick Flynn & Shirley McPhillips

STENHOUSE PUBLISHERS
PORTLAND, MAINE

Stenhouse Publishers, 477 Congress Street, Portland, Maine 04101
www.stenhouse.com

Credits are on page 239.

Library of Congress Cataloging-in-Publication Data

Flynn, Nick, 1960–
A note slipped under the door : teaching from poems
we love / Nick Flynn and Shirley McPhillips.
p.   cm.
Includes bibliographical references and index.
ISBN 1-57110-320-1 (acid-free paper)
1. Poetry—Study and teaching (Elementary)—United States.
2. Poetry—Authorship—Study and teaching (Elementary)—United States.
3. Mentoring in education—United States.   I. McPhillips, Shirley.   II. Title.

LB1576.F495 2000
372.64—dc21
00-030814

Cover and interior design by Catherine Hawkes, Cat & Mouse
Cover photograph by Teri Dixon from photodisc.com
Typeset by Technologies 'N Typography

Manufactured in the United States of America on acid-free paper
12 11 10 09 08 07   9 8 7 6 5 4

To the teachers and students who, over the years,
allowed us to be a part of their lives

Contents

Acknowledgments

Stanley Kunitz once said that the great poems of the language have no dates. They remain, "locked within the circulating energy, which does not leak out in the imperfections of the making." We think of this line when we think of the many poets who have contributed to the energy that has allowed us to write this book. This book is a tribute, in part, to their continued presence in our lives. We thank them for their grace and willing faith.

Also, because so much of our work takes place in the classrooms, alongside other educators, we want to thank them, collectively, for that part of their learning lives in which we were included, and for creating the kinds of classrooms that allow young poets to flourish. This partial list also includes the teachers whose students' poems are represented in this book: Dina Anzalone, Marie Catania, Reid Donnelson, Kathy Doyle, Doug Fedderman, Philomena Fonda, Bonnie Gabizone, Rosemary Harris, Bonnie Hayes, Stacy Frischman Lauber, Doug Linney, Christina Locke, Kathy Mason, Kim Corn Newman, Indya Phelps, Arlene Rabito, Shirley Raffaele, Melissa Rodrigues, Emilio Santiago, Joan Shayne, June Slade, Joanne Wisniewski. We particularly want to acknowledge friends and colleagues who helped in the search for student poets—tracking down numbers and addresses, assembling lists of possibilities—especially Sandy Woodson and Elsie Nigohosian. Thanks, too, to Holly Kim, whose love of poetry and wise teaching produced the poetry conference transcripts in Appendix B.

The Teachers College Reading and Writing Project at Columbia University, also, has been vital to our work with teachers. We thank Lucy Calkins and the many friends and colleagues we have been fortunate enough to work alongside over the years. This book would not exist without them.

Special thanks to Georgia Heard, Suzy Kaback, and Marjory Forbes, whose enthusiasm and critical eyes early on inspired us to steam ahead with purpose; to Brenda Miller Power, whose sharp insights helped sustain our belief in the work and affected the final shape of the text; and to Philippa Stratton, our editor at Stenhouse, who guided us throughout with a deft hand, with patience, and

[ix]

with kindness. Finally, we want to thank Naomi Shihab Nye, who has given unconditionally and inspired us beyond measure.

IN CLOSING

Shirley: Eternal gratitude to my soul sister in life, my greatest mentor, Thelma Plender. Thanks also to Patrick Westcott, Elsie Nigohosian, Marie Catania, Patty Vitale, Anna Reduce, Kathy Doyle, and Ella Urdang for professional company over the years and continuing friendship.

More personally, I am fortunate to live within the "circulating energy" of a family whose hearts are wide. My parents were bedrock. Now, thanks to my sisters, Phyllis Dodds and Eve Powell, who hold our family footing steady. To Edward, my prince of England, for devotion. And to Sean, our son, for fire.

I am indebted, also, to Nick Flynn, who has been closer in my thoughts than most over the last couple of years. We are proof of how collaboration can work in the age of cyberspace. From the beginning, for me, faith in my part in this project came with the knowledge that Nick would be standing alongside. His enormous writing talent, his discerning eye for excess, for precision of word, for the truth of a line, have instructed me well. Most of all, Nick's bold heart and his devotion to poetry as life have inspired me far beyond the work of this project. Still, whenever I repair to my small suburban study, light my aromatherapy candles, and settle down to work, for just a moment I picture Nick, already in his studio overlooking the dunes. I imagine picking up the phone again and his quiet hello. Lifelines.

Nick: I would not have undertaken this project without the boundless energy and limitless good nature of Shirley McPhillips. When my mind was elsewhere, Shirley was focused; when I came to the end of my attention, Shirley stepped in. After many years spent working together in New York City, the actual writing of this book took place when we were living far apart. Despite this, on many occasions we found the time to meet, to hammer out our early ideas. Many other times these meetings were thwarted—once by a killer heat wave, once by a flood, more than once by circling Teachers College searching for that elusive parking space. For the last year it has been faxes, FedExes, phone calls, and e-mails. Her persistent brilliance made it all worthwhile.

1

A Compass Through These Waters

These poems have come a great distance to find you.

EDWARD HIRSCH,

How to Read a Poem

KINGDOMS WITH LOVE

Some kingdoms can be buildings.
Small kingdoms are doghouses.
And really really small ones,
cat beds, these can be
cat kingdoms.

But I am just getting
to the beginning. Famous
people have really big kingdoms.
They have electricity
and lights.

People on the street have kingdoms
as dumpsters and they
have to eat out of them. But when
the garbage truck comes
their kingdoms are gone.

—*Shawndell Williams, grade 3*

How far has Shawndell's poem "Kingdoms with Love" come to find you, you now holding this book in your hands? Perhaps not as far as, say, Blake's "The Tyger," at least not if we are measuring distance by time. But if we are measuring the likelihood that a poem written by a third grader in a Harlem school at the tail end of the twentieth century would find its way into your hands, especially if you don't happen to be a New York City public school teacher, then the distance is great, perhaps greater even than from Blake. For by rights this poem should never have been written: its very existence is unlikely, given the forces against it. Shawndell's school was located in a neighborhood reminiscent of Beirut in the 1980s, with more than half the surrounding buildings abandoned, boarded up, and it's not all that different today. That poetry is able to come from such surroundings is a testament to several factors: a tight-knit community, some wonderful teachers, the inherent vision of children, and the power of poetry itself.

We begin this book with a poem by a young person, not someone more famous, because we believe a mentor poem can come to us from unexpected sources, that the first criterion for a mentor poem is that it be a poem we love, that moves us in some way, intellectually, emotionally, or spiritually. And, for us, Shawndell's poem does all three. Intellectually, it deals with a complex idea in a focused way, by using an extended metaphor to describe a specific part of the author's observed world. Emotionally and spiritually, it is understated, without judgment, yet it pulses with life, with understanding. It allows us a glimpse of the world through new eyes.

This book is written in the belief that the poems we need, even when we might not know we need them, will find us, if we are looking, if we are open. Writer Brenda Miller Power, in a personal communication, remembers when she was sixteen, "basically in a coma trying to get through the dreary horrors of a rural Midwestern high school," a poet visiting the school read a poem to her English class by Kenneth Patchen about how baseball was invented. "It was such an angry poem. I was stunned by it. For the first time in years I felt wide-awake in school. I remember the actual moment of lifting my head off the desk and listening. From then on, poetry mattered in my life." Rereading the poem years later, she was shocked that it didn't live up to the poem she had held onto for so long. "I couldn't believe the poem I was reading was the same one I experienced in high school . . . how could those dull words have changed me forever? I sat among the dusty stack of books and learned a lot about myself, and how much of my own anger I had brought to the poem, how ready I was for any lifeline to understand that emotion. Poetry provides insights and lifelines like no other form for many students."

Jack Kerouac was such a mentor for poet Naomi Shihab Nye. In an e-mail to us she wrote:

His motto about writing, "Rest and be kind, you don't have to prove anything" has served me for a long time. His energy and belief in the fiery passion of the writing life, his conviction that spontaneous wisdoms spring forth as one writes, through the writing act itself, his care for the seemingly incidental, his humor and fabulous weave—all of these things fueled me forward when I was in college, sagging under the dreary load of formal papers, research, projects—and still, whenever I read Kerouac, I feel heartened in the daily unexpected poetry of this life, as well as the rich narrative story of it all. Or the insights he had while hiking or being in solitude or driving across the country, the interesting ways he described everything—such vigor! Such joy and loss combined, ever and ever! Well, he has saved me many times in this life.

A couple of years back Eloise Greenfield spoke at Teachers College, and we mentioned that we were using her as a mentor for our students. Thinking we wanted her to visit a classroom, she apologized and said that she had other obligations, so we explained that though we would love to have her in person in each of our classrooms, what we meant was that her poems were our mentors, and thereby she was already with us each day.

This book is about mentorship, about the need, in any art, to study those who have come before. As U.S. Poet Laureate Robert Pinsky points out in his book *The Sounds of Poetry,* "Art is best understood through careful attention to great examples." By looking at Greenfield's *Honey I Love* with "careful attention," we were learning from it what we could of our craft. Stanley Kunitz, who has been a mentor to generations of American poets, has said, "I didn't learn from teachers, I learned from poets." He was talking not about the poets themselves in each instance, though he has known nearly a century's worth of them, but their work. Kunitz is a teacher as well as a poet, and what we hope is that this book will be a way we can continue to learn from both poets and their work.

As co-authors of this book, we want to mention some of our mentors, besides those found in the pages that follow. Remember though: these are today's lists—ask us tomorrow and they may have changed, for what we need today may be solved by the poems that find us.

Shirley: The 1960s. The Civil Rights era. Skinny, short-skirted and long-haired, I sit on the floor in a small converted theater in Washington, D.C., for an after-hours evening of poetry reading. Someone in the corner plays the bongo drums however the spirit moves him and the Chianti bottles work the crowd. Finally, a beam of blue light hits the floor, growing outward to a fuzzy haze at the center of the gathering. Into this circle of unclear light walks a middle-aged bearded man with dark glasses and strings of amber beads around his neck. He kneels down and looks straight out, just above our heads as if to a place farther off in the distance, for a long moment. Then from somewhere primeval he recites . . . "The Negro Speaks of Rivers," by Langston Hughes. At the end, the light snaps off. There in the dark, the earth shakes beneath me. How can a handful of words hold such power!

His voice, as deep as the rivers he spoke of. The voice of the words themselves, so proud, so timelessly wise. Forged out of hardship, fueled by the wisdom of endurance, they reached in and grabbed something of mine that I call soul. My God! There were people for whom poetry was something more than just the fanciful dabblings of the dilettante, more than mere versification. Poems could be history, proclamation, an outcry, life itself. Maybe it was the times, turned upside down as they were, chafing, buckling against my childhood in the South. Maybe it was me yearning for something more, something otherwise. I don't know. But after that I could never hear poetry in quite the same way again. And I could never seriously write without consulting the experience of my heart.

Still today, the words that find me come connected to the person I know or imagine behind them, whose words give voice to life experiences I yearn to understand and help me find something more of myself. I call upon them often. Gary Snyder is one such mentor, through his articulate love of the wilderness and the world, showing us something of the interconnectedness of things and how we might live. Nobel Prize winner Wislawa Szymborska is another. Her "View with a Grain of Sand" (1993) captures something of a notion I, too, find intriguing: that the things of the world don't pay any attention to us; they just exist. Mary Oliver's "The Summer Day" from *New and Selected Poems* sits framed before me as a daily touchstone for the curious and attentive way it reminds us to examine how we want to be in the world. William Stafford, walking the land, stopping me every few steps with all the truth there is.

I call upon Naomi Shihab Nye for devotion to a life with poetry at the center. For faithful attention to the moments of her life. For her kind of slow savoring of the silence that words give her, that we "may become a lily or pebble again . . . for just a minute." Growing poems "with that beautiful space around them—the way we would like our lives to be." She writes in "My First True Love," "Truly, I feel irresponsible when I don't notice things well enough, when I slide or slip through a day. . . . I want to hear the cat down the street turning the block."

A few years ago, feeling a gradual loss of self in my job at the time, asking myself if I had what my mother called "the strength of my convictions" to make yet another change, I received a postcard from Nye. "What a gift it is," she wrote, "to know when our own *times* are right for changing." Turning over the card, a photo of William Stafford—a kind, accepting smile, wise eyes, white blossoms circling his straight, brushed-back hair. Next to his picture, the poem "You Reading This, Be Ready" from *The Way It Is,* written just two days before his death. It stopped me cold.

> Starting here, what do you want to remember?
> How sunlight creeps along a shining floor?
> What scent of old wood hovers, what softened
> sound from outside fills the air?

Will you ever bring a better gift for the world
than the breathing respect that you carry
wherever you go right now? Are you waiting
for time to show you some better thoughts?

When you turn around, starting here, lift this
new glimpse that you found; carry into evening
all that you want from this day. This interval you spent
reading or hearing this, keep it for life—

What can anyone give you greater than now,
starting here, right in this room, when you turn around?

What greater gift—that our mentors, in turning on all the lights, allow us to see something of ourselves.

Nick: When I think of my early life, I cannot conjure much poetry. *Alice in Wonderland.* "Twinkle, Twinkle, Little Star." *A Child's Garden of Verses,* unopened. That's about it. I imagine my mother read to me, but I can't remember a particular instance. She was young, a single mother, working two, sometimes three jobs, so maybe she wasn't able to find the time. From childhood I can still bring forth sections of Poe's "The Raven" (memorized in a morbid phase), the lyrics to "Big Yellow Taxi" and "American Pie" (which a woman with a guitar had us sing along to in fifth grade), but true mentorship for me begins years later, with a book called *The Country Between Us,* by Carolyn Forché, which chronicled the time she spent in El Salvador, the years that country was at war with itself. I was introduced to this book in college, and was amazed, stunned really, that it seemed to prove that one could combine a creative life with a political life. This was the book I gave to friends when I said I wanted to write, the book that made writing make sense, have meaning, purpose. I'd read the poem "The General" to a girlfriend and await her response: if she wasn't moved, could I love her? By reading this book over and over I was able to enter into the world of the poems. And by entering into this world, I was able to begin to understand what poetry could do. Of course, so inspired, I inevitably tried my hand, which mainly allowed me to glimpse how difficult it was, could be, to write a poem, a good poem. By keeping Forché's poems beside me I was able to try to emulate them, over and over. So Forché feels like my first true mentor, who reminded me that writing poetry could be, essentially, a political act.

Now, after twenty more years of reading, I can list the deep well into which I return again and again, those poets who have become as essential to me as water: Gerard Manley Hopkins, whose struggles with faith were played out with breathtaking linguistic dexterity; Emily Dickinson, for her moving strangeness that somehow changed the world; William Stafford, who committed himself to writing a poem each day; and Rainer Maria Rilke, who asked questions of the universe. I want also to include here my teacher Philip Levine, who spoke to me

[6]

of his own mentorships, of those poets who had inspired and influenced him: of hearing Dylan Thomas when he first read in America; of sneaking into John Berryman's workshop when he didn't have the money to register for classes; of following Lorca's ghost to Spain; of his long apprenticeship to Keats. Even before I met Levine, he had been a mentor, through his poems. They spoke of what it meant to work, to be a part of a family, to be a man, to struggle with language, demonstrating through example and fierce commitment to his craft how to be a poet in the world, how to take the craft of poetry more seriously.

In the pages that follow are some of the poems that found us, those to which we have given our careful attention, and which in turn we have found ways to talk about. Each has helped us in our teaching, and in our lives, and in these ways they have become our mentor poems. Through this process of mutual discovery we have come to recognize the need to be able to talk about a poem in a way that can make it come alive, unlocking some of its insights beyond simply illuminating what we think the poet was trying to say. In each chapter we try to present a few of the ways we have used them in classrooms, as teachers and as staff developers, often to discuss some aspect of the craft of poetry, at times simply for the thrill of hearing them again, and to witness our students' responses. If poetry is, as Naomi Shihab Nye claims, a "bridge, a conversation with the world," then we hope that this book can, in some small way, add to that conversation.

Before we go much further, we want to say a word about our inspiration for this book and lay out some foundational underpinnings that we trust will be helpful to you in further navigating its waters. This book is a response to something we have encountered in hundreds of classrooms during our years of attempting to show teachers ways they might work with young writers. The concerns and desires we've identified include: how to read a poem; what to teach from a poem we love; and how to recognize and name what poets do in order to inform our writing, our teaching. Over the years we have also been part of a think tank at the Teachers College Reading and Writing Project at Columbia University in New York City, and this has taught us the value of staying with an idea over time in order to create new meanings. By thinking alongside other professionals, all of our teaching and staff development has taken place in terms of inquiry. Without this inquiry-based teaching, we would be left to deal with the surface of poetry, and our students' writing would also lack depth. We hope that by letting teachers in on the ways we have found to read poetry, and the lessons we have tried in scores of classrooms, we will open deeper discussions of what poetry can do and the ways it can do it. Ultimately, we hope you will feel more free to find, to talk about, and to teach from the poems you love.

How to Use This Book

We don't intend our book to be a blueprint for the teaching that takes place in the classroom, nor would we want it to disrespect the craft of teaching or of poetry by supplying prompts that attempt to cover all curriculum needs. We do not feel that type of book would encourage teachers or students to think for themselves. Rather, our book attempts to re-create in tone, structure, and practice what it's like to be part of an inquiry with other professionals. We invite you to think with us, to have, as readers, an interactive dialogue about poetry.

Although the content of the book is a result of our collaboration—arising out of a shared devotion to poetry and having worked together with teachers— each of us takes responsibility for writing certain chapters in our own voice. Each chapter begins with the mentor poem we have chosen to represent an element of craft or practice, followed by a discussion of what the central issues of this element mean to us as writers and as educators. We then discuss some of the ways we have used this and other similar poems in our classrooms. Each chapter provides several mini-lessons that could be taught from the mentor poem. The mini-lessons are clustered under four headings: Getting Started, Keeping It Going, Extending Our Thinking, and Mini-Inquiry. We hope this structure will help you see them as part of a thoughtful progression of instruction, though we would encourage each teacher to structure the discussions according to what makes sense in his or her own classroom. We don't intend teachers to try each mini-lesson we present, as that could lead to spending the entire year on one poem, which we wouldn't envision as helpful. Rather, we present a range of possible mini-lessons so two or three can be chosen that feel right, given the abilities of your students and the focus and aims of the inquiry. We do encourage teachers to try the lessons that make sense to them or that they feel an interest in, and to adjust those lessons to both their students' lives and their own.

Instead of the "tell-and-go-do" model, we present ways to stay with one poem or type of poem, to think about it over time, to practice in our writer's notebooks what we notice the author doing, to let it teach us what we need to know. Each poem we present could of course be used to teach any one of several aspects of craft. In fact, a poem we present in one chapter for one type of inquiry can be used to teach many mini-lessons in other chapters. Simic's poem in Chapter 4 on lists, for example, could as easily be used to look at sounds (Chapter 5) or sense of place (Chapter 9) or image (Chapter 2). For the sake of clarity we chose to limit our discussion of each poem to the inquiry that is the focus for that chapter.

Ideally, we see this book as a place to start you on the path to choosing your own mentor poems. Just as we cannot, ultimately, choose those poems that will move our students, we do not intend that these poems will necessarily be the ones to move others.

Inside the Classrooms

The classrooms we present here, the classrooms we invite you into, are at times composites of those rooms we've been lucky enough to work in. The examples we give are often put together from many sources, a re-creation of how it went in several classrooms and what we did over the course of many weeks, of what certain students said and how particular rooms looked. For this reason, while we acknowledge the deep debt we owe to so many fine teachers who have allowed us to learn with them, we don't mention them by name within the chapters, as if to suggest that all this work were happening in one room. When we quote directly what a student said or wrote, we are being accurate to the best of our notes or recollection. Usually, with written work, we are working from transcribed photocopies of students' writer's notebooks or finished pieces. In certain retyped versions of student work, we have done some minor editing to point up their best elements and to avoid distractions for the reader. In each case we have tried to locate the source of a piece of writing but have, alas, not always succeeded, because in the ten or fifteen years of our staff development work, young writers have grown and teachers have moved on. Please contact us if you are one of the writers we mention but have not been able to reach; we'd be grateful to hear from you and glad to give credit in subsequent reprints.

Terminology We Use

We also need to define certain terms we use throughout this book.

By **writer's notebook** we mean an actual notebook that our students use exclusively to gather entries during their daily writing—a place where once entries accumulate, writers can reread to find seed ideas and practice developing them toward a crafted piece of writing, where they can try out forms, techniques, and strategies for writing. But we understand that not all classes use this tool, and if your class is one of those, please simply substitute in your mind the term you use for wherever it is your students gather their daily or weekly writing, be it a folder, a portfolio, or whatever. Should your students not use a writer's notebook and you would like to learn more about that, we include, in Appendix C, under the heading A Short Professional Bookshelf, books written by colleagues whose work we admire.

The **mini-lesson** is a key feature in this book. In each chapter, headings describe the focus of the lessons that follow them. By *mini-lesson* we mean that period of direct instruction that often launches the daily writing workshop, though in practice it may come at any time during the workshop. We see a mini-lesson as a short lesson focusing students' attention on one issue or aspect of writing that advances our work together. Often one day's mini-lesson builds on observations and lessons that have come before it, the teacher always keeping in mind the purposes and aims of the ongoing work. Mini-lessons may take different tones and structures, sometimes including student/teacher demonstration; or everyone's doing a short tryout of a skill or strategy; or the use of literature as an example of a writing life or a craft issue.

As we mentioned earlier, each chapter of our book proposes an **inquiry** around a specific issue of craft or practice with respect to writing poetry. As you read our chapters, you will see that this work involves elements key to any good inquiry: exploration and observation, conversation with others, raising questions and wondering, following a line of thought, and changing or being changed as a result of the work. Ultimately, we hope that students, having taken part in a class inquiry around a mentor poem, will find individual ways to work with their own mentors.

Another term we use is **sketching.** Sketching is a technique for representing mental images, for allowing us to focus and sometimes to think in more detail (see Chapter 2). It is quick, not elaborated unless we go back to it specifically for particulars. When students **sketch off** a poem, they make a quick drawing of something that, after hearing or reading, stands out to them: something the poem causes them to think, to remember, to connect to, or to imagine. At times, we try to limit their sketches to the actual images presented in the poems.

Writing long asks the writer to push thinking past two or three lines, down the page, letting the mind cut deeper into the groove of thinking about the subject, coming up close to it and writing particulars, and perhaps carrying on some internal dialogue along the way.

There may be other terms in this book that will not seem clear to you. See A Short Professional Bookshelf in Appendix C for fine resources that will help you flesh out these concepts.

∽∾

Mentors, in the end, can help us identify who we are and what we are, and through poetry we learn that our voices can be larger than we are. Donald Murray says that through teaching and reading he has been "instructed in other lives." Naomi Shihab Nye says that she compiled her first anthology of poems as a direct result of the Iraqi War, that when the war began she was visiting schools and she realized that no one had any sense of the people who lived beneath the bombs we were dropping. So she included Iraqi voices in *This Same Sky* in order to humanize a people who were being presented to the American people only through bombsights and infrared.

Joseph, a fourth-grade student in the same school as Shawndell, once wrote,

When I look at the sky I see shattered blue colors that cross from one side to the other. Then I think about how it would be if I was an adult, and could tell my children about how it was when I was their age. When I look into the sky I think of creatures from different planets and spheres. They might not look like us, but they're still alive, and they're still God's creations. And I know God created these creatures for some reason. When I look into the sky I think of the year two-thousand. I heard that in the year two-thousand it will rain acid. I really hope it doesn't happen, because this planet is beautiful and glamorous and filled with wonders. This is how I feel when I look into the sky.

Joseph is a poet who has, like Shawndell, like Naomi Shihab Nye, like William Stafford, paid close attention, who has looked closely at his world and named it. And, through his writing, he has helped instruct us in the concerns of an eleven-year-old living in Harlem in the mid-1990s. What will change in the world if we take the time to look closely and learn about other lives? Impossible to measure. How does one learn this from poetry? By getting excited about something and wanting to learn, which, according to Donald Murray, is the fundamental way we learn anything.

Naomi Shihab Nye, clearly one of our inspirations for this book, writes, "I think of poets over the ages sending their voices out into the sky, leaving quiet, indelible trails." We, as teachers, also want to leave trails in our classrooms, trails that our students will be able to follow. Those trails may be footprints through a dark forest, or the path cut by a ship across an ocean. Imagine, then, that these few poems in the following pages have been making their way toward you from far away, some across centuries, using any available map, until somehow you find them now in your hands, in your mind, in your mouth. We hope this book will be a map to those footprints, and a compass through these waters.

2

Watermelons in My Grandmother's Car

THE IMAGE

Nick Flynn

*The image comes first and tells me what
the "memory" is about.*

TONI MORRISON,

in *Inventing the Truth* (Zinsser 1987)

IN PASSING
Alberto Blanco

The moon is only
dust in the curtains.

Blue clouds
in the mirror of the room.

When she looks at herself
she feels sad and sings:

Her voice guides
a cat's shadow.

I have an enduring image from my childhood, one that returns to me often, unbidden. It involves a plant that somehow took root in the backseat of my grandmother's car. Collected on the floor between the seats and the doors was a mixture of sand and dirt, carried in on our feet from the beach, and as mud on our sneakers on rainy days. No one ever cleaned the dirt, not from the back-seat—my grandmother never gave it much thought. When I was young I sat in the back with the groceries, watching the trees pass, pushing her dog away with my feet. The dog smelled; if you touched it, your hands smelled like dog. Over the years the soil that gathered in the space between the seats and the doors grew deep, deep enough for a seed of an unspecified plant to take hold and send up a shoot. I'd chart its growth in private, checking on it whenever we went for a ride. I don't think that I ever told her, for fear she'd uproot it. My secret, this plant, growing in my grandmother's car.

Near the end I drove more than she did. I drove her into town for groceries or to go to the bank, I drove her to the dump and to the vet's, and if it was spring the plants would send up their green leaves, for by then there were more than one, and by the leaves they were identifiably watermelons. By then I felt safe to talk about them with her, and we'd laugh together at the weirdness of it all.

Without this image, how else can I hold her now? Her voice? (like sandpaper and smoke). Her hands? (gnarled from tending her roses). Her roses? (in the summer they nearly swallowed her porch). All of these, too, are images, and all images are containers for meaning. Images hold the meaning of our lives. Without images we have no memory; they give the past shape, keep the memory. It makes sense, then, that the image is one of the poet's most reliable tools, the foundation of many poems. Toni Morrison, in her essay "The Site of Memory" (Zinsser 1987), writes,

> *It's a kind of literary archeology: On the basis of some information and a little bit of guess-work you journey to a site to see what remains were left behind and to re-construct the world that these remains imply. What makes it fiction is the nature of the imaginative act: my reliance on the image—on the remains—in addition to recollection, to yield up a kind of a truth. By "image," of course, I don't mean "symbol"; I simply mean "picture" and the feelings that accompany the picture.*

Morrison is talking about the image as central to her fiction, but she could just as well be talking about poetry. Poet Barbara Esbensen writes, "I think about the image first and the rhyme only incidentally." Poet Ellen Bryant Voigt, in her essay on the image in *Poets Teaching Poets* (Orr and Voigt 1996), quotes M. H. Abrams' description of the image as "a picture made out of words," and "the sensuous element in poetry." By *sensuous* Abrams was referring to the use of the senses, which Voigt goes on to clarify: "While most textbook definitions of the image acknowledge all five senses, the primary—that is, the most effica-cious—sense is sight, and the sister art to poetry is painting."

The ability to write so the reader can see what it is that we see is the one skill that seems essential to any good writing. What are the ways a writer does this? Many teachers use the term *the senses* to define what an image is, telling their students to write "using their senses." While this is an important branch of imagery, it is only one branch of a rich tree. We can also explore, for example, "sketching," in order to go deeper into an image, to focus us, and to determine if what we are writing is actually image-based. Or we can practice writing "observations," maybe five a day for a week, and then read them to our partner to see if she can see what we saw. Even writing about a moment from our lives can be image-based, the difference between "I love my cat" and "My cat makes a circle when she sleeps." T. S. Eliot, writing on *Hamlet,* said, "The only way of expressing emotion in the form of art is by finding an 'objective correlative'; in other words, a set of objects, a situation, a chain of events." Eliot was describing image making.

This chapter comes early in this book because Shirley and I recognize the central importance of image making. This is not to say that all writers or writing begins here, but we feel that any poem that inspires and moves us maintains a tension between the concrete world and the transcendent, between the image of watermelons growing in the backseat of a car and the larger question of what that could possibly mean to an eight-year-old boy. We will look closely at a mentor poem that is image-based, and discuss how the poet crafted that particular image, along with other examples of crafted images.

๑๑ *Getting Started*

DEFINING WHAT MAKES AN IMAGE

The first week of October, my third year in this Lower East Side school, my third year with this particular group of teachers, but the students in the classroom we'll be working in as our "lab site" are, for the most part, new to me, though a few familiar faces from last year's second grade smile when we enter, knowing what to expect. As we usually do, we begin our writing workshop by gathering on the carpet for the mini-lesson, which I will lead while the teachers take notes. The students, at the direction of their teachers, have been reading poems on their own, informally, for about a week now, setting up the poetry center, gathering poetry books from the class library, from the school library, from home, and it is time to turn our attention toward our inquiry. In our planning meetings outside of class the teachers and I have already decided that the focus of our inquiry will be the image. For the mini-lesson on this first day it seems important to simply introduce the concept of making images. We do not expect each student to leave today with a complete sense of what it means to write using imagery, but to begin to question what it means, what it could be, and to begin to look for writing that is image-based.

There are many ways to name the idea of writing that uses images. We could call it writing with description or with details. We could call it writing so that the reader gets a picture in her mind. We could call it writing using our senses. It could be the act of paying close attention to the world, of writing observations of what we see rather than our reactions to what we see. It could be writing so the reader could sketch out what we are describing. Images can be created through descriptions of places, of actions, of dialogues, of objects. All of these definitions fall under the larger concept of imagery. For today, I decide upon one of these definitions to begin our discussion.

I begin by introducing myself to those students I haven't already worked with by asking those I have worked with if they remember what it is we do when I'm in their classroom. "We work on our writing process," one thoughtful girl responds. The teacher has already introduced this concept of a writing process to the class, so the other students are excited to get started. I then tell them that today we are going to talk about one thing a poet does that seems so important that we've decided to look at it closely and practice it ourselves for the next few weeks. I start by saying that writing with an image can give us a picture in our minds. This feels concrete, solid, something our students can hold onto. I tell them that a poem that uses imagery can lead us somewhere unfamiliar or somewhere recognizable—into a room or a city, onto a tabletop, or into a garden—and allow us to see this place with new eyes. After a brief discussion (I remember to try to keep my mini-lessons to under ten minutes so we have time to practice what we have discussed), the students are sent off to look for poems that have images in them.

CHOOSING A MENTOR POEM

For this inquiry, the mentor poem we want to choose will be one that gives an image, ideally in more than one way. There are many ways writers give us images, and we will want to look at a few of those ways closely. The class has read and reread the poem "In Passing," by Alberto Blanco, which one student discovered in *The Tree Is Older Than You Are* (a title I now see as a slant description of the plants that grew in my grandmother's car), one of Naomi Shihab Nye's wonderful anthologies. This anthology is a collection of Mexican writers and artists, and each piece of writing is presented in both the original Spanish and in translation. We have already read "In Passing" as a class more than once, and have decided to include it in a folder for image-based poems in our poetry center.

As a class we decide, for several reasons, to choose "In Passing" as one of our mentor poems. First, for this inquiry, it feels very image-based, each stanza creating a picture, a different picture than the one that came before (it should be noted here that many poems feel more thought-based, abstract, communicating primarily by revealing the way the poet's mind moves). And not only is this poem image-based but there is a certain simplicity to the images it presents, so we hope it will be easy to picture. Also, we notice that it creates a narrative, not a chronological narrative with a beginning, a middle, and an end, but more the outline of a narrative, the suggestion of a narrative. Yet it is open to various interpretations (Is the girl in the room? Is there a girl at all, or is *she* the moon? How does the room become a mirror? and so on). Though we could have chosen a poem more grounded in one interpretation, we like that this one is somewhat open and mysterious, though still image-based. It is also important to remember that, at times, a poem that may seem daunting to us as adults can be more easily accepted by children, perhaps as a result of our less-than-positive experiences with studying poetry in school, and a lack of experiences with poetry in later life. Children, we find, can be accepting and receptive of a poem if we approach it in an open, interested way—not thinking we have to know what everything means.

Today is the day we need to choose a mentor poem, and since "In Passing" is a poem that moves us, that we like and have enjoyed hearing again and again, and that is image-based, we decide it would be a good choice. We write Blanco's poem on a chart and hang it in our poetry center, or somewhere else prominent, so we will have a chance to notice and discuss it. While we are gathered, we read Blanco's poem together and mark the places where he has given us an image.

SKETCHING OFF THE MENTOR POEM

Until now, our mini-lessons have been, for the most part, nondirective, allowing the students a wide range of possible ways to begin exploring this idea of the image. Today, we decide to direct our attention to looking at the way Blanco has created images in this poem. This is what Lucy Calkins has called "directed looking," where the students are directed to look closely at something specific. I read the poem out loud again, asking them to imagine the picture the author is creating for us. Some of the students close their eyes, some read along silently with the poem on the chart. When we finish, I remind them that one thing a poem can do, an important thing that all writers practice, is to give us a picture in our minds. I ask them to imagine what they would include if they were to sketch this poem. (*Sketch* is a term that may need to be defined for your students—I usually define it as a quick drawing made to capture the information we want to write about, so we don't spend time with elaborate coloring or backgrounds unless they are important to the story. See Chapter 1.) I am ready with a marker at a clean flip-chart. The students raise their hands and name what we should include in our sketch—a moon, a window, the curtains at the window, a girl in a room looking out the window, a cat, the shadow of a cat. Sometimes our students see a word in a poem and name that, which doesn't necessarily mean they are getting an image of what they name. Sometimes what they first name isn't directly in the poem—"I see a man walking alone outside"—but I try to hold that type of comment accountable, by asking, "Where did you see the man? Is he in the words the poet gives us?" Sometimes the student is reading into the poem at this point, which is a good skill to develop, but for this lesson I try to steer the student back to the images the poet's words have created directly. I sketch these out quickly on our chart, and we look at the image we've created and remind ourselves that it has all come from this small poem, these few words, and that this is one thing Alberto Blanco intended, for us to get a picture from his words. I send the students off to mark places in their notebooks where they have written so that it gives us an image. They are then to choose one and sketch it out.

DISCUSSING OUR SKETCHES

The next day the students come back to share the places they marked in their notebooks that give us an image, and the sketches they drew off them. We have a discussion about what they chose, and why. We do this for two reasons: first, so the students can expect that we'll follow up when we ask them to try something; and second, in order to notice the difference between the ideas that are in their heads and the images they have written out for us on the page, which is often an enormous difference. The students could do this in partnerships before we gather again, or as the teacher I could choose two or three students who seem to have a good sense of the concept of the image and use their work as models. Often the pieces they choose from their notebooks are actually not image-based at all—their first attempts may be based on something they saw or experienced but that they have not yet translated into words.

Today, one student raises his hand and says he has marked "My brother bothers me" as one of the images he has written in his notebook, and he shows us the sketch he made off this image. Now, "My brother bothers me" is not yet a fully formed image, but when we look at his sketch we can see that he has drawn his brother with something on his head. "It's a pot," he tells us. "My brother comes into my room with a pot on his head yelling about robots." I write what he just said ("My brother comes into my room with a pot on his head yelling about robots") on the chart beside what he first said ("My brother bothers me"), and we all agree that the longer version does seem like something we could all make some sort of sketch from. The shorter version is more the *seed* of an image, something the writer can see but has not yet translated into language. I tell all of them to turn to a partner and discuss whether the image they have marked is the seed of an image or something we could all make a sketch from. For the beginning of this inquiry into what an image is, which is a complex concept that writers struggle with throughout their writing lives, I am satisfied that we have started to question what makes an image.

LOOKING AT OUR MENTOR POEM SKETCHES

As a class we may want to go back to the sketches we've made of Blanco's poem at this point, and try to imagine how it would have been if he had written it in a way that hadn't given us any images. During our mini-lesson we rewrite his poem as a group, rewriting his lines, trying not to use images:

The moon is nothing.
There are clouds.
A girl sings.
There is a cat.

We agree that it would be harder to make a sketch off this version of the poem, because there aren't as many details in it for us to turn into pictures. The students go back to their own entries off which they made sketches, and discuss with a partner whether their words line up with their sketches.

WRITING LONG

One of the essential components of any writing workshop is whether our students can stay with an idea over time, to write about it in different ways while "staying in a groove." Included later in this chapter as a mini-inquiry is a discussion of writing long, but Shirley and I want to bring the idea up in this Getting Started section because we both agree that it is central to any writing workshop.

CONFERRING ON IMAGERY

Our conferences at the beginning of an inquiry into imagery are often the same conference. I kneel down beside a third grader who has chosen for his image, "My mother is nice, I love my mother." Since this is the fourth student I have come upon today with essentially the same limited idea of what makes an image, I know what my mini-lesson will be tomorrow. I will explain again the difference between "My mother is nice," which we, as readers, can't see, and an image. In order to set up this mini-lesson for tomorrow, I decide it would be worthwhile to get this student to try writing a more concrete image now, while I'm beside him, so tomorrow I can model his entries for the whole class. I ask him if there is one thing his mother does that lets him know how nice she is, that will let us see how much he loves her. He looks at me blankly. I try again. I ask if there is one thing he remembers his mother doing that he always thinks of when he thinks how nice she is. A light goes off. "Yes," he nods, "she made me a pie last week because she knows I love pie." This is the moment I knew he had in him—the moment I can imagine seeing: the image. I ask him to close his eyes and go back to that moment when his mother is making the pie. After his eyes are shut for a few seconds I ask if he can see his mother, and he smiles and nods yes. I begin to ask a series of questions, slowly, taking notes on his responses: "What room is she in? Is she standing or sitting? What are her hands doing? What is the light like in the room? Is she saying anything to you? Are you helping? What are you doing?" The boy smiles and says, "Yes, she is in the kitchen, standing at the counter, and I am sitting at the table, and she is rolling the crust out, she lifts it up and turns it over, telling me it is going to be the best pie yet, and that's how she is nice to me." I read back to him the notes I have taken, and tell him to write it down just as he told it to me, and show it to me when he finishes, and not to forget how she lifts the dough up and throws it down. I will use this conference tomorrow to start our writing workshop, gently discussing his initial confusion on the concept of the image while praising him on the fine image he finally created. (See Appendix B for examples of one-on-one writing conferences with students.)

⟨∿⟩ *Keeping It Going*

During the course of the next week we continue honing our ideas of what makes an image. We continue going back into our notebooks and questioning whether the places we marked the first day actually gave us images, or if we need to modify our choices. Usually, simply sketching out the places we believe we have written using images, even if these places are not technically image-based, will have focused us enough to move on. By creating a sketch we have by definition created an image. On another day we can add more details to our sketch, by including objects, characteristics of the setting, or actions the people in the sketch might be doing, all of which will deepen the image.

MODELING OUR NOTEBOOKS

As teachers we can also model our own writing by showing the places in our notebooks where we thought we wrote using images, and model how we would

The case was made of black velvet on the outside with red velvet on the inside. The corners of the case were battered, as if he had dragged it all over the world. Inside the red velvet was a package of extra string, in case he broke one. He had a photograph of himself as a young man, propped up on the lid. In the photograph he was playing the violin to a young girl, who was smiling into his face.

FIGURE 2.1   Entry from Nick's notebook showing man playing violin.

include the necessary details when we sketched them out. Figure 2.1 shows an entry from my notebook, based on an observation I made one morning on the subway platform of a man playing a violin. I like to model with a sketch like this because it shows how simple our sketches should be. I point out how I included those details I thought I would write about later (his violin case, his long coat, the passing people), how I was using my sketch to plan what I would write the next day.

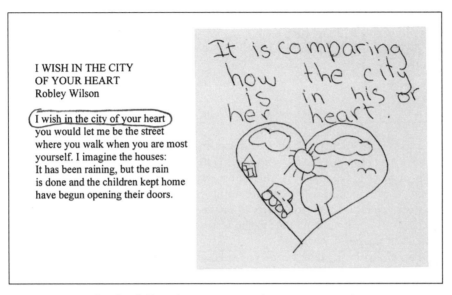

FIGURE 2.2   Student's Post-it comment on how a poet uses images.

USING LITERATURE

As a class we continue hunting for other poems, looking for places where authors have written using images. At this point in our inquiry we try to name the strategy the author used to create that image. We mark where we notice an image, and name what we notice on a Post-it (see Figure 2.2).

It is important to mark the exact passages in the poems we have chosen that give us an image, so we can begin to sort out which writing is image-based and which is something else, and to see the various ways authors write using images. From looking at and naming how authors create images we can begin to list the different ways we notice that images are created.

ᘐᘐ *Extending Our Thinking*

As mentioned in Chapter 1, we cannot possibly do each mini-lesson that is presented in this book. It is necessary to choose those that feel right for where the class is, and to linger on two or three for the length of the inquiry. At this point in our inquiry, as a class we are beginning to get a better sense of what it is to write with images. We have looked for examples in literature, we have searched in our notebooks and folders for places we have already written with images, we have begun to name the ways writers create images, we have practiced sketching those places that seem to give us a picture. Now it seems like a good time to model, in more depth, a few of the different ways images can be created.

USE OF PLACE IN THE MENTOR POEM

As a class we turn again to our mentor poem. If we look at the first and second stanzas, we notice that one way to read them is that both are essentially descriptions of place. "The moon is only / dust in the curtains. / Blue clouds / in the mirror of the room." As yet, there are no people in the poem, and no actions have yet taken place. We are given an image of a room with a curtained window looking out on the moon. This is the setting. This is another way a writer can give us an image.

The students by now have chosen one of their sketches they think they can write more about. We direct them to turn to their partner and talk briefly about the setting where their image is located: Is it the brother's bedroom that is always a mess? Is it Grandmother's house by the highway you visited once five years ago? Is it the concrete steps you sit on while watching your friends on the playground? After five minutes or so of discussion we come back as a group, and a few students relate how it went, especially those who think they might write an entry today where they describe their setting. We remind them to make the setting so we can see it. Some students feel they have already written a setting that gives us an image. They read their entries to the group, and the students decide if they get a picture of the setting or if something else is needed.

As with all mini-lessons, if we want our students to really get a chance to explore what it means to write about place so that it gives us an image, we will have to present the mini-lesson to them in different ways and give them different opportunities to explore this idea. We can, again, search literature and our own writing for examples of good writing about place. Here's one from Patricia MacLachlan's *What You Know First*:

> Or maybe
> I'll live in a tree.
> The tall cottonwood that was small
>   when Papa was small,
> But grew faster than he did.
> Now it has branches
> And crooks where I can sit
> To look over the rooftops,
> Over the windmill,

Over the prairie
So big that I can't see
Where the land begins
Or where it ends.

USE OF ACTION IN THE MENTOR POEM

Another way writers create images is through the use of action, using language to show what the people they are writing about are doing and how they are doing it. Action also gives us a picture—it's the difference between "we had fun" and "we ran three times around the tree before falling in a pile laughing." As a class we again return to "In Passing" and look closely at the last two stanzas, which create an image for us primarily through action: "When she looks at herself / she feels sad and sings: / Her voice guides / a cat's shadow." The girl in the poem is looking, feeling, and guiding: all verbs, all actions. We go off to read through our entries, to mark where we have used actions or to find any places we'd like to add some.

OTHER WAYS WRITERS CREATE IMAGES

Besides action and setting, some other ways writers create images are through dialogue, by close description of an object or objects, by using the senses, and through the use of comparisons, sometimes by using similes and metaphors. If we look again at "In Passing," we see that the first stanza, along with being a description of a place, is also using a metaphor. Blanco compares the moon to dust in the curtains. If this concept has not yet been introduced in the class, this could be a time to do it. Or if it has, this could be a time to reinforce it. Either way, as a class it is time to make a list of the ways we've noticed writers create images:

- Action
- Setting
- Dialogue
- Metaphor/simile
- Objects
- Comparisons

We choose one or two of these ways and go back into our original sketch and write long off it (see next section).

◦◦ *Mini-Inquiry*

We have spent two or three weeks now considering images—discussing whether the parts in our notebooks we've marked give us an image, looking for images in poems and other literature, sketching out two or three of our images, choosing one sketch and adding details to it, maybe adding some more words if we notice the sketch has more details than our words. Depending upon the amount of time we have set aside for this inquiry, we could use the work we have done to begin crafting poems, or we could choose to begin a mini-inquiry. A mini-inquiry is a short-term focus on some aspect of our work that intrigues us, sometimes taking place within a larger inquiry. For a mini-inquiry we want to clear some time—two or three days, a week—to follow this interest. Sometimes the whole class can work on a mini-inquiry, sometimes just a few students.

Now it is time to try writing long, to stay with a piece of writing over time in order to deepen the images. One way we can try this is by focusing on one part of our sketch (the setting, an object, a person) and staying with it for as long as we can, for a few days, or for just the length of an entry. In the primary grades the expectation of what constitutes "long" might be different, though we have been in many first-grade classes where, by spring, many of the students were able to fill up half a page or more. But the trick with writing long is not just filling a page, even for a first grader. The trick is to write long with focus, to stay on a topic or in a groove. The thinking behind this is that in order for us to develop an image, to make it as vivid as we possibly can, to make it so the reader sees what we saw, we need to practice focusing on one aspect of our image and staying with it.

IMAGINING BLANCO WRITING LONG

We return to our mentor poem at this point, and imagine how Alberto Blanco's notebook might have looked (assuming he even used a notebook), the places where he may have written long about his image, before distilling all his words into the poem we have before us. It is important to point out that this is what all writers, especially poets, do—they push themselves to write more, knowing that many words will be cut so they can come to the best words. We take the first stanza of the poem and write it at the top of a blank piece of chart paper, then ask for other possible ways the poet might have described the moon, the curtains, the room in which it is all taking place.

MODELING STUDENTS' WRITING LONG

We now want to practice writing long off one of our sketches. Again, there are many ways I could model this, but for this mini-lesson I decide to use a student's writing. (Any one of the following student entries could be used to model this mini-lesson, or another student's work from the classroom could be developed and used.) With the students gathered around me, I read an example of a second grader's entry written long to give the reader an image:

> *When I was jealous I screamed all over my room, my eyebrows went up and my eyelashes went down. I was crying. My mom couldn't stand my crying, so she said, "It will be fun," but I didn't listen, so she had to pull my hand and I jumped so hard that she had to carry me.*

This entry goes on for another page or so, but we discuss only this excerpt because it is focused enough so we can picture the scene and sketch it. As we've done in previous mini-lessons, the students raise their hands and tell me what it is they see, and I sketch it out in front of the class.

The next example is from a Manhattan fifth grader named Alex:

> *My mom told me to try to get a good loaf of bread. When I went in the store it smelled like wetness after rain and warmth. I saw a good big warm bread but I couldn't reach it. A lady helped me and I said thank you. I gave a Russian dollar to the cashier and ran home with the nice warm big bread.*

Again, we quickly sketch out the image this gives us.

The final example of a student's writing long comes from Shawanna, a Brooklyn kindergartner (Figure 2.3):

I had a seashell.
My baby brother broke it.
The song came out.
The song won't come back.

The expectations we had for these three students were different, since each was a different person and in a different grade, but we still expected each to attempt to stay with their image and develop it over time. For today, several students agree that they will attempt to write long off one of their sketches.

FIGURE 2.3   A kindergartner's writing long.

MODELING OUR OWN WRITING LONG

Alongside or instead of the previous mini-lesson, either the teacher or I could use an entry from our own notebooks to model what we mean by writing long. On this day I decide to go back to the entry from my notebook where I sketched the man playing the violin in the subway, and talk about the different ways I could have written it long. I could have written long off how the man looked, the way the violin was tucked under his chin, his eyes shut tight and his coat buttoned all the way down; or I could have written long off the place he chose to play in, the way the lights in the subway tunnel flickered above him, how the walls were tiled like those in a bathroom, how the ceiling was arched slightly as if water had once passed through it; or I could have written long off the people who were listening to him play, how some hurried past without looking, how some slowed down and glanced at him, smiling, how some nodded and stopped, grateful for the music. What I did choose to focus on for this day was his violin case; I show them how I circle it in my sketch before I model writing long about it in front of them on a chart:

[28]

His violin case is black leather on the outside with red velvet on the inside. The corners of the case are battered, as if he had dragged it all over the world. Inside the red velvet is a package of extra strings, in case he breaks one. Propped on the lid is a photograph of himself as a younger man. In the photograph he is playing his violin to a young girl, who smiles up into his face.

I write this slowly, to show the students my thinking, to talk out the choices I am making as a writer.

While the students are still gathered, I direct them to go back into their sketches and choose one part where they will try to write long, whether it is from an object in the sketch, as I have done, or from the setting, or from a description of someone, or from something else we haven't yet discussed, which I am always open to considering. After they have marked what they will do today, a few tell their choices to the group, and I lead them into telling us how they will write long about them. We will continue to practice writing long throughout the week, reinforcing the idea of focusing in and staying in a groove.

REFINING A STUDENT'S NOTEBOOK ENTRIES

Eric was a struggling fourth grader with whom his teacher and I were able to confer closely, and who was able to write several entries using different strategies we had studied in order to give his readers an image. We had used "In Passing" as a mentor poem in his class, and had noticed the ways Blanco gave us images. Eric's notebook entries, before we began our inquiry into the image, were all very similar, variations on

> *Today I went to church. I like going to church because God protects you. When you go to church you need to pray. I love going to church.*

and

> *Today I went to church. I like going to church because God helps you. When we go we talk about God. And we like God. And you need to go on Sunday. I had a nice day.*

Eric had at least twenty entries that were basically the same as these two. It was clear that he liked church, and also that he was limited in his ability to write about the experience so others could see it. After our mini-lesson on sketching out an entry that gave us an image, he went back to one of his church entries, almost identical to the first example here, and underlined the sentence "Today I went to church." We had him choose just one sentence because even in his short entry there was a different image for each sentence. He then did a sketch off that sentence (Figure 2.4).

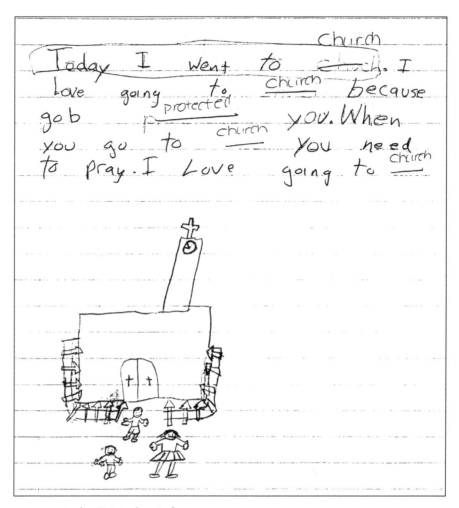

FIGURE 2.4   Eric's sketch from one sentence.

Eric could have sketched almost anything from his line "Today I went to church"—his family getting ready for church, his family on the way to church, the neighborhood of his church. What he chose to sketch was the outside of the church, with details about how it looks—the heavy wooden doors with crosses on them, the steeple with a clock on it, the pointed cast-iron fence. During our conference the next day I direct him to focus on one part of this sketch and write about that, keeping in mind our discussion about how a description of place can give us an image. He could have chosen to focus on that pointed fence, or on the people standing outside the fence, but he chose to focus on a general description of how the church looked:

My church is dark red. My church is kind of big. But when you go inside it looks so little. It has a clock high on the wall.

Already an improvement over the entries he had been writing. As readers we are beginning to get a picture of his church. In his next entry he takes us inside the church, this time using a list of actions to create an image:

When I go inside I need to find a chair. Then I get ready to pray. The mass finishes at 1 o'clock. When we go to church we get the bread and wine.

Below this entry Eric has made another sketch, this time of four pews with himself sitting in one of them. His teacher and I are thrilled that he seems to have internalized one of the ways (sketching) we have been modeling to create an image. In our conference the next day we notice that this last entry of his is essentially a list of actions, and suggest that he might try focusing in on just one so that we really get a picture of it. He agrees that this might be a good idea, and he chooses the action of "praying":

When we go to pray we fold our hands and start to pray. We look straight and not sideways. We pray the Our Father. We pray in our minds.

Eric's teacher and I are able to see real improvement from the repetitive way Eric had been writing. As with all writers, there is still work to be done, but we want to be sure to celebrate the moves he has made and the effort he has put into these entries. Since many of his classmates have not written off their sketches in several different ways like Eric has, we use his entries to model how they could try. Modeling the work of someone from within the class can be very powerful, especially if he is a struggling writer, like Eric. While the other writers in the class are trying their entries in different ways, we give Eric another direction in our conference. We have him divide his page into two columns, the word *ordinary* on top of one and *interesting* on top of the other. We have him find a line from his entries where he wrote something in an ordinary way. He chooses "I love church" and writes it in the Ordinary column. We then leave him to write that same idea in interesting ways, as many as he can. At the end of our writing time he has come up with this list:

Church is where God protects you.
When I'm in church I feel like I can do anything.
The church is like a red turtle.
There is some music. It sounds like somebody dying.
God doesn't look like nobody.

Again, Eric, our "struggling writer," has done so well with this that we will use this entry tomorrow to model the difference between ordinary and interesting language, which is another way a writer creates an image.

TURNING THE ENTRIES INTO POEMS

By now we have practiced how to gather images, and how to write long about them. In our notebooks we have the sketch we made from one of these images, and we have tried to write long off this sketch in three or four different ways. At this point these entries could be turned into almost anything—a picture book, a memoir, a letter. We have not yet gone over how a writer could turn these entries into a poem, though we have been looking closely at many examples, and many of our students have already tried their hand at crafting their entries into poems. Again, one of the best ways to model what we'd like our students to try is by example, either from ourselves, from literature, or from another student. It is up to each of us, each day, to decide how we are going to do this. For today, I decide to go back to Eric's entries, in order to show how he carefully read through all the entries he had gathered, chose what he thought were his best lines, and then made a draft of a poem from those lines:

> I love going to church.
> My church is dark red.
> When I go inside I need to find a chair.
> Then we need to pray the Our Father.
> We fold our hands, we look straight, not sideways.
> We pray in our minds.
> My church is kind of big
> but when you go inside it is so little.
> It smells like a cold wind.

This is a far cry from Eric's first entries in his notebook, but we don't expect every student to come this far, and even Eric, unless we reinforce what he has learned throughout the rest of the year, will likely backslide and forget. I have used Eric's work in other classrooms in order to model the idea of focusing in on something and then writing about it in different ways. Ideally, we want to find and develop the Erics in each classroom, so that their work can help us to teach. Writing so our readers can see what we see is so basic that it needs to be practiced again and again.

A poem of images is rich with the things of this world—with refrigerators and missing teeth, with the steam coming off each spoonful of soup that is blown away before it is allowed into the mouth. We can get an image from re-membering a grandmother's hands, from sketching the floor plan of the house we grew up in, from describing the seashell we carried home from the beach. But it isn't usually enough to simply name these things. We can't say "my grandmother's hands" and expect anyone else to see what we see. Perhaps we need to include the actions her hands performed (crewelwork as she sat before her soap operas), or describe them at a certain time of the year (aching in the winter or on rainy days; gnarled from thorns and from crushing Japanese bee-tles), or compare her hands to something else (my hand in hers was like a spider in its web). We begin to see her hands in relation to the world, and from this we begin to move a little closer to her as well.

I imagine the plants in my grandmother's car would have borne fruit by now, if the car were still running (a green Corvair like on the television show *Get Smart*), or even if it is now in one of those car graveyards I used to come upon sometimes in walks through unknown woods (across from the house where I lived in Amherst, cars from the 1940s, the 1930s, from the beginning of cars, now with trees growing up through the driver's seats); maybe her car is resting there now, the backseat filled with watermelons.

3

It Gets Late So Early

EAVESDROPPING

Shirley McPhillips

ᕫᕬ

*(Poems) For you must kneel down and explore
for them. They seep into the world all the time
and lodge in odd corners almost anywhere, in
your talk, in the conversation around you.*

WILLIAM STAFFORD,

You Must Revise Your Life

THE TIME
Naomi Shihab Nye

Summer is the time to write. I tell myself this
in winter especially. Summer comes,
I want to tumble with the river
over rocks and mossy dams.

A fish drifting upside down.
Slow accordions sweeten the breeze.

The Sanitary Mattress Factory says,
"Sleep Is Life."
Why do I think of forty ways to spend an afternoon?

Yesterday someone said, "It gets late so early."
I wrote it down. I was going to do something with it.
Maybe it is a title and this life is the poem.

Tonight, on PBS television, musician Wynton Marsalis is talking about his yearly schedule. To most of us it sounds like a grueling impossibility. He tours three hundred days a year, continually writes new music, puts in numerous personal appearances, and acts as Artistic Director of Jazz at Lincoln Center. He smiles easily as he enumerates his awesome musical responsibilities. His mother is a little concerned about him. She says, "I hope you'll stop someday and smell the roses a little more." "Man," he replies, "This is the roses!" *This is the roses.* I am delighted by the twist in Marsalis's view of what it means to "smell the roses." I reach over to my notepad and my favorite purple pen. Marsalis will have other intriguing things to say. And so will his mother.

Poets live wide awake in the world. They "eavesdrop," watching and listening in the moment, letting things catch their attention. They wonder and ask questions, letting what they see and hear inform their lives. Sometimes a poet will notice the exact words that people use. These "found" bits of speech can be a springboard for new ideas or a backboard against which to bat ideas and test them further. Just by listening closely to what people say, to the very words they use in their everyday speech, the world around us can be revealed. We can be moved by the words themselves at the moment we hear them, yet we don't know why. But, as poets, we keep them, believing these words can hold new meaning.

When Naomi Shihab Nye spoke at Teachers College, she told about taking in the sights around the city with her son. One afternoon, they stood in a long line waiting for the ferry to take them across to the Statue of Liberty. Right beside them spectacular gymnasts leaped, flipped, and jumped onto one another's shoulders. They, and some others, watched, mesmerized by these artists and their antics. But many paid no attention at all, fretting about the line, deploring the wait, craning their necks to spot the boat that would take them to their destination. All of a sudden, one of the gymnasts broke ranks and yelled to the crowd: "We are doing something you cannot do. Please watch us and enjoy this! Take your mind off that boat! It will come, I promise you it will come!" Nye was deeply moved by the words "Take your mind off that boat." She held onto them, as poets do. Later, as she was thinking about the importance of pushing the "pause button" in today's busy world, she wondered how many of us miss what's right around us all the time because our minds are far off, elsewhere, hectic, distracted. When the gymnast said, "Take your mind off that boat!" he wanted people to forget the boat and watch them. It was Nye who remembered the line and let it deepen her thinking about the human condition.

Naomi Nye knows to hold onto the exact words she hears. The gymnast didn't say, "Boat's gonna be here soon. Y'all look over here, please." The sound and position of the words can make all the difference to the poetry and its significance. Like Nye, when I eavesdrop, I make sure to pick up the exact words people say. I use whatever paper I have handy, but I keep notepads, Post-it notes, and little pots of pens on the telephone tables, by my bedside stand, and in the car's dashboard organizer, just in case. If I can get to the small notebook in my bag, I'll scribble a phrase there. Later, I can put it in a more permanent place, my book of special lines or my writer's notebook where I work out ideas.

Driving home one day from a school in the Bronx, for example, I turn on National Public Radio. Playwright August Wilson is asked how he, a school dropout, could have become a renowned playwright. "I dropped out of *school*," he said. "I didn't drop out of *life*." I like the rhythm of these words, the authority and wisdom that come from the phrasing, the emphasis. And on the phone to Uncle Jim one night, after he reports on the people I might remember for whom the death knell had sounded, he says, "You know, people are dying today that never did before." His placing of the serious and the comic side by side amuses me. And last spring, while visiting our old homestead in Virginia, my sister Phyllis and I stop by to see Mr. Garnett, an octogenarian who used to work with my dad. As memories come flooding back, he realizes that all the people he mentioned are dead and that he has no one left to talk to who has shared a certain way of life with him. "They've all passed," he says, then pauses. "Nobody's left alive who knows what I know." A very modest man, delivering a poignant line at the moment he thinks it. The simple poetry of his line, what it conjures up, moves me deeply. I don't know what he made of my scrambling for paper to write it down.

Often, the lines I hear have no significance for me at the moment, but I like the sounds of them and I believe I am hearing something in a new way. Outside Teachers College one morning, I stop at the breakfast cart across the street to get a drink. I say hi to the vendor and order a hot tea with a "few grains of sugar and a dollop of skim milk." He repeats this colorful request, and as he measures out "grains" and decides on "dollops," he shakes his head and says, "This is good. This is going to take us through some strange streets today. Yes, this is good." He hands me the hot brew and says, "Travel straight, now." I thank him and head across the street to the Horace Mann Auditorium, rehearsing his musings over and over, commanding my temperamental memory to hold out across that "strange street" until I can get to my notebook. I love the playful exchange we've had. I love his words. To me they are packed with potential. "Strange streets . . . This is going to take us through some strange streets. . . . Travel straight, now." Later, I can savor them all by themselves and try writing off them, or I can put them next to a line or entry in my notebook and think between them. I can put them next to the poem I'm already working on and see what results.

Sometimes I even eavesdrop on myself. When I pull up next to Angel, a first grader in a bilingual class, his teacher whispers that he doesn't communicate. "He is afraid of everything—other kids, school, himself." I notice that I say the word *great* to him a lot. I try to make him feel that he is doing interesting things, intriguing enough for me to scribble notes on them. I hand him my favorite purple pen. He seems surprised, but he takes it. "Great," I say as we find the letter *i* and he laboriously draws it. "Great," I say as he points to something in the tangled lines of his picture and I suggest, "Love?" He points vaguely to a list of little words on the wall. "Great! You found it." I put my finger on the word. "You keep going." I say. "I expect you to do great things. And I'll be back to see them." Such commonplace, even empty words. Reading them again in my writer's notebook one evening, deep in my thoughts about Angel and kids like him, I write, posing the question, "What if we really believed that our very words can shape what a child believes about himself?" I start sketching out some early lines: "Today I expect you to do great things, she said to the boy, scared of himself, and I'll be back to see them. The boy has made a nest of everyday nightmares on the inside of his life, and he hunches there like a skinny bird."

ᏣᎳ *Getting Started*

TUNING OUR EARS TO THE WORLD

I heard the heart of each of them somewhere. A grocery store line. A beauty shop.
The emergency room. A neighbor across her clothesline to another neighbor.

—Jo Carson, *stories i ain't told nobody yet*

When I arrive at the school on this rainy winter morning, the fifth graders are already spread out around the room reading poems with their reading partners. As I drop my bags, one child runs over. "Look," she says, "our folders have about thirty poems in them!" To give you a little background, the teacher has been reading aloud a range of poetry all year (in addition to other short pieces and books), encouraging students to build up a friendship with poetry, especially poems they may not always select to read on their own. Copies in hand, they talk—flexing their listening minds, filling up with sound, mining ideas, finding, as Mary Oliver says, their "second nature" with poetry. Often they reread to react and prepare for discussion—making marginal notes, underlining, writing lines in their notebooks—then collect their notes in their personal folders for future reference. For these students, poetry is ongoing. By the end of the year, each student's folder is a personal repertoire representing a long investment of attention and apprenticeship.

This particular class has already studied images (see Chapter 2), and the students have drafts of several poems in their notebooks. Some have crafted a poem for their writing celebrations in the fall. After reading quite a few of Naomi Nye's short pieces and poems, they have identified her as a person who seems to "soak up the world." So we have decided to look at the poet-as-eavesdropper.

I sit in the white rocking chair. The children gather around me on the carpet with their poetry folders and writer's notebooks. They know to bring these in case we need to refer to a poem, jot notes, or pause to try something in our notebooks. We talk about what we think poets have to be able to do well. To their list, I add that poets—like all writers, like scientists, like artists—are alive in the world, tuning their eyes, ears, and hearts to the particulars of things around them, like striking a tuning fork to the world and hearing it resound.

Naomi Nye's poem "The Time" (*Fuel* 1998) is on a chart near us. The class has already read it with their teacher and had some conversation. We read over it again and notice that the narrator of the poem is remembering the exact words she has overheard and also noticing an advertisement. This kind of eavesdropping is one way of tuning our ears to the world. "Eavesdropping is listening carefully," Eric says, "like spying with your ears." I give them a picture of how this happens for me by telling the story about listening to Wynton Marsalis, being fascinated by his words, writing them down exactly as they were said. I read from my notes about Naomi Nye's being struck by the words of the gymnast and holding onto them for later. This is enough to get the students started thinking about letting language catch our attention as we go about our daily lives. I ask them to look through their poetry folders and classroom library collection during the week for other signs of poets eavesdropping, and to be alert for language as they watch TV or chat at dinner.

LISTENING FOR LANGUAGE, FINDING POSSIBILITIES

I was that little girl, sitting in the corner of the kitchen, in the company of poets.

—Paule Marshall, in *The Open Door* (Gilbar 1989)

As the class is becoming more interested in listening for language, I think it is important to emphasize further that we can find possibilities in ordinary circumstances, ordinary speech. I read some quotes from my special lines book (Figure 3.1) and show the students how they look on the page. I tell them stories around the lines to give them a context, how I came to be hearing those words and what I thought when I heard them. Yesterday, at lunchtime, for example, I heard a teacher at a Bronx elementary school say to a friend, "You work too long. You need to learn how to say no." The friend hunched her shoulders, looked at her colleague in surprise and said, "Well, look who's talking!" Such an ordinary line, "Look who's talking." But it interests me for the possibilities of looking at it in different ways. Wanting them to imagine how one might hear something ordinary and find possibilities, I ask the students, "What might this

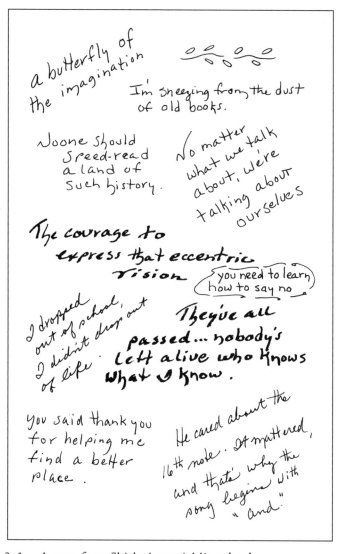

FIGURE 3.1   A page from Shirley's special lines book.

line mean to us?" Emily says, "We've been reading essays and magazine articles, and looking at things from different points of view. Maybe 'Look who's talking' could be about different people having their say." Paul remembers a former classmate who rarely said anything out loud but who wrote in moving ways and with a passionate voice.

We try another line. I tell them that last night I listened to (then) New York

City's Chancellor of Education, Rudy Crew, speaking at a press conference to unveil his plan for supporting city charter schools. He explains that the plan is about decentralizing decision making, empowering individual schools and communities to hire staff and design effective programs to improve student achievement. "This is about finding a way to let go," he says. I challenge the students: "What if we take that line for ourselves and think about it in connection with our own issues, our own lives?" Hands go up tentatively. Then Adi says softly, "I left Israel and when I knew I'd be leaving, I had to find a way to let go . . . of my friends, my land . . . my language." "My uncle died, of lung cancer," Katie says. "It's hard to let go."

Sensing how they can hear an eavesdropped line and give it meaning, the students are excited about eavesdropping now, so the teacher and I ask them to mark off a section of their notebooks for their own collected lines. We decide we'll need a week or so to get better at it. The teacher sends them off to draft ways they plan to eavesdrop. At the end of the workshop, we share a few plans. Like Jo Carson, quoted at the beginning of the Getting Started section, some want to take their notebooks to the cafeteria, some to the supermarket, others to the dinner table, to karate, and so on. *With a reminder that eavesdropping is really a metaphor for being awake in the world, not for intruding on people's private conversations,* we decide to begin eavesdropping for homework.

THINKING ABOUT THE BIG IDEAS

While students are eavesdropping and collecting lines and stories around them, we look again at our mentor poem. We plan to read and reread this poem over time, to deepen our thinking about it, and eventually to put it alongside the work we're doing in our writer's notebooks. But on the first and second readings, we just want to see what we can notice and what that makes us think.

"She wants us to think about spending time wisely," Adi says. "To be a kid is a short time. If we keep missing things, it adds up to a lifetime."

Paul adds, "I think she's saying you have to enjoy your life. Life's like a poem."

"Then the words 'It gets late so early' *persuade* her," Shayne says. "It doesn't mean it gets late early *just that day.* It's like things change so quickly. She wants us to capture the moment. Don't let it go by."

Samantha admits that she didn't get the last line at first. "Now I think she took bits of her life which is the title. The poem is the beginning of her life."

Students spread out around the room, alone or with their partners, with copies of "The Time" and their notebooks, to think further about what they notice and what they think about the mentor poem. Several jot down ideas they want to remember.

ᕫᕬ *Keeping It Going*

SHARING EAVESDROPPING

The teacher and I think it's important after a few days for students to check in with each other on how their plans for eavesdropping are working out. How are they positioning themselves for eavesdropping, and what are they jotting down? One or two share their lines with all of us (Figures 3.2a and 3.2b) and tell the stories of how they were gathered.

Then students go off in twos and threes to share the context within which they overheard their lines, as I have modeled, and what about their lines seemed to catch their attention. If they hear something from someone else that they can imagine trying, they jot this down in their notebooks. Each day, when they share, the teacher adds new ways for eavesdropping to the flip-chart. The habit of listening for and collecting overheard lines, both in speech and from being read to, continues over a week or two (and, ultimately, throughout the year) even when the mini-lessons change to focus more on the mentor poem.

TALKING OFF A LINE

After practicing eavesdropping and looking more closely at the mentor poem, we can help the students begin to make connections between a line and the stuff of their lives. We have touched on this in a previous mini-lesson, Listening for Language, Finding Possibilities. To demonstrate further, I read Mr. Garnett's line from my writer's notebook (see the beginning of the chapter): "Nobody's left alive who knows what I know." I tell the story of where I heard it and why, as a poet, I want to keep it. First of all, I am listening intently. Here is a man who was, for many years, a close working companion of my dad. He represents the most active years of my dad's life. When I listen to him, I am hearing my dad, envisioning him. The sound of his words strike me first: the musical ring of the line, the satisfying rhythm. *Nobody's left alive who knows what I know.* The words of a simple man holding a world of wisdom beyond what he is thinking at the moment. His words come after a reflective pause in his story, giving the effect of a profound instant realization. The line has the weight of something big, especially as it is connected with my dad's life. When I write the line in my notebook and start to write off it, I think about what Mr. Garnett might have meant. Not only were his comrades gone but a whole way of life had disappeared. He can tell his stories now only to people who nod nicely and indulge an old man. The tools and talents of the watermen in his day go unnoticed because the industry, the very landscape, has drastically changed—the roads and buildings, inlets and shores. I think I know something of what he is feeling. In a

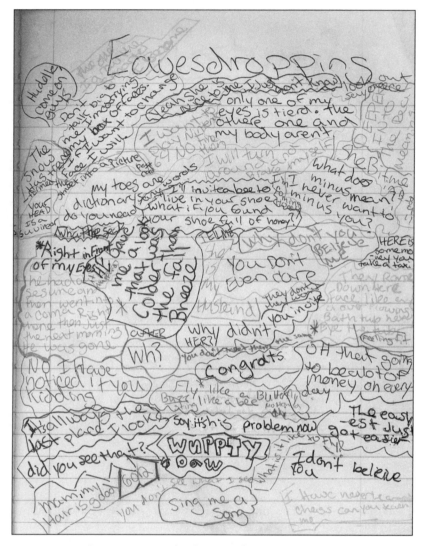

FIGURE 3.2a   Samantha's notebook page of "eavesdropped" lines.

small way I've felt some of it, too. His words remind me of another line in my notebook, another time. The day I took my dad for a ride down to the old points of water he used to know well. The riverbanks were so developed by urbanites building homes along the waterfront for recreation that we couldn't find a public road to get anywhere near the serious water of his lifetime. After repeated attempts, we pulled over to the side of the road to renegotiate. Daddy could only murmur, "Can't even get down to the water." A severed lifeline.

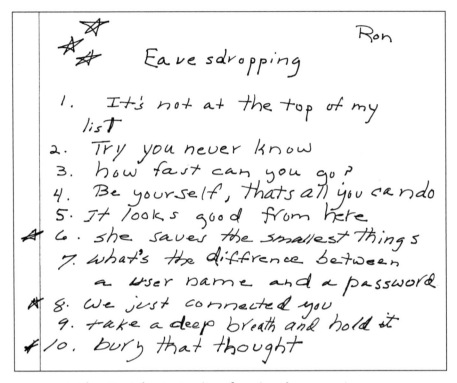

FIGURE 3.2b   Ron's beginning list of overheard conversations.

I show the students how I might explore several aspects of Mr. Garnett's line, and my dad's line, because of their deep connection to my life. But I also want students to know that I sometimes note lines that have no obvious meaning at the moment I hear them. I just like the sound of them or think they'll have some potential when I get to thinking about them. I read out one of those, too. Now I ask the students to pick one of their overheard lines, make notations about what it's making them think about, then go off with their partners to practice telling the stories of their lines and what connections they are making. Oral storytelling, saying the memory out loud as a narrative, perhaps using a storyteller's voice, can help flesh out details and subtleties for writing to come.

QUICK WRITING OFF AN OVERHEARD LINE

Write luxuriously, abundantly, fill whole pages, making little notes to yourself in the margins. Don't worry about saying it perfectly in a condensed way.

—Naomi Shihab Nye, *speech at Teachers College, Columbia University*

We hope that by telling stories off an overheard line, students will begin to feel more comfortable with generating thoughts, thereby making some interesting connections to their lives. We also want them to practice doing that thinking on paper. So we ask them to look over their collected lines and to star one or two that stand out to them for some reason, that maybe connect to an image or memory (see Figures 3.2a and 3.2b). Then write that line at the top of a notebook page, writing rather quickly without pondering too much. Just "write abundantly," filling a whole page or more, staying with the image or memory (see Chapter 2). We think it's important for the writers to get the feel of writing quickly, so we stay together in the meeting area for a few more minutes than usual. After six minutes or so, enough for many to get started, Samantha has written almost a page about how her mother's friend Ms. Glantz told them about her experience at the hospital when her husband passed away. She writes the overheard line and a retelling of Ms. Glantz's account (Figure 3.3). Samantha happened to choose a line that came connected to a story, an image, that is still clear in her mind. So she has used the line as a springboard for retelling this experience as Ms. Glantz told it to them, as if in her voice. In another class, Tao, with a line more isolated from a story, let it make her think something new:

I get lost in a book.
in another world,
in my own dream,
in circles of words,
all together like a maze you can never get out
never want to get out.

It's time now to work on our own. Some who were unable to write as much as they would like in the group setting continue to write off their lines. Others, like Samantha and Tao, might want to extend work they've started or practice writing off other lines: narratives, lists, images. As we confer, we try to help writers see what they have so far and make plans for what they want to try.

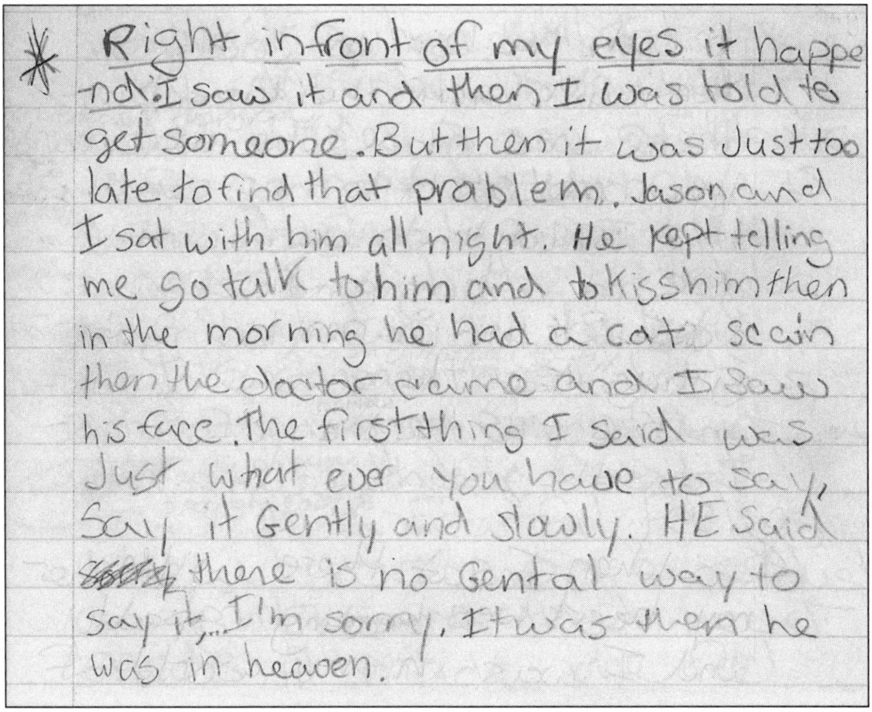

> ✳ Right infront of my eyes it happend. I saw it and then I was told to get someone. But then it was just too late to find that problem. Jason and I sat with him all night. He kept telling me go talk to him and to kiss him then in the morning he had a cat scan then the doctor came and I saw his face. The first thing I said was just what ever you have to say, say it Gently and slowly. HE said there is no Gental way to say it,... I'm sorry. It was then he was in heaven.

FIGURE 3.3   Samantha writes quickly off overheard line.

❧ Extending Our Thinking

COMPARING ACROSS THE MENTOR POET'S POEMS

I prefer the idea of being invisible, traveling through the world lightly, seeing and remembering as much as I can.

—Naomi Shihab Nye, in *The Place My Words Are Looking For* (Janeczko 1990)

Having collected and read a number of Naomi Nye's poems and short pieces, the students think that eavesdropping on the world seems to be "second nature" to her, though they haven't particularly looked for examples of this. So, with their partners, they look through pieces they have collected and select other examples of Nye's work to put against "The Time." Today, we gather to talk.

Katie says, "In 'Valentine for Ernest Mann' [Janeczko 1990] Naomi Nye says you can find poems in surprising places, like a sock drawer. She's this awake kind of person. So when she hears 'Sleep Is Life,' I think she kind of disagrees with that. If you sleep you'll miss everything."

"I think she's been eavesdropping all her life," Joel says. "In 'Mint Snowball' [Kitchen and Jones 1996] she remembers all the little things her mother told her about her great-grandfather's drugstore. 'The Mint Snowball tasted like winter.' And the Swiss village when she closed her eyes."

"In 'One Boy Told Me' [Nye 1998]," Katie continues, "she writes down all the sayings of her little boy. She had to write them down. She wouldn't just make them up! In 'The Time' she writes down 'It gets late so early' and says she's going to do something with it."

"I think she wants to enjoy her life," Jenifer says. "She doesn't want it to get too late to do that. She writes things down so she can remember them. In 'So Far' [Nye, ed. 1999] she's noticing the names of signs people put up on poles when their pets are lost."

James says, "She's a smart person. My dad says if you ask a lot of questions you're smart. Not what people usually think. She asks a lot of questions and she puts them in her poems. In 'The Time' she's wondering about what's important to do with her time. In 'Mint Snowball' she's wondering if there's another land for her. In 'One Boy Told Me' she writes all her son's questions, too."

Listening to just a few minutes of dialogue about Naomi Nye's work, we realize that this is a way for students to gain more of a sense of how one poet lives wide awake in the world; how this everyday attention, this thoughtfulness, finds its way into her poems. Reading across several works of one author, we think, brings students back to the mentor poem with deeper insight and can give them a better understanding of a purpose for eavesdropping. So we make plans for them to continue this kind of discussion with their partners periodically. Some go on to do a mini-inquiry (see later in the chapter).

LOOKING AT THE MENTOR POEM THROUGH THE LENS OF EAVESDROPPING

After talking more about the "big ideas" we are finding in "The Time," we want to reread the poem, paying particular attention to eavesdropping. We have already noticed that one of Nye's lines is an advertisement and the other is a bit of overheard conversation. LeShaun wants to know, "Why did she decide to use two quotes in the same poem?" We wonder how the two might be connected. One makes the poem's narrator ask a question and the other the narrator wrote down, in order to "do something with it."

Dimitra notices that the quotations are farther down in the last two stanzas. Why aren't they up front, the poet saying what she overheard and then writing off it, the way we sometimes do?

These observations and questions seem like enough to stimulate discussion. In partnerships, the fourth graders talk further about what they notice and what they can imagine was in Nye's mind as she thought about the overheard lines in her poem. They try to connect more closely the overheard lines with the big ideas they talked about a few days ago (previous mini-lesson, Thinking About the Big Ideas).

NAMING HOW THE POET IS USING EAVESDROPPING

We remind the students that "The Time" is a *crafted* poem. This is the end of a journey filled with lots of writing. We ask them to reread the poem and imagine what the poet-as-eavesdropper is doing in this final poem with regard to the quotations. We have noticed that two quotations are positioned farther down in the poem, after Nye lets us in on what is already on the narrator's mind. The narrator seems to be saying, "I have this idea, this thing I'm noticing about myself, about life, and here's how these words I overheard fit in with that." As Jeong Hye says, "I don't think she picks a quote and tries to fit a poem to it. I think it's the other way around." Dimitra agrees. "She doesn't keep looking for quotes. She looks into what she finds and it connects with what she's thinking about." Using our own words, we name this "fitting a line to an idea" and write it on a chart entitled Some Ways Poets Use Eavesdropping. We will be naming and adding other ways to the chart during our study.

The students go off to fit a line to an idea. They reread some of the entries in their writer's notebooks and pick one where they're thinking about something in particular: a moment, a memory, an image. They look at their collected eavesdropping and find a line that could fit with their entry in some way. Or, they might put a line with *any* entry and try to "force a connection." They can write the line in the margin next to the entry or on a Post-it note and attach it to the entry. Then they talk with their writing partners about what they were thinking in this entry and how this quote could fit in with that.

For homework, and during daily writing workshop, students can find other connections between eavesdropping and entries.

EXTENDING WRITING OFF A LINE

As Nick discussed in Chapter 2, sometimes we want writers to write long: to try writing something in a different way, from a different perspective, to stretch their thinking. And we'll use a student's work to show how that played out for one person. We'll also want to hear different strategies and results from others. Samantha works on extending her initial retelling by putting herself in the picture. Where is she in this? She continues the entry shown in Figure 3.3, focusing exclusively on Ms. Glantz, giving us the particulars:

I sat there on the couch not able to imagine somehow at the worst times doctors lose all their humanity. I just could not understand. The tears were streaming down her face like an overflowing bathtub. She was quivering and seemed lost. She needs now to have something to do. Her fingers scrambled as she tried to open the box of cookies. Her nail struck the tape but there was more. . . . She was scared. You could see it in her eyes. All I wanted to do was just give her a hug and when I did I felt this warm, loving, comforting hug. Like there was a monster and she was the woman of armor and I was the queen.

On another day, Samantha, having moved closer to Ms. Glantz, now moves in on herself, stretching out her own reactions. In a new entry, she writes as if talking to herself:

My heart was beating rapidly. I was in my world of wonders. What should I say? Should I talk about him and remind her, or should I get her mind off of it? What would happen if my father died? Could I imagine? Why does she have what looks like a piece of black tape on her shirt? Why is there a sheet over all the mirrors? What is she feeling? Is it like that guilt feeling when you know you did something but you can't tell or a fearful feeling like a horror movie or just a nightmare that never ends?

She ends this entry with a personal meditative thought:

Maybe God needs a person so you can't have them anymore.
    Take advantage of the time you have with people and do things with them. They might not even always be there.

We notice that across her entries, Samantha, though not even thinking about drafting a poem at this time, is using some strategies that will serve her well as a writer, especially as she nears a draft: getting in close and writing a scene, internal conversation with herself (questioning, wondering, posing possibilities), meditation.

LOOKING DEEPER INTO HOW THE POET'S OVERHEARD LINES FIT INTO THE MENTOR POEM

Conversation about the lines Nye used, fitting lines to our own notebook entries, and writing off lines get us looking more closely at the quotes in the mentor poem to see how they fit into the whole of the crafted poem. Why did Nye include these particular lines? Are they part of the central image, or an aside? Do they reveal something unique about the author? The way the lines are put together suggest a paradox—words that jog themselves out of their usual places, putting them almost into reversal. How can sleep be life? Are we living when we sleep? How can late be early? This kind of line seems to set the narrator thinking about life in that same quirky way when she suggests that maybe "It gets late so early" is like a headline for our lives; that our engagement in life, our wide-awakeness to life, is the ultimate poem, or the nourishment out of which poems come.

Students read back over their notebook entries and flag those where they think they are showing a wide-awakeness to their lives: observations, detailed images, memories, questions, and wonderings. On a blank page, they take one of their collected lines and try their hand at rewriting the entry (or some part of the entry) with the overheard line in mind. Looking back and forth between the two, writing another entry, they can force themselves to think something new.

ZOOMING IN ON AN ENTRY

Students are talking and writing off lines, writing long. Sometimes within all this lies a seed, some essential kernel of an idea, or an image. So we might ask students to imagine they are holding a camera. Zoom in on some part of an entry that seems to be where the main action is, or where they feel something bubbling up, some spark in their minds or emotions. We'll write that part on a clean page and extend it, staying in the groove. Before going to write, we ask students quickly to reread their entries off a line and tag such a place.

Samantha zooms in on Ms. Glantz's face and her reaction to it:

> Once I saw it, her hand swiping her face, her tears streaming down like white water. I had never (even) seen my mom cry. I didn't know grown-ups could have such fears and sad emotions. Once and only once did it take for me to realize it all. Her hands were guarding her face from fright and she was closed in like a dark shadow. Then out it came like the sun that swept away a fierce shadow and it all spilled out like a soda machine that's busted. It was not organized flow. Just a mess of letters and words of expressment.

Although Samantha isn't looking at ordinary and interesting words the way Nick did with Eric in Chapter 2, by moving in close to some part of an image and focusing, she has written some revealing particulars using active verbs, internal dialogue, similes, even an extended simile. By tightening her image, the writing here has a different rhythm, a flow, that begins to sound more like a poem. She may or may not decide, in the end, to turn this into a poem. Or she may take something from this to use in another draft. She won't know yet.

A year later, when Samantha moved on to the middle school, she went back to reread her notebook and craft a final poem, "Right Before My Eyes," included now in Appendix A. It could also be read within the context of spirituality (see Chapter 11) as it leads her to a question as large as life: "What's death? Words. These words. / Words that eat away at my heart. / Too many. Too harsh."

LOOKING CLOSELY AT THE STRUCTURE OF THE POEM

Once students have had, over several days, opportunities to write long and extend some of their eavesdropping, we will want to let the mentor poem help us look more closely at some craft issues. One of these craft issues is structure. We want to look at the mentor poem line by line and name what we see the poet doing, name its structure in our own words. These will be the words *we* use; others may name it differently.

In "The Time," Naomi Nye starts with *a thought* about the best time to write. In the rest of that stanza and the next, she uses clear *visual details* that ground the poem in reality. Then she writes her *eavesdropped line* and *meditates* about it. She adds the second *overheard line* and ends with a final *meditative thought.* Students jot this structure in their notebooks, and the teacher writes it up on chart paper for later reference.

Our Naming of the Structure in "The Time"

- A thought (something narrator tells herself)
- Visual details
- Overheard (eavesdropped) line
- Meditation on overheard line (questions)
- A second overheard line
- Meditative thought (ponders)

In writing workshop students reread their focused writing off an overheard line (earlier mini-lesson, Extending Writing Off a Line). In their notebooks some try their hand at pulling out bits and writing a poem draft, using elements of Nye's structure as we named them or as they make sense to them: for instance, a thought, visual details, an overheard line; or, an overheard line, visual details, some meditative thought. We will hear one or two at the end and continue writing for homework. Tomorrow, we will share what more people tried. Figure 3.4 shows how Michael tried out elements of the structure we named after rereading "The Time."

We will want, along the way, to help our students notice other issues of craft and apply them to their writing. See Appendix B for a chart used to get classes looking closely at a mentor poem, Valerie Worth's "Sun," from *all the small poems, and fourteen more.* They reread "Sun" to notice what Valerie Worth is doing and to find possible reasons and names for that. Writers can then select one observation or strategy and try it out in their own poems as it suits their purpose.

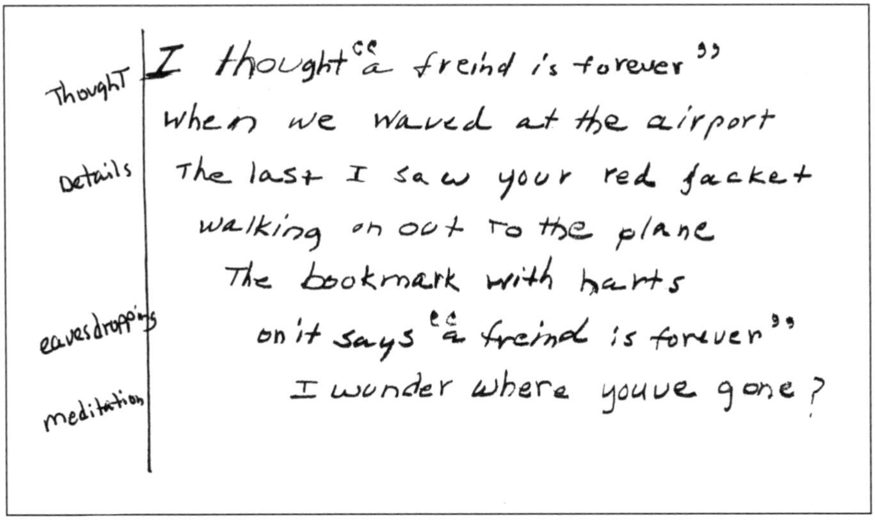

FIGURE 3.4   Michael tries out elements of structure of "The Time."

You will find more discussion of how to use this chart in Katie Ray's book *Wondrous Words*.

PLAYING WITH THE ORDER OF OVERHEARD LINES

Because we are using mentor poems to inform our own writing, the teacher and I realize that we need to talk with students about the fact that where lines appear in poems is not random. Poems are crafted, and therefore the poet has thought carefully about the placement of each line in the poem. When we are reading poems with eavesdropped lines, we want to look at where these lines are and what the impact of that is on us, the readers. We remember in "The Time" the lines are farther down in the poem after the poet has posed a thought and given some visual details. That gives us the sense that the narrator has been thinking about something and is using the lines to further meditate about it. We look at "One Boy Told Me," another Nye poem (see complete poem in Appendix A). The snippets of conversation may look random, but they are not. Why these twenty-five utterances? Why does she begin with this one? How do they connect one with the other? She decides to end up with "I do and don't love you— / isn't that happiness?" It's not by chance that she lands on those two lines. What do we make of that?

The writers look at their own lines they have selected and play around with the order in their notebooks. In which order do I create an image? suggest an idea? In which order do I take the reader by the hand and think with her down the page? What if I begin with this line? end with this line? Which way does it sound better (see Chapter 5)?

On another day, we can go further. What if I add something in between each line: a meditation, a question, a repeating line? What if I repeat one of the over-heard lines? What if I try a question-and-answer poem like Naomi Nye's "Boy and Mom at the Nutcracker Ballet," from *Fuel*?

In "Great Aunt Matty" (Figure 3.5), Morgan decides to land on his over-heard line at the end of his image. When we read it, we can't imagine the line being anyplace else. But Sarah's is part of a narrative, an internal thought set-ting us up for the flashback memories she has of the great oak tree (Figure 3.6).

FIGURE 3.5   Morgan lands on his overheard line at the end.

Nightfriends

Sitting at the window
staring out upon the grave
of the great oak tree
when it was there
we feared it
"Gosh if that thing falls"

But now that it is gone forever
I miss the things we did together
I never swung
I never climbed
I didn't even touch it
But at nighttime,
in my bed of dreams
We played
and guessed
and thought together

I'd make up pictures
with the branches
and then
When we were done
the wind would shake
and rearrange them
and I'd
Have
Lots
More
Fun!

— Sarah Winfield

FIGURE 3.6   Sarah's overheard line is part of the narrative image, an internal
thought.

∾ *Mini-Inquiry*

IMAGINING THE PERSON
BEHIND THE LINES

Reading through some of the students' notebooks one day, we noticed Cassie writing a cluster of quotes from her younger brother: "You're being Mom again"; "I'm not going to let you see me laugh"; "Cheerios would rather swim in sweet milk." The lines make us laugh, imagining the delightful five-year-old behind them. We ask Cassie to tell the class the stories around these lines. Why do these lines stand out to her? Where was she when she heard them? What was her brother doing when he said them? What do the lines make her know, want to know, about her brother? How do they affect her?

A few other students say they have noted more than one line by someone. So we suggest that some of them might make a project of observing someone over time who they think says things in interesting ways: a little brother or cousin, a friend from another part of the world, a grandmother. They could write down exactly what that person says, what she tends to say, words or phrases that are just "her." What is she wondering about? What interests her? What is she "having her say" about? What happens when we string some of these quotes together? when we reorder them? What happens when we select a quote and write long off it? when we put a line next to something we're already thinking about this person? next to something we're thinking about ourselves?

IMAGINING THE LIFE OF THE POET

In one class, after a mini-lesson on Comparing Across the Mentor Poet's Poems, the teacher and students want to spend more time reading Naomi Shihab Nye's poems and short prose pieces, and through them, to be instructed by her in living more like poets. They look closely at one piece next to the mentor poem, then later across several pieces of her work, talking across them.

As the teacher and children read Nye's work, they try to imagine the kind of life she lives in order to write these pieces and collect these poems for her anthologies. What does she tend to notice, to value? What are her sensitivities, her issues? How does she tend to use words? Are there lines that are "just Naomi Nye"? Looking at the poet behind the poems will be a support to students as they use the mentor poem, not only as they try on some of the writerly habits of the poet but as they start to craft their own poems. In one class we collect a variety of her work, then decide which *three or four pieces* we will study. Students can read others on their own.

Some of Naomi Nye's Works We Collected

- Short prose pieces: "Mint Snowball" from *In Short* (Kitchen and Jones 1996), "Looseleaf" from *Words Under the Words* (Nye 1995)
- Poems: "Valentine for Ernest Mann" from *The Place My Words Are Looking For* (Janeczko 1990), "The Rider" from *The Place My Words Are Looking For* (Janeczko 1990), other poems from *Words Under the Words* and *Fuel*
- Picture books: *Sitti's Secrets, Lullaby Raft*
- Essays from *Never in a Hurry: Essays on People and Places,* "My First True Love" *from CBC Features* (1999)
- Collections edited by Naomi Nye: *This Same Sky, The Tree Is Older Than You Are, The Space Between Our Footsteps, What Have You Lost?, Salting the Ocean: 100 Poems by Young Poets*

As we read and discuss each of our three or four pieces, students underline and make marginal notes in response (on photocopies), or they use Post-its to mark and respond. Then they make a list in their notebooks about what they are noticing, perhaps longer entries about what they are coming to know about Naomi Nye. They might mark or respond next to exact parts of her work that make them think this way. During whole-class discussion, the teacher may write what they intuit about Nye's habits and craft on a flip-chart so that they can talk further and discover something they will want to practice. One class generated this chart over, perhaps, a couple of weeks' time.

What We're Learning About Naomi Nye

- Has a deep interest in people and cultures
- Is sensitive to ordinary people, to the smallest details of everyday life
- Reads and collects poetry from other poets and has favorites
- Lets herself be "struck" by things that others might just pass by
- Finds her own special meaning in what she sees and hears, and makes new ideas grow
- Asks questions and sometimes thinks about possible answers
- Uses ordinary language but puts words and lines next to each other in ways that surprise us
- Listens for "fresh" and ordinary ways people say things

To extend this study, and because he expects his students to work purposefully, one teacher asks his students to write down a plan in their notebooks showing what habit or technique they're learning from Naomi Nye that they want to try as they work on their own writing. They post their plans up in the room for the community to see and learn from. In a teacher/student conference and in discussion with the class, writers show what's working for them.

LOOKING ACROSS ONE POET'S POEMS FOR SIGNS
OF EAVESDROPPING AND HOW LINES ARE USED

Since Naomi Nye is a poet who exemplifies a wide-awakeness to life, it can help the writers to find examples of eavesdropping in her other poems and study these in the same way they studied "The Time." Looking across some of Nye's poems, we find her eavesdropping in different ways. In "One Boy Told Me," we notice, she lists twenty-five exact snippets from conversations with her son over time. Reading these lines, one after the other, with nothing else to hold them together, gives us a startling image of the world being created by this little boy. One third of the lines are questions, most of them asking for his mom's reactions or, perhaps after hearing her answer, making up his mind about something. We talk about what role eavesdropping plays in this poem and how this compares with "The Time."

After identifying other ways in which Naomi Nye uses eavesdropping in different poems, the writers can look back through their lines and try some of the ways. When they notice, for example, that she strings quotes together to create a boy's picture of the world, they can pick out quotes from their collections that they think might go together for some reason, write them on a page in their notebooks, and try a draft.

In "So Far," from *What Have You Lost?*, Nye clumps together messages tacked on telephone poles from sad and frantic owners of lost pets. She follows these by an extended, meditative image, then another clump of messages, ending in a repetitive plea. If it seems to fit with their lines, some students might like to try clustering their lines on a variation of this structure.

Some Poems by Naomi Nye That Include Eavesdropping

- "Boy and Mom at the Nutcracker Ballet," from *Fuel.* A mom and her son, in a poem-for-two-voices with a question-answer structure, have a conversation during the performance. It's amazing to see what happens when the outside story of life meets up with the imaginary story in full view on the stage.
- "The Rider," from *The Place My Words Are Looking For* (Janeczko 1990). Something a boy says about trying to outskate loneliness causes the narrator to think about that next to her own life.
- "The Man Who Hated Trees," from *Words Under the Words.* The narrator observes and listens to a man who takes pride in cutting down trees and wonders what manner of man he is.
- "So Far," from *What Have You Lost?* Messages tacked on poles alerting passersby to lost pets cause the narrator to ponder lost things.
- "Messenger," from *Fuel.* The narrator notices a spray-painted phrase on the backs of bus benches and muses about the painter and his life.

LOOKING ACROSS DIFFERENT POETS' POEMS FOR SIGNS OF EAVESDROPPING

Just as they did with Naomi Nye's poems, young writers in one class search for poems in their classroom library, or among the poems they are collecting in their folders, that demonstrate a poet's eavesdropping on the world. We take our mentor poem, or another one of Nye's poems that we know well, and put it beside, say, Janeczko's poem "Section 7, Row 1, Seat 3" and talk about the evidence of eavesdropping and the different ways poets use their overheard lines. Students go off to have the same kinds of conversations with their partners using the poems they have found.

Some Poems from Other Poets That Include Eavesdropping

- "Section 7, Row 1, Seat 3," from *That Sweet Diamond* (Janeczko 1998). An old lady comes to the game as she has all the years of her life. What she says at the end of the poem is a testament to her devotion.
- "Chester's Wisdom," from *Spin a Soft Black Song* (Giovanni 1991). Chester gives a boy some advice about fishing.
- "Weights," from *Nathaniel Talking* (Greenfield 1988). Nathaniel ponders something he heard his grandma say.
- *Mornings Like This: Found Poems* (Dillard 1995). The poet looks through a variety of print material and pieces together poems from "found" lines.

The habit of tuning their ears to the world—of being intrigued by language, of expecting the things they see and hear to hold promise—is a habit we want students to practice through all their days. Listening for lines, searching for our own and having them find us, we are reminded of what Annie Dillard says in *The Writing Life:*

One line of a poem, the poet said—only one line, but thank God for that one line—drops from the ceiling . . . and you tap in the others around it with a jeweler's hammer.

4

A Note Slipped Under the Door

Nick Flynn

Poets think they're pitchers, but they're really catchers.

JACK SPICER

Collected Books of Jack Spicer

NOTE SLIPPED UNDER A DOOR
Charles Simic

I saw a high window struck blind
By the late afternoon sunlight.

I saw a towel
With many dark fingerprints
Hanging in the kitchen.

I saw an old apple tree,
A shawl of wind over its shoulders,
Inch its lonely way
Toward the barren hills.

I saw an unmade bed
And felt the cold of its sheets.

I saw a fly soaked in pitch
Of the coming night
Watching me because it couldn't get out.

I saw stones that had come
From a great purple distance
Huddle around the front door.

I make lists of those who have called me and those I haven't called back, mundane lists of what I have to do each day, each week, of letters I've written, of poems I've sent out into the world. Some of these lists are single words—*laundry, stamps, swim;* some are whole sentences or parts of sentences—*drop off keys, Tad coming this weekend, revise third section.* Many of these lists are in a code known only to me, like the list of titles for poems that have never been written: *Heroic Uses of Concrete, My Brother Waits for the Tiny Machines.* Time lines of where I've been and what I've done for the past ten years, the past twenty, are also in the form of lists. Before me is a list of books I've read and books I mean to read, and another of books I've loaned out and may never see again. These sit beside the list of things I need to buy in order to fix my bicycle, of what I need to have looked at in my car, of what could possibly go wrong (*back up all files, weatherstrip the door, check the spare*). And those friends I've lost track of, whom I haven't seen in a long time, and those projects I hope to start or plan to finish, these are the anxiety-producing lists that never seem to get checked off. Then there's the lists of places: of houses for sale I should call about; of things I could do to make life easier in New York (like move out of New York); of places I could possibly go away to this winter, which leads to a list of my daily expenses and whether I'll have the money to take any trip at all. Being unable to pass a body of water and not jump in, I even have a list of some of the places I have swum in the world: off the Aran Islands; in a green river in Northern Vietnam; in a granite lake in Vermont; in a communist pool complex on the outskirts of Prague; in a hot spring outside Taos; in a lake fed by a glacier in the Rockies; in a subterranean bathhouse below Budapest; beneath a waterfall on the coast of Big Sur; in the North Atlantic. This connects with the list of ways I have injured my body over the years, which is helpful to remind myself to be more careful, as I can be somewhat accident-prone.

I believe that making these lists fulfills a vital function, that of clearing out my mind, of making room in my head for other thoughts. Look at what I've done in the preceding paragraph—yet another list. The physical act of writing, of putting pen to paper (I never start with the computer) takes the words out of my head and anchors them someplace; my obligations are now there on the page rather than popping up every five minutes in my head, asking, Haven't you forgotten something? When are you going to get to this? Now—why don't you make that phone call now, before you forget? Unfortunately, it seems list making is an endless process, a Sisyphian-task, with precious little satisfaction in accomplishing what is listed: check off the names of those called and they are forgotten, instant candidates for a new list of those yet to be called. Each day like this—buy batteries, *check,* the batteries safely inside the flashlight and forgotten; letter to X, *check,* letter dropped into the box and forgotten; oil the chain, *check,* the grinding sound behind me now and forgotten. And yet, still, I believe the lists help, not knowing what I'd do without them, how I'd order my days, how I'd get anything done or clear out my head to even know what has to be done.

I feel an intimate bond with all list makers. In perfecting the epic poem, which often incorporated extensive lists, the ancient Greeks proved themselves to be epic catalogers as well. Epic poems were passed on orally, and along with the rhyme patterns, the lists were mnemonic devices—they helped the poet remember the poem, often by repeating a word or a phrase, so that the poem could be passed on through the ages. Look at epic poems, from the Finnish *Kalevala* to Homer's *Odyssey,* with whole passages detailing the food eaten at banquets, lists of battles fought, lists of ships sunk, lists of plunder and of those lost, of who begat whom. These early poems were a means to keep track of a culture, of the things and events that were deemed important, that made up the culture. The novel has been called the modern version of the epic poem, which would suggest it has survived these millennia.

List making, then, along with being an aid to shopping and organization of one's mind, is one of the oldest forms of art. Here is an example of an early genesis myth from the Kato Indians, found in Jerome Rothenberg's anthology *Technicians of the Sacred:*

> *Water went they say. Land was not they say. Water only then, mountains were not they say. Stones were not they say. Fish were not they say. Deer were not they say. Grizzlies were not they say. Panthers were not they say. Wolves were not they say. People were washed away they say. Deer were washed away they say. Coyotes were not then they say. Ravens were not they say. Herons were not they say. Woodpeckers were not they say. The wrens were not they say. Then hummingbirds were not they say. Then otters were not they say. Then jack-rabbits, grey squirrels were not they say. Then long-eared mice were not they say. Then wind was not they say. Then snow was not they say. Then rain was not they say. Then it didn't thunder they say. Then trees were not when it didn't thunder they say. It didn't lighten they say. Then clouds were not they say. Fog was not they say. It didn't appear they say. Stars were not they say. It was very dark. (7)*

Try reading this out loud in order to fully understand the incantatory power of this list. Rothenberg goes on to give one definition of the list, commenting that

> *What's of interest here isn't the matter of myth but the power of repetition and naming (monotony, too) to establish the presence of a situation in its entirety. This involves the acceptance (by poet and hearers) of an indefinite extension of narrative time, and the belief that language (i.e., poetry) can make things present by naming them. The means employed include the obvious pile-up of nouns (until everything is named) and the use of "they say" repeated for each utterance. (441)*

The poet, then, in this belief system, can make things present by naming them, another useful function of list making. We can get things out of our heads by putting them down on paper, and by putting them down on paper they become real. So the list is an ordering principle and a creation principle. To add to this, Confucius claimed that one purpose of poetry is to teach the names of birds and plants to a nation's children. In the Old Testament, a list begins the creation story, a list of what God did on each of the seven days of the week, which I imagine God also had to create. This device has also proved effective for beginning writers of poetry. The listing, for example, of what they eat on each day of the week—*Monday I eat apples, Tuesday I eat spaghetti,* and so on—can clearly, then, be classified as biblical.

This is not to claim anything epic about my compulsive list making, simply that, perhaps, it serves a similar function—to hold information in a simple syntactical form, a form that is not as rigidly tied to sentence structure and grammatical conventions. What we do know is that by teaching the possibilities inherent in list making, hopefully there can be more room for risk taking by struggling writers, and for surprise by those more accomplished.

⊙◟ *Getting Started*

Today's classroom is in the Bronx, a sun-drenched mid-November morning. This is my first year in this school, with these teachers, but already we've had a few small in-class authors' celebrations, and one larger one that involved several classrooms. This classroom has been working in notebooks since September, and nearly every student has published a memoir, along with one or two quick, one-page publications. Most of the class has begun to shift to poetry—reading poems on their own, having informal poetry talks in small groups—while a few stragglers finish up their memoirs. Now we are ready to begin an inquiry into the use of lists in poetry.

To begin this inquiry we need to first discuss what makes a list, how we can identify lists, where we've seen or used lists in our lives. Once we gather I begin to talk about some of what I've mentioned—about the long history of lists in literature, about how lists seem to be a part of every culture. I then mention my own relationship to lists, the reasons I keep and use lists, from the mundane to those in my poetry. Then I have the students turn to a neighbor and discuss when they have used or seen lists in their lives, and after a few minutes we come back as a group and share what was discussed. What has come up, I'm pleased to find, are shopping lists for groceries or for holiday gifts, lists of the names of members of our families, lists of the places we have lived, of friends we have or have had, lists of what we eat for breakfast, of the music we listen to. Before they go off to write today some of them raise their hands and say they are going to work on lists.

For the next few days the teacher decides to read some list-like entries from her notebook to the class during her mini-lesson, or some poems that feel list-like, in order to continue and deepen the discussion.

FINDING LISTS IN OUR WRITING

On my next visit we decide to expand our search for types of lists by looking for them in our own writing. I begin by looking at an author's page (Figure 4.1) that I have transcribed onto the flip-chart I usually keep beside me during my mini-lessons. This author's page, I point out, was included as the last page of a memoir written by Ryan, a third grader in another school:

About the Author

When I grow up I'm going to be a boss.
When I become a boss I am going to be happy.
When I get old I'm going to play the numbers, like my Grandma.

I remind the students of what an author's page is, that it often comes last in a book, though when reading we may, if the work interests or confuses or irritates us in some way, turn to this page sooner than if we had read the book straight through, to get a sense of the person who wrote it. I then point out that Ryan's author's page is also a list: it is a list of how Ryan expects his life will turn out, his plans. I ask, "How do we recognize it as a list?" One student, tentatively, says that, first of all, it looks like a list, and I agree that that is always a good place to start. I take a marker and number each sentence 1, 2, 3, so that it looks even more like a list. Looking closer, we see that he has even separated each line with a space and a period, making it akin to both list making and poetry. Also,

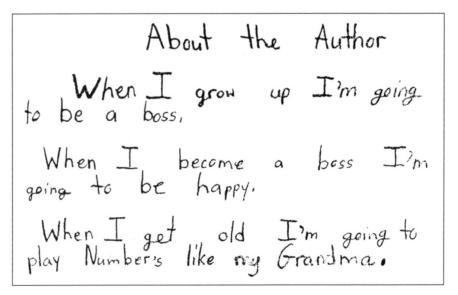

FIGURE 4.1 Ryan's author's page.

each sentence begins with the repeated phrase "When I . . . ," which, I point out, often signals that what we have before us is a list, using the syntactical device of repetition to move us between each item. Before we return to our writing this morning, the students agree to take a few minutes to find and mark places in their notebooks where they have already written, using lists.

We could have used Ryan's author's page to begin the chapter on time (Chapter 8), to notice how effortlessly he moves through time in this short piece. We could show how he begins with where he is now, and projects his desire to be a boss into the future. By the next line he is in that future, and has attained his goal, and it has made him happy. And by the last line he has moved beyond his desire, he has retired, and it ends with his plans for how he will spend his retirement. So Ryan has also given us a fine example of how a writer can compress an entire lifetime into a few lines, by using a list.

INTRODUCING THE MENTOR POEM

We are several days into our inquiry on lists by this point. We have been thinking about the different types of lists, trying to find examples from our lives, from our notebooks, and in literature. It is time for us to look closely at one poem that can be said to be, among other things, list-like. In our inquiry into how writers use lists, Charles Simic's "Note Slipped Under a Door," from *Unending Blues,* is one of the poems we have come across, and one that has stayed with us. We have been reading it out loud and having informal discussions about what we notice in it for a week or so, leading up to its being chosen as one of our mentor poems.

DISCOVERING HOW THE MENTOR POEM IS MADE

As with all our mentor poems, we have chosen Simic's poem primarily because we love it. It is full of vivid images, mystery, and beauty. For our inquiry into lists, it seemed fitting to pick a poem that is, essentially, a list. In this way it is similar, we notice, to both Kenyon's "Let Evening Come" and Blake's "The Tyger" (see Chapters 5 and 6), but we will talk more about those similarities on another day. We decide to limit our discussion today to noticing how our mentor poem is put together. Unlike in Blake's or Kenyon's, in Simic's poem, we notice, each stanza starts the same, and each stanza is made up of only one sentence. Six stanzas, six sentences, all beginning with *I saw.* It is also similar to Ryan's "About the Author" page in that we could number each stanza and make it look even more like a list. Taking this idea a bit further, we notice that the order in which Simic put the stanzas seems deliberate, not random, that if we change the order of the stanzas the meaning of the poem changes, not in an obvious way, but in subtle ways. For example, if we try to start the poem with the last stanza, the whole poem seems to then be about those stones huddled around the front door. We decide that this is an important thing to notice when we are looking at lists and trying our own, that we try each item on the list in different places to see if the meaning changes.

When we teach "list books" we often tell our students that we can put the pages in any order and it doesn't matter, it won't change the meaning, although many list books end with a page that summarizes the pages that came before it. This may be a way you want to begin your inquiry into lists, in which case you will choose a poem where the order of the lines feels less important than in Simic's.

ᕳ꙳ Keeping It Going

A LIST OF IMAGES

As we gather a couple of days later, I want to continue our discussion about Simic's poem, this time wondering if we can name, generally, what it is that he has listed. A few hands go up, and a student points out that each stanza begins with *I saw* and then follows with detailed examples of what he saw. Each stanza, the student goes on, is like a photograph; we can see each in such a way that we could sketch it out. We are thrilled that the lessons from our very first inquiry back in October, on the image, has stayed with him, and use this as another opportunity to reinforce our inquiry into the image. I say, yes, I can see each stanza clearly, too, and remind them that we call this an image, and that I feel Simic's poem is essentially that, a list of images that seem somehow, mysteriously, connected. We decide to sketch off one (or as many as we want) of Simic's stanzas, in order to see how effective he was at creating a picture for us through words.

LOOKING CLOSER

We decide to look closely at each image Simic has created, first going back to our sketches. Why are these images together, what is this a list of? We break into small groups to discuss this for a few minutes. When we come back together, our attention forward, a few hands go up. A girl says her group noticed that all the images seem to take place inside a house, that each stanza feels like a different room in that house. We look at the poem again on the chart, and the girl comes up and points out what room she sees in each stanza. The first is at a window, the second is in the kitchen, the third is looking out the window, the fourth is in the bedroom, the fifth, well, the fifth is harder to place, and the sixth is at the front door. We can all see what she means, and we praise her group for noticing this, and agree that perhaps the fifth stanza is a leap, the place of mystery, which we have already discussed as something vital to any poem. A boy raises his hand and says that the person speaking in the poem is like the fly in the fifth stanza—they are both trapped inside the house. We decide, for today, to call Simic's poem a list of a place.

OTHER POEMS OF PLACE

On another day we decide to look back at our mentor poem of place, Marie Howe's "The Copper Beech" (see Chapter 9), and to see how Simic's poem compares to it, remembering that Howe's entire book, *What the Living Do,* seems to walk us through the floor plan of a house, its yard, its neighborhood. I also remind them that the word *stanza* is an Italian word that translates as *room,* which makes sense in Simic's poem, because it seems to move us through different rooms.

COMPARING THE MENTOR POEM WITH OTHERS

We line up the Simic poem beside our two other list-like mentor poems—Blake's "The Tyger" and Kenyon's "Let Evening Come." We can either do this in small groups with photocopies of each poem in front of us and Post-its to mark what we notice, or as a whole class with the poems written out on flipcharts. We are looking for the similarities and the differences. We begin with "The Tyger," which we have already decided is essentially a list of questions, whereas Simic's is essentially a list of images. We also notice that where each of Simic's stanzas starts with *I saw,* each of Blake's starts differently, although he uses the word *what* over and over to ask his questions. Also, Blake seems to be talking to a character in his poem, while Simic seems to be talking to us, the readers. We notice that they both have the same number of stanzas (six), but that Blake's stanzas all have four lines, where Simic's have anywhere from two to four, making Blake's poem longer. This seems enough for today, though we could go on. We return to our desks and get back to our writing, keeping in mind the many ways we are noticing in which poets use lists.

Depending on time, we could then partner up to discuss the similarities and differences between Simic's and Kenyon's poems. What we might notice is how both Simic's and Kenyon's are lists of images as well as lists of places, though different places. Simic seems to stay inside the house, whereas Kenyon moves all through the farm. Again, both have six stanzas, but Kenyon's is more like Blake's in some ways, as each stanza is more regular, with three lines in each. These few observations are merely a beginning to what we can notice.

ᕼᕼ *Extending Our Thinking*
LOOKING FOR OTHER LIST-LIKE POEMS

All during our inquiry we have been searching for and finding other poems with lists in them. In Naomi Nye's anthology of Mexican poetry, *The Tree Is Older Than You Are,* we find several, including this one:

DUCKS
Homero Aridjis

1
On cold mornings the ducks
slide across the ice
after the dry bread
thrown to them by the little girl

2
In the afternoon
the hungry ducks
cross the street
against the traffic

3
At night the ducks
nestle beside the frozen canal
they scarcely move
their green heads

4
At dawn the ducks
sleep beneath the mist
which cover the man
the dog and the stone alike

We notice that Aridjis has arranged his poem as a series of moments, each describing a different time of day, from morning to the next dawn. Each moment is also set off by a number, not just a space, which, we agree, makes us pause even longer between stanzas, as if each were a poem in itself. One boy raises his hand, a boy who usually doesn't say much, and slowly points out that he thinks the man and the dog in the last stanza are hunting and that they are about to kill the ducks, an insight into the poem that none of us, not even I, who had read this poem dozens of times, had noticed. And we see that he is right, they do seem to be hunting, why else would they be out there at dawn, although the poet never comes right out and says it. Another place of mystery. So, not only is this an example of a list of moments divided by time but it is also a list that is about more than it seems to say directly. We decide to add both these new strategies to our list of lists (see mini-inquiry later in this chapter):

- A list of moments divided by time
- A list about more than it seems to say directly

Before returning to their desks, some students decide to try writing a list that doesn't say what it's about directly, as in Aridjis's poem.

Another poem we looked at was Gwendolyn Brooks's "We Real Cool," from *Selected Poems.* We notice that in this poem Brooks has used a strategy similar to Simic's (although, technically, it's the other way around, because Brooks wrote her poem first), starting each sentence with the word *We.* But where Simic uses a list of images, Brooks uses a list of actions, mostly, and seems to depend more on the way her words sound together.

Finally, we look at Naomi Nye's "One Boy Told Me," from *Fuel,* which is a list of the amazing things that come out of one little boy's mouth (see Chapter 3).

LISTING TYPES OF ONE THING

In Rothenberg's *Technicians of the Sacred,* there is a poem entitled "1st Light Poem: for Iris—10 June 1962," by Jackson Mac Low, which is a page-and-a-half-long poem of some of the different sources and types of light in the world. One of the stanzas reads

> Evanescent light
> ether
> the light of an electric lamp
> extra light

After reading this poem we decide to find other poems of this type to study how a poet could list as many attributes and types of just one thing as possible.

LOOKING IN OUR NOTEBOOKS

We gather with our writer's notebooks, and I talk about how, since our inquiry is on lists, it is helpful for me to look through my own notebook for examples of writing that feel list-like. Being, as I've pointed out, a serious list maker, I can do this easily. I've marked some passages that are lists or the beginning of lists, in order to point out the types and ways I've done it. I read these out loud and hold my notebook up so they can see what I've marked, as well as how I've marked them (I prefer circling passages with a blue pencil—we each have or need to find our own system). If I hadn't been able to find any lists in my notebook, I would have written a couple of list-like entries before class in order to prepare for this mini-lesson, consciously writing entries in different forms, not simply one-word lists. But I did find some. We each then turn to our own notebooks and mark examples of passages or entire entries that feel list-like. After a few minutes we turn to a neighbor and discuss what we found, and I eavesdrop on some of these conversations, so I can ask two or three to share with the whole group. Before we go back to our seats I ask if anyone thinks they might try one of these entries as a poem, using one of our mentor poems as a model, and a few agree they will. I jot down who is planning to try this and will check with them during our conferring time.

MODELING OUR LISTS

We can also model the work of other students who have written list-like entries, either from this year's classroom or from another year. Here's an example of one such entry (Figure 4.2):

> I will be a leader, not a follower.
> I will be a leader, not a follower.
> I will be a leader, not a follower.
> I will be a leader, not a follower.

and so on, for two full pages. We discuss whether this is another type of list or something else. Most lists contain some variety, we agree, and this is repetition for its own sake, this is writing as punishment, which many students feel already about any writing. We decide that this isn't a type of list we will include in what we will try.

Another entry we discuss is this one, which was written by Francisco, a sixth grader:

> *Riding the Horses*
> *When I go to ride my horse first I feed her, and give*
> *her water. I put on all the safety tools, then I get the*
> *saddle and put it on her. Then my father gives me tips*
> *about what I need to know about riding so I don't get*
> *hurt. After that I go and sit on the horse and say ya*
> *and she walks off. First we go in circles for awhile,*
> *nothing serious for an hour or so, then we go to the*
> *jumps. I love the jumps. I do the one with two poles,*
> *once I tried the three poles but I fell.*

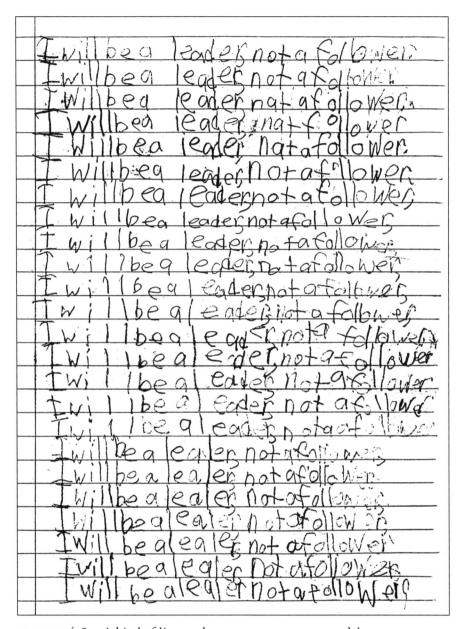

FIGURE 4.2   A kind of list we do not want to use as a model.

We notice that Francisco has listed each step he needs to take before he can get on his horse. This is another thing listing can help us with—it can cause us to slow time down (see Chapter 8) so that we can get a better image of what is happening in any given moment. We decide to call this a step-by-step list.

ᏉᏉ *Mini-Inquiry*
MAKING A LIST OF LISTS

It seems time to gather what we've noticed onto a chart, a list of possible types of lists, as it were. We begin by reading from an example of a poem by Cassandra, a fifth grader in another school:

HOW TO MAKE DEAD DEVIL SOUP
In order to make dead devil soup
follow these 8 easy steps:

First, do something very bad, like kill someone.
Second, jump off the roof of the Empire State Building.
Third, go to where the devil lives.
Fourth, kill the devil.
Fifth, boil a pot of water.
Sixth, put him in the boiling water.
Seventh, wait 3 minutes.
Eighth, enjoy.

We decide to call this a recipe list. I jot that down on our chart under the heading Types of Lists We Could Try in a Poetry Workshop. We follow this with what we've noticed so far in our mentor poems and in our notebooks.

Types of Lists We Could Try in a Poetry Workshop

- A recipe list (Cassandra)
- A step-by-step list (Francisco)
- A list of images (Simic)
- A list of a place (Simic)
- A list of questions (Blake)
- A list of commands (Kenyon)

This seems enough to begin. We put this chart in our poetry center, which is now focused on lists, complete with list paper, list poems, examples of different types of lists (shopping lists, wish lists, to-do lists, etc.). We will add to this list as we discover other ways poets and writers use them. Before we break today we decide to try a draft of a poem using one of these list strategies.

ADDING TO OUR LIST OF LISTS

We may decide to add to this list during subsequent mini-lessons. Some of the types of lists we might add include

- A list with repeated words or phrases
- A list of moments
- A list of the attributes of one person
- A list of the types of one thing (e.g., *light*)
- A list of definitions
- A list of actions
- A poem that has a list in it, but the list is not the whole poem
- A list using single words
- A list using phrases
- A narrative list, a list that tells or suggests a story
- A list about more than it seems to say directly

Each of these listing strategies would, of course, need to be demonstrated in the context of our mini-lessons, and time would have to be set aside for our students to try each in their writing. As each is added to the list an example should be given, using poems or notebook entries, in order for the strategy to have any meaning for the students and for the students to be able to apply, and hopefully internalize, the strategy.

At the Writing Project there have been heated debates recently around the question of what are the essential structures in literature. Some have proposed that there are just two—the story and the list. While I am undecided if I can agree wholly with this paradigm (Where does an image-based poem fit into this? or a sonnet? What about Stanley Kunitz's proposition of three essential structures for poetry—linear, circular, and didactic? Or Gregory Orr's "Four Temperaments": story, structure, music, and imagination?), it does point to the essential nature of the list.

From our inquiry, we have discovered that lists do not necessarily have to be made up of one word followed by another. We've read and tried writing a whole range of different types of lists, and tried incorporating these into our poems. If this is one of the basic structures of all literature, we feel satisfied that we have begun to explore it deeply.

5

Let the Cricket Take Up Chafing
SOUNDS OF LANGUAGE

Shirley McPhillips

You must love the words, the ideas and images and rhythms
with all your capacity to love anything at all.

WALLACE STEVENS,

"Adagia," in *Opus Posthumous*

LET EVENING COME
Jane Kenyon

Let the light of late afternoon
shine through chinks in the barn, moving
up the bales as the sun moves down.

Let the cricket take up chafing
as a woman takes up her needles
and her yarn. Let evening come.

Let dew collect on the hoe abandoned
in long grass. Let the stars appear
and the moon disclose her silver horn.

Let the fox go back to its sandy den.
Let the wind die down. Let the shed
go black inside. Let evening come.

To the bottle in the ditch, to the scoop
in the oats, to air in the lung
let evening come.

Let it come, as it will, and don't
be afraid. God does not leave us
comfortless, so let evening come.

When Miss Bessie Mae Brown, on that hot too-near-summer day in the Virginia Tidewater, opened her book and started to read Longfellow's *Evangeline* to us raw seventh graders, we thought then it was because she'd done it every year (as everybody in the county who had been a student of Miss Bessie's pointed out). We thought that because it was near summer vacation she needed a heavy dose of Longfellow to keep the educational lid screwed on just a bit longer. We even thought reading this long saga every torpid afternoon entitled Miss Bessie to believe she was teaching 'til the bitter end when really the last of the year's sentences, surely, had been diagrammed and the "My Life as a Piece of Chewing Gum" treatises had long been molded. Only years later did I realize that, the engraved curriculum notwithstanding, Miss Bessie read *Evangeline* year after year because she *loved* reading it. As testament to her devotion, she didn't even ask us to do anything with it, just be quiet and let her read. She loved the orator's stance. She loved saying, "We will commence with stanza 16." She loved the melodrama of the love story (we said then it was because she never got married) and the drama of the lines that carried it. She'd saved the best for last.

I don't know that Carlyle or Edwina or anybody else in the class knew any more about what was happening along the trail with poor Evangeline and her lover than I did. We never spoke of it. All I know is that in the euphoria of being force-fed Longfellow with no strings attached, we listened. And as we did, the voice of Miss Bessie, and Longfellow, was heard in the land.

> *This is the forest primeval. The murmuring pines and the hemlocks,*
> *Bearded with moss, and in garments green, indistinct in the twilight,*
> *Stand like Druids of eld, with voices sad and prophetic,*
> . . . .
> *Loud from its rocky caverns, the deep-voiced neighboring ocean*
> *Speaks, and in accents disconsolate answers the wail of the forest.*

In May of seventh grade, I became aware of the sound of something sacred. Something that in its ability to confound could also elevate one to the ethereal. I was transported on the weight of words.

As I think about it, it was as if all the daily scramble of random language in a Virginia countryside came together, allowing me to recognize the art of *Evangeline,* its rhythms and sounds all compact and perfectly placed. After all, I had an Aunt Eva who once said to her son, pronouncing his name like the great Barrymore, "Lionel, go down to the to*may*to patch and bring me a to*mah*to!" She knew the value of emphasis and the singular color that word needed depending on its position in her spoken command. Uncle Larkin warned us about the perils of "single courtin'" (going steady), and Uncle Jim, observing some skimpy portions on our plates, would quip, "That'll take you but it won't bring you back." And when you asked him how he was feeling (which you did with trepidation knowing you would get more of an answer than you bargained for), he might say, in the metaphorical vernacular of local watermen, "Oh, my anchor is dragging in the shoals today."

In the Tidewater, words were colored differently for different occasions. Whenever the doors of the Glebe Landing Baptist Church cracked open, we stood on the threshold. Here, on Sundays, a perfectly humble and sensible country parson every other day of the week became a "preacher." At the agreed-upon chord from the organ, he would rise from the pulpit, like Proteus rising from the sea, and harpoon his words directly into the souls of us sinners—soothing, admonishing, cajoling, sympathizing, challenging, warning, and sometimes, redeeming, his voice a whirligig—whispering, fluttering, thundering in an electric undulation of words, rising and falling with unabashed emphasis and passion. Bracing these ceremonies like stays were the hymns: voices lifting up poems, in anguish, in jubilation, timeless, worn. And that's where I think I caught it, the dynamics, the rhythms, the language of old, the parable and the poem:

> *The time of the singing of birds is come, and the voice of the turtle is heard in our land.*

> *Though I speak with the tongues of men and of angels, and have not charity, I am become as sounding brass, or a tinkling cymbal.*

> *To every thing there is a season and a time to every purpose under the heaven.*

> *Amen, brother.*

Is it any wonder, then, that at age nine, in the midst of all this excitement, when the words of the final hymn were sung—"Just as I am without one plea"—I waded out into the sea-nettle-infested Rappahannock and let Preacher Herndon, his hands unsteady in the stablest of times, duck me in the muddy undertow?

Such is the power of the sound of words.

So many writers attribute their listening to the sound of words to their love of language and to their desire to read and write. Poet Paule Marshall, daughter of immigrants to the U.S. from Barbados, traced her love of words to her mother and friends who carried on endless and passionate conversation while they worked. "I was that little girl," she says, "sitting in the corner of the kitchen . . . seen but not heard, while these marvelous poets carried on" (Gilbar 1989). From way back, she wondered if she could "capture some of the same power on paper."

Jo Carson collects stories of people in her native Tennessee and turns them into poetry. She tunes her ear to everyday situations, to particular words and cadences. She tries through sound to capture their essence: "I heard the heart of each of them somewhere," she writes in *stories i ain't told nobody yet*. "A grocery store line. A beauty shop. The emergency room. A neighbor across her clothesline to another neighbor."

And journalist Robert MacNeil, in his memoir *Wordstruck*, tells how, being raised on a regimen of stories both read aloud and told, he developed a lifelong love for the spoken word. Later in his life, listening to poet Dylan Thomas reading aloud from his own works, startled by the "extraordinary resonance and richness" as he gave voice, "I listened as though my whole body were ears. . . . I had never heard such a tumble of wonderful words." Then, "Something began to come together for me that had taken all the time from childhood to understand: it was the *sound* of English that moved me as much as the sense, perhaps more."

There is much we can say about what makes words hang together in memorable ways. There is much we can say about the other aspects of what gives a poem a particular sound. In this chapter, I talk about how we can help young writers listen for sounds of language, notice ways in which sound matters, and use what they are noticing in crafting their own poems. We could consider such things as breaking down lines into metrical structures, stresses and syllables, or syntax. But while these are worthwhile inquiries, going too deeply into them does not suit the scope of this space or our purposes. There are other books that do this, and much more, interestingly and well. *The Pleasures of Poetry,* by Donald Hall, I have returned to over the years. Recently, I have read and reread the following newer books and refer to them often: *The Sounds of Poetry* by U.S. Poet Laureate Robert Pinsky; *A Poetry Handbook* and *Rules for the Dance* by Mary Oliver; *How to Read a Poem* by Edward Hirsch, and Bill Moyers's *Fooling with Words*.

๑๏ *Getting Started*

TUNING OUR EARS TO LANGUAGE

Failing to develop the conscious ear that becomes the unconscious, governing ear . . . the more disconnected, the more remote from the sound of our language and therefore from a feeling for the weight of words.

—Robert MacNeil, *Wordstruck*

This class has been building up a friendship with poetry—reading poems aloud and silently, collecting ones that resonate, writing off them a bit. Now we want writers to listen more intently to poems, to savor their taste, to feel the weight of words in their mouths. I tell them something more of Robert MacNeil and his lifelong love of listening to the sounds of words, to voices as they read words; how he said he listened "as though my whole body were ears." That's what we want to do over the next week or so. Tune our ears—our outer ears to the spoken word and our inner ear to that voice inside as we read. I show them my special lines book (see Chapter 3), where I collect bits of language that resonate for me. I read them a few lines: "Nobody's left alive who knows what I know" (Willard Garnett); "Streams became lively with the tumbling and gurgling of meltwater" (Bill Bryson); "The expectancy of Spring and the hard facts of fall" (Ken Burns). I read one or two again, slowing them down, giving emphasis to certain words, as if I'm thinking while I say them. We talk a bit about how the lines sound and how I decide how I read them. I show some different ways I can read the lines and talk about what happens to me when I read them. I invite the writers to go back to an assortment of sources—their collected poems, other writing and reading, eavesdropped lines—to find a few phrases that, when read aloud, they like the sound of. Students designate a page in their writer's notebook (or writ-

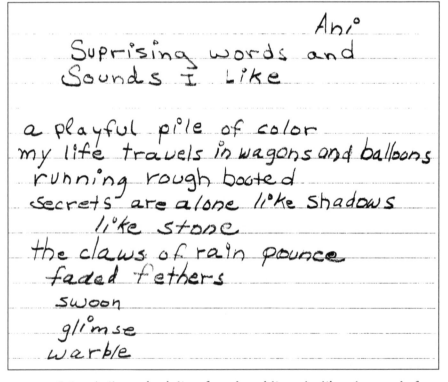

FIGURE 5.1   Ani's notebook list of words and lines she likes the sound of.

ing folder) for recording these lines and practice reading them aloud, hearing themselves give voice.

We hear two or three today at the end of workshop. And over the next few days the students practice reading selected lines aloud to their partners, perhaps coloring them in different ways with their voices (cadence, voice variety, tone), paying attention to the different ways they are reading.

Ani practices reading a list of collected lines (Figure 5.1) from her notebook with her writing partner, Jewel. They talk about what they notice and why they like the sounds.

When we confer, the teacher and I talk about the importance of filling up with sound, with rhythm—that this may not affect writing at the very point of hearing it but can lay a pattern inside for writing to come. The teacher says she wants to be more of a student of words herself. She understands that she is one of the chief demonstrators of what it means to be affected by language. When she reads aloud, for example, she will be aware of reading well, of giving words their weight, without affectation or outsized drama, (i.e., without exaggerating for effect). She will want to let the import, the tone of the whole piece, her sense of it, dictate how she reads; not one presentation fits all. She realizes now, she says, that prose, as well as poetry, has a shape, a rhythm, a well-defined line. She will want to let language affect her and to share language stories with her students.

WHAT SOUNDS BETTER?

Poetry is a vocal, which is to say, a bodily art.

—Robert Pinsky, *The Sounds of Poetry*

As I move among the writers sharing lines or poems, I hear them saying things to each other like, "It sounds better when you read it this way" or "That doesn't sound right." And sometimes a student will say to the teacher or to me, "I like the way it sounds when you read." They already have a feeling that some things sound more delectable than others and that the way we read them affects how they sound. So the teacher and I think it might be helpful to get the writers listening for what "sounds better." We are prepared to accept what they think at first, even though we might disagree. The point now is that they begin to develop more of an awareness of the sound of words as they come together in a line; that they will take part in conversations around what makes phrases and lines sound the way they do.

I tell them about our friend Katie Ray, who says in her book *Wondrous Words* that she likes the sound of part of the Miranda warning that police say to people about to be arrested: "You have the right to remain silent." The line rings with strength and integrity. We like it in the ear. It's the part of the warning that we remember. How different than if it had read "You don't have to say anything right now if you don't want to" or "You have the law's permission not to speak up at this time."

I take another example from the primary grades. Ally, a first grader, has written a poem about the late autumn trees she's been observing outside her classroom window (Figure 5.2). She tried to find a way to show how they look and sound as a brisk wind blew them about. She talked with her friend at the windowsill and drew a sketch to get herself going. I show them her sketch and say that what we're about to do is an exercise, that I'm holding the poem Ally has already written, and I'm not sure how she arrived at her word choice, but I will write up several lines that we might consider if we were looking out at her trees. And we'll see what we think. I read them aloud, giving each one its due:

The leaves are flapping up against each other in the wind.
The trees shake hands with their branches. They sing a song for you.
The branches hit each other and make some kind of noise.

Writers turn to their partners and discuss which ones "sound better." Gerard likes "flapping up against each other" because it sounds sharp like "slap each other" and the wind is blowing kind of hard. Celine thinks "hit each other" sounds like they're having a fight. "But it could be that if it was a hurricane." And "some kind of noise" is too vague; what noise? Gerard thinks trees shaking hands is a little weird. Adam disagrees. He reads it out: "The trees shake hands with their branches." He can picture that, he says, and shaking hands is what people do, but trees can *look* that way if we imagine the wind's not doing it.

Intriguing stuff, we decide. Then I show them Ally's poem. We say it together—feeling the words in our mouths—and marvel at her words. I admire the way the students listen, coloring the words with their voices, giving the poem a mood.

As the students go off to write today, we ask them to try taking a line or two from something they're working on—an eavesdropped line (Chapter 3), a line from an observation (Chapter 10), or an image they've tried (Chapter 2)—and try rewriting it to make it "sound better." They can try a line in several different ways, reading it aloud to get the feel of it, to hear it as it rings out.

In her notebook Tamika has written a previous entry about moving to the music she likes: "I turn up the radio. I like to dance to it. I dance around in my room." Her first rewrite: "I turn up the radio. I dance around and around to the rhythm of the music." Slightly more focused. Beginning to think about some alliterative sounds (radio, around, rhythm). Later she will return to this for another rewrite (see later mini-lesson, Feeling the Sounds—Alliteration).

FIGURE 5.2 Ally's poem: "The trees shake hands with their branches. They sing a song for you. Shsh. Their leaves look like ghosts."

TURNING TO THE MENTOR POEM

*It's what you hear that makes your heart thump or
make you feel a little giddy and out of breath.*

—Scott Elledge, "Preface," in *Wider Than the Sky*

Any poem we love, surely, can teach us about sound. Poems that are steadily rhythmic with dependable rhyme, joyful poems that make us want to clap them, chant them. Eloise Greenfield's "Things," in *Honey I Love,* is like that. When Greenfield reads aloud her "Honey, I Love," she *sings* it. Arnold Adoff says in *A Jar of Tiny Stars* (Cullinan 1996), "I want my poems to sing as well as to say." And they do. Some poems work up a frenzy and hurl sounds at us, like A.J.M. Smith's "Sea Cliff" (Booth, ed 1989). So many poems, so many sounds for our poetic palates.

"Let Evening Come," from Kenyon's book of the same name, might seem at first too sophisticated in form, too adult in content, to use with some young writers. And we would want, of course, in selecting any literature to use in the classroom, to be attentive and use our best judgment according to our aspirations and purposes. But generally Nick and I, and many of our colleagues, reject the notion that students can't hear poems they may not "get." Because it's not about "getting it." Poems are mysteries and come from our deep places. We can be amazed or moved without always being able to explain why. We reject the notion, too, because we believe that the sounds in poetry are like music, that by hearing we build up layers of memory that create a critical ear. And because we remember Annie Dillard's story about a joyful painter she knew, who when she "asked him how he came to be a painter" said, "I liked the smell of paint" *(The Writing Life).* We hope young writers will like the smell of poems. And because poet Scott Elledge reminds us, in *Wider Than the Sky,* of what it's like to hang on to a poem by pure sound. He says, "You may occasionally discover that you are being attracted to a poem before you have quite understood it. . . . After all, there's no law that says you have to understand people before you fall in love with them."

These are some personal intuitions that guide us in choosing a poem. Other reasons we choose this poem as a mentor poem concern certain technical devices that Jane Kenyon uses having to do with sound that we can learn from: its tone, its rhythms, its shape. And the emotional weight of its words taken together has the power to make us weep and sing.

LETTING THE EAR SPEAK

I feel words creating a rhythm, a music, a spell, a mood, a shape, a form.

—Edward Hirsch, *How to Read a Poem*

As the last students are finding a place on the rug, I study the chart of listed lines they like the sound of. I see that they are responding to the musicality and surprise of lines, alliteration and some rhyme:

> She had a thousand rivers in her voice (*Sitti's Secrets,* Nye).
> Brushing the bright lemons (*Sitti's Secrets,* Nye).
> A wonder of wings and things (from a student's notebook).

This is good information for me as we start to look at our mentor poem. Students have brought their poetry folders, which include Kenyon's "Let Evening Come." Before today, the teacher has read it aloud to them, and they have talked about it with partners. They have had that crucial first opportunity to receive the poem in their own way, to talk with others about what impact it has on them. Now we want to give our attention to some things the poet has done to make us feel the way we do.

I ask students not to take out the poem just yet. Today we're going to try on Paul Valéry's poetical attitude, "the ear speaks, the mouth listens." They've already begun by collecting read and heard lines and saying them aloud (earlier mini-lesson, Tuning Our Ears to Language). Now I want them to listen to the whole mentor poem again, to feel it move, to hear it speak. I read, and wait, clearing space around the poem. I nod to a boy who has raised his hand. He says he hears a lot of repeating words. Several others chime in, "Yeah, lots of *let*s." Then, "'Let the' starts almost every sentence. . . . 'Let evening come' is repeated, too." Someone says, "It's like she's made a long list of things she notices happening in the evening. And she says them over and over."

Since repeated words seem to be the outstanding thing students hear at the moment, we decide to look at the poem and explore what such repetition might have to do with how poems sound. We notice that "Let the" starts the first two stanzas, followed by extended images. In the third stanza there are two *Let*s, each with a slightly extended line. And in the fourth stanza there are three shorter "Let the"s capped with "Let evening come." "And then it stops!" someone says. Before we go on, I suggest we read the first four stanzas and get the feel of what happens when the repetitions accumulate that way. A long sound as our voices stretch out with the beginning images, building to a mild staccato with "Let the wind die down. / Let the shed go black inside." Then, our voices settling, "Let evening come." "*To* the," someone rings out, almost as if she's seen it for the first time. We notice two even shorter "to the" phrases, which quicken the pace. We feel a sense of urgency. The last stanza is different, we think. *Let* is there but it's more like, as one boy says, "a repetition of all the repetitions." And the stanza ends with "let evening come," as do the second, fourth, fifth, and sixth stanzas.

We think this is a good place to stop. We've begun to make some interesting observations about repetition in this poem. We decide we will look for repetition in our poetry collections and in other touchstone poems. We can think about what it does to the overall tone of the poem, how it sounds when we read it out loud, and what it makes us feel inside.

Ꮼ *Keeping It Going*

THE OVER-AND-OVERNESS IN THE POEM

All musicians know, it's more fun to master a rhythm by tapping your feet than by counting on your fingers.

—Dana Gioia, in *The Practice of Poetry* (Behn and Twichell 1992)

As we linger with this poem, we extend our observations about repetition. We've already noticed that as the poem unfolds, when the *let*s become more frequent and the phrases shorter, the pace seems to quicken. What else are we noticing about repetition, besides the words *let, let the,* and *to the?* I refer to the girl who said earlier that the poet is "noticing things that happen in the evening . . . and saying them over and over." I say she's right in a way. There is an "over-and-over" feeling, a rhythm created by a repetition of three-word phrases—"Let the light," "Let the cricket," "Let the stars," "Let the fox," "Let the shed"—that gives the "over-and-over" feeling. There's also "to the bottle," "to the scoop." And others: "in the ditch," "in the oats," and "Let it come, as it will." Sort of mesmerizing, we think. "Like a chant," a boy says. The line "Let evening come" has a four-beat rhythm and is repeated, we notice, only at the end of a stanza. It stops us for a moment, "sort of to keep us from going faster and faster," someone says.

The teacher and I are interested in the comment of the boy who felt a chant-like quality in the poem. We think we know what he means. I ask if anyone has read or heard anything that is like this, where we get that feeling of being drawn in because of continual repetition of a word or phrase or line. Nothing comes to mind at the moment. Then a girl points to a poster on the wall of a poem she has printed and illustrated—another of their mentor poems, Langston Hughes's "April Rain Song." Spontaneously, the students break into a chorus.

They know it by heart, their voices rising and falling with the mesmerizing repetition that Hughes uses to begin his first two stanzas. In the echo of this loved poem, we go off to work on our writing. We will think about the quality of "over-and-overness" as we continue our study.

I am reminded of the structure and tone articulated in the lines of biblical verse that I mentioned at the beginning of the chapter. Lines run about the length of a spoken phrase—eight or so syllables—making them recitable. Repetition of words and phrases gives them a rhythm, a lyrical quality, that when spoken seems almost sung and has the power to move us, to move inside us, and even to make us move. Walt Whitman, we are told in Gross and McDowell's book *Sound and Form in Modern Poetry,* showed us how feeling could be communicated by manipulating words. Using what is called "syntactical parallelism," each line "comprises a rhythmical unit whose grammar is precisely echoed in subsequent lines." "Like music, these lines affect the reader (or listener) by movement of sound; they offer the structure of feeling without denoting the human problems that gave rise to the feelings," and achieve a "density and urgency of emotion."

"Let Evening Come" reminds us of a sermon or a prayer. That's one reason why we're struck by the student's feeling of a chant. But the teacher and I have to decide how much of all this we will take up with the students and how that might go.

BRINGING THE SOUNDS INSIDE

When I recite a poem I reinhabit it, I bring the words off the page into my own mouth, my own body. I become its speaker and let its verbal music move through me as if the poem is a score and I am its instrumentalist, its performer.

—Edward Hirsch, *How to Read a Poem*

When I return to the class, the students can't wait to show me what they've found. They've even practiced in order to read a few lines aloud for me: the "I Have a Dream" speech Dr. Martin Luther King, Jr., delivered on the steps of the Lincoln Memorial in August 1963.

Let freedom ring from the mighty mountains of New York. . . . Let freedom ring from the snowcapped Rockies of Colorado. Let freedom ring from the curvaceous peaks of California. . . . Let freedom ring from every hill and . . . molehill of Mississippi. From every mountainside, let freedom ring.

They read it chorally, a group chiming in on "Let freedom ring," a single voice on the rest of the line. We talk about how the sound of the rhythms, created by a choice of words and repeating phrases and delivered with the passion of conviction, deeply moved and inspired a nation during those turbulent times. The sound of them, the passion, resonate still. That's why they last.

We look back at our mentor poem. What if we try reading it in a more participatory way, just as they did with Dr. King's speech. But, we agree, the texture is not the same. These two texts were written in different ways for different reasons. "Let Evening Come" doesn't feel like a rousing speech to us, though it speaks to us in a powerful way. It feels intimate, more like a prayer or an invocation, so we will want our voices to reflect that; we will not want to ring it out loudly. We decide to let a different voice take each line up to a comma or period—"Let the light of late afternoon shine through chinks in the barn" (one person); "To the bottle in the ditch" (another person); and so on. A group comes in softly each time on "Let evening come." We've caught a mood, and now our poem feels different. We feel different. In the silence after the poem, we move off to write on our own.

In Appendix A are works by three students who let the verbal music run through them. Influenced by Byrd Baylor, first grader Emily, in "Desert Voices," gives us that "over-and-over" feeling by repeating "I hear," "I feel like." In "Trees," Vanessa's lines evolve one from the other with the phrase "remind me of." And Reina, filled with the spirit of her girls' club, "gathers up hands" in a rhythmic ritual.

ᎪᏜ Extending Our Thinking
FEELING THE SOUNDS: ALLITERATION

Students have already noticed alliteration in their collected lines, in other touchstone poems, in the memorable writing of Dr. King. We've noticed, too, that the writers we admire use alliteration in subtle ways, so that often we're not even aware of it: "notices flutter / from telephone poles / until they fade . . ." (Nye, ed. 1999). Now we look back at our mentor poem to see how Jane Kenyon has used this tool.

"What stands out to me," Shawna says, "is all the words with *l*." Interesting, I say, that Shawna doesn't limit her observation to words *beginning* with *l*, though that is how alliteration is defined—"Let the light of late afternoon." She includes the sounds of *l* repeated *within* words, called *consonance*. Quite a few words in this poem contain *l*, giving a fluid feeling to the movement of the lines. We notice the position of *l* in different words, then we say the lines in order to feel the sound, in a natural way, not with affectation: "Let the light of late afternoon"; "Let dew collect . . . in long grass"; "Let . . . disclose her silver horn"; "To the bottle . . . to air in the lung let evening come"; "Let it come, as it will . . . God does not leave us comfortless, so let . . ."

We notice other alliterative combinations: *barn, bales; needles, evening; stars appear; silver horn;* and so on. We don't want simply to point these out. We go back and read the lines again, to get the feel of the sounds in our mouths, to hear them; to catch the tone of the whole stanza.

During workshop, the writers look for places where they've already done some alliterative work. They can revise these or they can find new lines and play with alliteration for a while. It's a useful device, and so worth experimenting with even though once they're focusing on it some students will tend to overdo it at first. We'll share some "befores" and "afters" at the end and talk about the difference, deciding which "sounds better." Through our ongoing poetry reading, writing, discussions, we will come to a better understanding about what might be too much alliteration, resulting in sounds feeling forced, drawing too much attention to themselves.

Tamika returns to her "dancing" lines, quoted earlier in the chapter. We've challenged her to try writing an even clearer image, to play with more illustrative and surprising words. She writes, "I turn up the sound. And jiggle to the wrinkled up rhythm. Circling my favorite song." An interesting juxtaposition of words: "wrinkled up rhythm"; "circling my . . . song." Some nice alliterative sounds, unobtrusive, and some internal rhyme.

LaToya shares her "before" and "after": "Waves rolling to the sea" becomes "Waves splashing on the sand, falling back into the sea." Raymond's line gets a laugh when he reads it out one day: "It's spring. I want to take out my old legs and run in the sun." Though he liked the good press he got, he was willing to play with it: "It's spring. I want to stretch out my old winter legs, too white, for too long, until they are toasted. Then pick them up and run. So turn up the sun."

Mary Oliver (1994) reminds us that a "rock" is not a "stone." They can mean the same thing, but the tone of each is very different. She, as wordsmiths have over the years, points out some reasons why. The sounds of *l, m, n,* and *r* are called "liquids." Teachers can get the writers looking for others of these in the mentor poem. At a glance I see many of these particular letters, accounting in part for the fluid feeling of the poem. The "liquids" and other letters such as *s, v, z, y* coming at the end of a syllable lengthen the sound, the voice sustaining the sound a bit: *"bales as the sun moves down"; "sandy den."* "Mutes" such as *k, p, t* at the end of syllables stop us suddenly: *cricket, collect, black, scoop,* in the mentor poem. These make a livelier sound, perk up that place in the line.

In a spirit of inquiry, putting it out there as something fascinating to notice, to give it a try in their own work, young writers like Tamika, LaToya, and Raymond can enjoy manipulating words and noticing what happens to the sound of their own work as they hear it out loud or in the inner ear as they read. Charleze, a fourth grader, hearing language, playing with sound, finds a surprising combination of words. Notice the consonance and assonance (next mini-lesson).

POEM COMING

Wind crimps
new fallen snow
Like fresh ideas for a poem
buckling
onto my paper.

FEELING THE SOUNDS WITHIN: ASSONANCE

Often, one of the first things students will notice in a poem is whether or not it rhymes. The writers we're working with today have noticed that our mentor poem doesn't rhyme. And Joel has announced that he can find only two rhyming words in the entire mentor poem, *barn* and *yarn,* and "Maybe you didn't see them because they aren't at the end, like usual." They aren't even in the same stanza! Ariel challenges him: "*Lung* and *come* rhyme and they're at the end." "Well, sort of, but not quite." He concedes little.

We talk about rhyme, and the poems we know that rhyme. I tell the class another story about my Aunt Eva, who loved to write long poetic stories in which every other line rhymed. She was great at it, weaned on the long masterful sagas of Kipling and Coleridge—"You're a better man than I am, Gunga Din!" and "Water, water, everywhere, / And all the boards did shrink; / Water, water, everywhere, / Nor any drop to drink" ("The Rime of the Ancient Mariner"). She spent hours getting the story straight, the rhythm steady in every stanza (the same way she would smack out the beat on your back at the piano until you got the rhythm of the hymn right). And sometimes she would engage us kids in a mental search for the rhyming word that would make sense.

Joel is right. "Let Evening Come" doesn't rhyme in a strict "true" way. (He has noticed an "internal rhyme.") But there is a repetition of vowel sounds within words and lines *(lung, come)* that we hear almost as rhyme, and that is called *off-rhyme* or *slant rhyme.* So Ariel is right, too.

I might, because we are conducting an inquiry, and because it will be easier for us to talk about the concept in the future, mention that the term for what Ariel has noticed is *assonance*—not because we are learning rules or memorizing terms here, but because to know the names of poetry's devices might take us, as Edward Hirsch says, to "deeper levels of enchantment."

I point out a few off-rhymes in the first stanza: the long *u* sound in *afternoon, through, moving, moves;* long *a* in *late, bales;* even *barn* and *down* give us a feeling of similar sounds.

The students turn to their partners to find other examples and jot them in their notebooks. Instantly, ordinary conversational sounds of a minute ago turn into a sea of babble as they say out words in an effort to find a near match. It's not as easy to "see sounds" as they thought. They can't rely solely on their eyes.

Perfect. I suggest they take one stanza and concentrate on it, line by line. Stanza 4 yields to Matt and Chris *back, sandy, black,* and *let, shed, den.*

We read the fourth stanza together to hear how those words, intermingled, purposefully placed, affect the tone. That seems enough for now. Perhaps they'll go back to their own writing and reading with a bit better sense about the placement and role of rhyme. And we'll give our attention to it again as we go.

THE VISUAL AND AURAL RHYTHMS OF FREE VERSE

"Let Evening Come" is written in free verse (rhythmic, musical writing free of strict metrical structure). Free verse has a kind of verbal music, at times letting in a little conversation. In order to help writers get a sense of words moving down the page, to feel phrases, lines, growing out of each other, I ask the writers to do what Richard Jackson calls "stretching the syntax" (Behn and Twichell 1992). I say, Imagine yourselves immersed in something you love doing (or remember a time when you were doing something that still evokes a strong feeling). I ask them to get an image of this in their minds, right now. What are you doing? What are you thinking, wondering to yourself as you do this? What do you wish? hope will happen? After helping one person stretch his thinking aloud in front of us for a few minutes, I ask the writers to try writing a one-sentence poem about this image, stretching it, keeping that sentence going for six lines, or more if possible. They may use commas, repetition, other devices within the line. I show them an example of a sentence I have "stretched" so they have a better idea. They go off to try this just for the experience of it. The teacher and I circulate, helping a few students think about their images. Perhaps we'll retire to a corner to write, too, or just observe, letting the soft busyness of the room support them right now.

Reina's crafted lines about reading to her aging grandma come out of this experience:

> I sit beside you in your chair of dreams,
> reading the curling pages you cannot see,
> and wonder if I have the keys to unlock
> your invisible door, the door to your
> lonely house, the door which you used
> to open on your own and let me in,
> smiling from all the new words you could say.

When we share our work in progress, we notice that sometimes our words tend to spill over from the end of one line to the next, a phrase sometimes ending not at the end but in the middle of a line. In Reina's poem: "to unlock / your invisible door, the door to your / lonely house, the door which you used / to open on your own." This spilling over, called *enjambment,* causes our voices to want to, as Mary Oliver suggests, "jump over the ditch," thereby quickening the pace of the poem.

SHAPE AND SOUND OF FREE VERSE

For more experience in weighing the possibilities for the shape and sound of free verse, we choose a contemporary poem the students haven't seen and type it up

FIGURE 5.3   Andrew's poem shows careful attention to words and the sounds of language.

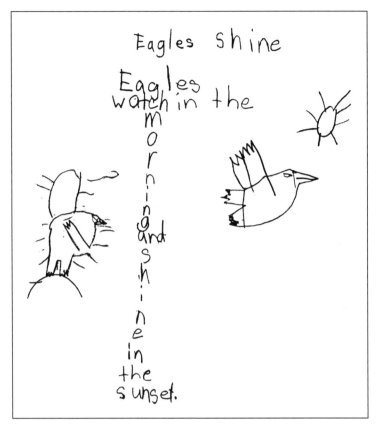

FIGURE 5.4   Matthew's carefully shaped poem for sound.

as prose (or copy a paragraph from a magazine, newspaper, or book). We read it several times (aloud, they with each other), then try writing it with different line breaks and lengths. Writers try variations and compare theirs with other people's versions to notice the *visual and aural differences.*

It's interesting then to write different versions of one of their own poems, changing only the line breaks and lengths. We read them aloud and ask ourselves, Which version do I like? Why?

Andrew's crafted poem (Figure 5.3) shows a careful attention to words, the color of words, the line breaks, the placement of words as they sit side by side. I have returned to this poem over and over again, mesmerized by its sound and rare energy. You might want to read it keeping in mind some of the poetic devices we've been discussing in this chapter.

Matthew's poem (Figure 5.4) shows particular attention to the visual look of his image. If the poem were written a different way, one might miss the stunning beauty of the words for their brevity. He has the sense, too, that a word like *watch* has a striking sound and needn't be drawn out, whereas *morning* and *shine* have those liquid sounds that ask us to sustain our voices.

௸ *Mini-Inquiry*
SOUNDS OF LANGUAGE AND WHY THINGS LAST

We decide to take a week or so to consider why some things stick with us, why they resonate through time. We begin by inviting students to join us in thinking about stories, poems, songs that we remember. I recite Rupert Brooke: "If I should die, think only this of me: / That there's some corner of a foreign field / That is for ever England" ("The Soldier"). Not only do I remember this line but, all by itself, it has the power to make me swallow hard. And I'm not English. Winston Churchill's "We shall fight on the beaches, we shall fight on the landing grounds, we shall fight in the fields and in the streets, we shall fight in the hills; we shall never surrender," from his speech on Dunkirk in June 1940, galvanized England under the threat of Nazi Germany in World War II. A student remembers a line from Jane Yolen's *Owl Moon:* "The snow below it was whiter than the milk in a cereal bowl."

We might tell students the story about the Gettysburg Address, how Edward Everett, a celebrated orator of the day and the invited keynote speaker at the memorial ceremony dedicating the national cemetery, thundered on for two hours. How President Lincoln, not expected to attend, not even invited at first, spoke at the end of the proceedings (with no amplification and not in top voice, apparently) for two minutes. Lincoln, believing his speech to be a failure, as did important newspapers of the day, was surprised later to receive a letter from Mr. Everett, who, prophetically, wrote, "I should be glad, if I could flatter myself that I came as near to the central idea of the occasion, in two hours, as you did in two minutes." The Gettysburg Address is regarded as one of the great speeches of our nation's history. For all his prodigious craft and eloquent presentation, no one can remember a word of Mr. Everett's.

One day, I read the class a quotation from my small brown-and-blue treasure, Strunk and White's *The Elements of Style:* "Who can confidently say what ignites a certain combination of words, causing them to explode in the mind?" But we know that words arranged on paper in a certain way have a certain sound. Because of that sound, some of these arrangements have lasted for centuries. In order to see this more clearly, White suggests, take a long-lived line and rearrange it. He uses Thomas Paine's "These are the times that try men's souls" as an example:

Times like these try men's souls.
How trying it is to live in these times!
These are trying times for men's souls.
Soulwise, these are trying times.

No comparison. Each of these lines is correct, grammatically, he points out, but it is the arrangement of words that makes all the difference. Though part of a prose piece, Paine's line has the ring of poetry—*is* poetry.

We notice some of the technical devices Paine uses, which are also used in poetry: the rhythm, brought about by heavy stresses on important words such as *these, times, try, souls;* the alliteration of *these, the, times, that, try;* the repetition of the long *i* sound in *times* and *try;* the repetition of the liquid *s* sound in *these, times, men's, souls.* Although the exact conditions and issues that inspired Paine to write these words no longer exist, for me the words still carry an emotional weight, maybe because the felt notion of "trying times," the universal struggle of dealing with them, in any day, is something our heartstrings can attach to. My emotional response is triggered and carried on sound.

Together, we decide the students will select one or two lines (not to belabor it) like this over the next week and try rearranging them to notice the difference. The important thing, besides hearing and feeling the difference, is to try to articulate what they think the difference is, as we did in this inquiry. We suggest that today they take a line from something they're working on in their notebooks or from one of their poem drafts and try finding new words, new arrangements for the words. Read them aloud; feel the rhythm; hear the sound. They will share their findings with each other during the week.

GOING FURTHER INTO WHY THINGS LAST

Sometimes, a mini-lesson, a certain discussion, a "try it," can spark an interest that doesn't die down. In some classes, teachers and students decide to get deeper into this inquiry around "why things last." They collect memorable advertising slogans, nursery rhymes, sayings passed down by Grandma or Uncle Herman, lines from songs, lines from poems. They interview family members, friends in the community or at school, to find out what lines they still remember from their childhood and growing up. We celebrate the art of speaking. Some students research memorable speeches throughout our nation's history to see why they "stick." "Orators" (a parent, grandparent, principal, librarian, town official) come to the class to recite favorite lines (poems, songs, parts of speeches). These orators tell the story of how they came to remember these lines. Students practice performing favorite poems, including their own, and parts of historical speeches, then make audiotapes for themselves or other classes to use.

LOOKING AT RHYME

There is much to say about *rhyme.* In some classes the word is synonymous with *poem.* In other classes, teachers feel that students have become so saturated with the notion of rhyme that they avoid it altogether. I'm betwixt and between, as my Uncle Wilber used to say. We look back to past masters and see their inventiveness, feel their brilliance (in more than just rhyme, clearly): Browning's "Pippa's Song," in which each word ending the first four lines rhymes with each word ending the next four lines; Masefield's "Sea Fever," rhyming in couplets; Stevenson's "Requiem," the first three lines rhyming in each of two stanzas, the last words of each stanza rhyming with each other. And Shakespeare—

In *How to Read a Poem,* Edward Hirsch says, "Rhyme has the joyousness of discovery, of hidden relations uncovered. . . . It creates a partnership between words, lines of poetry, feelings, ideas." Gerard Manley Hopkins, he tells us, "called rhyming words 'rhyme fellows.'"

In some classes, we want to broaden our awareness of rhyme beyond what we may have come to know. The teacher and I talk about some ways we might shape a journey of discovery. We could, through our reading and conversations about poems, note our biggest questions, such as how rhythm and rhyme combine to make music, to get inside us. Or where rhyme is found besides "at the end" and what this does to the *feeling* of sound, the tone. Do they know that there are *masculine* rhymes and *feminine* rhymes? *Slant* rhymes and *half* rhymes and *full* rhymes and *true?* Why can we remember and recite some poems more easily than others?

As a class, we pick out three or four poems we love that rhyme in different ways and read them well, looking closely at what the poet is doing in each and trying out what we are learning in our own poetry. We also try writing one of our own poems more metrically, using "true" rhyme, then as free verse, using what we know about consonance, assonance, and alliteration, off-rhyme and internal rhyme, and asking ourselves which works better and why. Along the way, we say what we are coming to believe—that not just any words will do just because they rhyme; that we wouldn't want to rhyme for rhyming's sake (unless we were doing the important work of playing around, having some fun to see what happens); that, with poet Stephen Dunn, we think "Poems have a governing intent which permits them to be more than just verbal play."

With our emphasis here on recalling words tucked away in our individual and cultural memories—with saying them aloud for sound—teachers often want to know, "What do you think about asking children to memorize poems?" And everybody has a story. Poet Dana Gioia reminds us that "Poets weren't always writers. Like musicians, they were originally performers as well who created invisible worlds out of sound" (Behn and Twichell 1992). My husband tells me of an actress friend who works at learning from memory a poem a day, she says, to keep the mind alive. My daddy one day looked up from his chicken soup—one of the few things left, by the end, that he could eat—lifted his eyes beyond our gaze, and quoted eight stanzas of a poem we had never heard of, then resumed eating, more proudly, I thought. Aunt Eva up and said snippets of poetry in old stories conjured from her youth—at wedding celebrations, in the middle of snapping peas. To know her was to know her passion. As Virginia Woolf said of the Elizabethans, it was as if "thought plunged into a sea of words and came up dripping" *(The Common Reader)*. With a dramatic sweep of his arm, my son, Sean, used to bellow forth whole stanzas of Chaucer's *Canterbury Tales,* in Middle English dialect, so enchanted was he with this newsprung river of sound and his newfound ability to swim in it. Dr. Stein, his professor, wanted his students to wake up with it in their mouths. Our friend Frances Richard has fifty-plus poems patterned inside her that she can cue up at any time. Long ones, too— Keats, Whitman, Hopkins.

But not everyone has the fortitude or passion to memorize lines, especially if they do not ring or resonate for them in some way. For some, memorizing is a meaningless challenge perpetrated upon them, often with lingering negative aftereffects—like another friend who said the only thing he remembers about poems in school was the agony of having to commit them to memory. As teachers and lovers of language, we couldn't bear that someone would set the word *agony* down next to *poetry* (unless it were the agony of the ecstasy).

And so we are ambivalent. Poet Octavio Paz says of a poem, "The poet creates it; the people, by recitation, re-create it." Paz may not have meant memorizing necessarily, but there is something noble about the calling up and casting out of the words we love. Noble, too, to lodge them, mumbling and howling, in the odd corners of our heart, even if we never say a word.

To be transported on the weight of words. And where will our students find the power of the sound of words so put together that they might read, that they might write? For teacher and writer Mem Fox (1993), "It came from the constant good fortune of hearing great literature beautifully delivered into my ear, and from there into my heart, and from my heart into my bones." When it came time to write, all the sound, all the rhythm was deeply there. And there, she says, they remain, "in the marrow of my memory."

6

What the Hand Dare Seize the Fire?

QUESTIONS AND WONDERINGS

Nick Flynn

Be patient to all that is unsolved in your heart
and try to love the questions themselves.

RAINER MARIA RILKE,

Letters to a Young Poet

THE TYGER
William Blake

Tyger! Tyger! burning bright,
In the forests of the night;
What immortal hand or eye,
Could frame thy fearful symmetry?

In what distant deeps or skies
Burnt the fire of thine eyes?
On what wings dare he aspire?
What the hand dare seize the fire?

And what shoulder, & what art,
Could twist the sinews of thy heart?
And when thy heart began to beat,
What dread hand? & what dread feet?

What the hammer? what the chain,
In what furnace was thy brain?
What the anvil? what dread grasp,
Dare its deadly terrors clasp!

And when the stars threw down their spears
And water'd heaven with their tears:
Did he smile his work to see?
Did he who made the Lamb make thee?

Tyger! Tyger! burning bright,
In the forests of the night:
What immortal hand or eye,
Dare frame thy fearful symmetry?

As a child some of my favorite books were the now near-classic nonfiction set beginning with *Tell Me Why*. It was the first of a series by Arkady Leokum, followed by *More Tell Me Why,* and *Still More Tell Me Why*. For Christmas three years running I was given the next volume, and I held onto each for a long time, pored through them and their dark pen-and-ink illustrations, until one day I had enough, they suddenly seemed too childish, so I passed them on to a younger friend. A loss, during one of the great purges leading into adulthood, that I later came to regret, along with the emptying of my Led Zeppelin collection and the banishment of white jeans. Happily, I came upon *Tell Me Why* in a friend's bookcase recently, and was thrilled to find it still had the power to fascinate me. Here are samples of its chapter titles, each chapter less than a page or two in length:

Does the air have weight?
Why do we walk in circles when we're lost?
What would happen if there were no dust?
Why is the crow a harmful bird?
Do fish have hearts?
If molecules move, why can't we see things change?
How did music begin?
Is there any group of people who are giants?
Who started short haircuts for men?
Can salamanders live through fire?
Who made the first movie?

The titles alone still have the ability to get me to wonder about things I've never even considered, to excite me with possibility. *Can't* we see things change? What *would* happen if there were no dust? As a child I had never considered the possibility, never really thought about dust at all, beyond the mundane fact that it was my job to dust our house, a chore I came to like: the outline of my mother's eyeglasses on mahogany; how much could gather in a week—the smell of Pledge and Endust still makes me nostalgic. But I had never really considered dust; it just was, everywhere. Embedded in the chapter title is the question of what constitutes dust, what it's made of, where it comes from ("particles of earth light enough to be raised and carried by the wind," according to this chapter). Also implied by the title is the idea that dust can have a function, beyond keeping an eight-year-old busy on a Saturday morning or selling lemon-scented cleaning products. This was when I first learned that without dust there would be no rain, for each raindrop forms itself around a particle of dust (I'd subsequently forgotten this fact, and was grateful to be reminded of it). So there I was, making a connection between something in a book and the chore-filled life I was living. A child begins by mindlessly dusting the living room, moving the dust from the television back into the air, one of the lowliest of household tasks, and that child ends up changing the weather. Rain. A miracle.

Other questions that form the chapter titles I simply liked the sound of, such as Do fish have hearts? or Why is the crow a harmful bird? or Can salamanders live through fire? Beyond where these questions could lead me, there was something about the way they were asked that managed to excite me, and still does. Each question arrives in a different form, using a different syntax, and, of course, the syntax can and must change the meaning, as for example, the difference between Can salamanders live through fire? and Why is the salamander in the fire in the first place? Beyond the syntax, these titles/questions feel open-ended in some way, in that they do not lead to one-word answers, but to more questions, to wondering about the power of wonder, to a journey somewhere unexpected. I don't know the answer to the salamander's fate, but I am made curious about whether or not it will live. Other titles, far from leading us to one-word answers, can lead us into imagining entire narratives, such as Why do we walk in circles when we're lost? which, for me, conjures those moments I've been lost, or just felt that way, and the story that goes along with each moment. These books led me to the possibility of questioning the world, even the simplest parts of it, and considering how to ask the questions and which questions to ask.

❧ Getting Started

The point is not to believe or to express one belief but to live in the contradictions, to live in the questions. Poetry can help us stay awake to the possibilities.

—Mark Doty, *Heaven's Coast*

To begin an inquiry on questions and wonderings we decide, as is often the case with any inquiry, to start by looking closely at literature, at poems. In the first few days of our inquiry we send our students off to the library or to the poetry center in our room, preferably in partnerships, to begin looking for poems with questions in them, with the expectation they will bring their discussions and what they've discovered to our next writing workshop. It will be important in follow-up mini-lessons to listen to some of the poems we've found that have questions in them.

OPEN-ENDED QUESTIONS

Often we need to introduce early on the idea of the ways writers ask questions, and maybe name a few ways questions can be asked, so that as we look at poems we will begin to know what to look for, or what we are looking at. How I usually begin is by telling my students that we are looking for questions that we don't necessarily know the answer to, not those questions where the answer is already clear to us. The reason I begin here is that I've found that many students believe all questions have either one-word answers or only one possible answer. It is important to let them know up-front that these are not the types of questions we are necessarily looking for, and I give an example of the difference between the two, such as the difference between What color is my cat? and Does the cat remember its mother? We then try generating a few of our own examples of open-ended questions, first on a flip-chart as a class, then in partnerships, or on our own.

REINFORCING THE IDEA OF OPEN-ENDED QUESTIONS

During our next writing workshop, often I feel the need to reinforce the previous mini-lesson before introducing a mentor poem. One way I could do this is to make a chart—Simple Questions/Open-Ended Questions—my intention being to simply get my students to focus on the nature and types of questions possible. I point out the difference between asking a question for a science report (What color are the fish?) and asking a question in a poem (Are the fish listening for rain?). In the first one, it is assumed there is one correct answer and that this report will answer it correctly. It is important to remind the students that this is a good skill to work on when we are doing science reports, keeping in mind that in science, too, the truly significant questions are anything but simple. In the second, the question is more open-ended, meant to send our minds into new places, to stretch what we already know, to see something with new eyes. Brainstorming and charting out the difference between the two can clarify this for our students.

The previous mini-lessons are presented as ideas for possible first, introductory steps, which would need to be built on and reinforced later. Depending on how our initial conversations go, once we have assessed how sophisticated our class seems, we may decide to push them a bit faster.

INTRODUCING THE MENTOR POEM

The poem we have chosen for this inquiry is William Blake's "The Tyger," from his *Songs of Experience.* We introduce the class to Blake's poem, as we often do, by reading it out loud to them. We may even do this a week or so in advance of any discussion of it, letting the students know that we are considering it for a mentor poem, that we will be leaving a copy of it in the poetry center if anyone would like to look at it more closely. Students may have already had informal discussions as to what they think of Blake's poem, what image it gives them, what it's about. Only then do we gather and begin looking at it as part of our inquiry into questions and wonderings.

Besides being one of the ten or so most anthologized poems in the English language, "The Tyger" is also a poem that is often taught, or at least once was, and not always to good effect. It is, like many great poems, difficult at times, mysterious in places, and often the teaching around it has fallen to attempts at clarifying these mysteries, or to reducing it to simply an "animal poem." Robert Frost said that a poem should "ride on its own melting," which can be taken as a reference to the mystery and the tension that are necessary for any poem to work. In the mini-lessons that follow I hope we can allow much of that mystery and tension to remain, focusing instead on the various ways poets like Blake fill their poems with questions and wonderings.

NOTICING BLAKE'S QUESTIONS

Since our inquiry is about how authors use questions and wonderings, perhaps a good place to start is with what we notice about Blake's questions. Depending on the class, we might first direct the students to notice something very basic, such as simply counting how many questions they notice, just to get them to begin looking closely at the poem.

In this class, what we notice is that nearly every line in Blake's poem is a question. Most of us have never seen a poem made up entirely of questions, or at least never noticed one. In looking at poems so far, mostly we've found that poets put one or two questions into a poem, if they use questions at all, and then answer those questions, in some way, within the poem. Blake's poem, we notice, seems to ask a series of questions that have no one answer, questions that for some of us don't even make sense. But we all agree that we like the sound of them, and that they give us several images we could sketch out. Though we aren't necessarily looking for answers, one girl says she thinks the answer is "God," especially to the question that makes up the first and last stanzas. But she wonders why Blake doesn't use the word *whose* instead of *what,* as in, "Whose immortal hand or eye." We laugh that there doesn't seem to be one answer for this, and decide to look at all our poems more closely to see how the poets have asked their questions.

DIFFERENT WAYS TO ASK QUESTIONS

If this class had been somewhat further along, we could have begun by looking at the different ways Blake chose to ask his questions, and begun a discussion on why he might have made those decisions. We could have tried to ask a couple of his questions in different ways ("Whose hand got burned?" instead of "What the hand dare seize the fire?") to see if this changed the poem for the better or for the worse. (I would guess that, unless we had a class of poetic geniuses, it would be difficult to improve upon Blake.)

AN ALTERNATIVE BEGINNING: PREDICTING

As a class, before we begin to look closely at questions in poems, we may decide to first make a list of the types of questions we expect to find, and then compare that with what we do find. This could be a good way to assess what our students already know so that, as teachers, we can develop our mini-lessons accordingly.

⟡ *Keeping It Going*

DIRECTING OUR CONVERSATIONS OFF LITERATURE

We are two weeks into our inquiry, and already the idea of questions and wonderings has become the lens through which we are looking at poems, at least for now. We send groups of students out looking for specific types of questions, such as those that ask the same question in several different ways, or poems for two voices that alternate question with answer. Once they have found other examples, the teacher and I direct their conversations into noticing how the poet asked his or her questions, and to speculating on why and what it might mean.

HOW QUESTIONS ARE ASKED

In our next mini-lesson, we look again at "The Tyger," this time to name how Blake asks the questions that make up the poem. We go over the first stanza in front of the group, and decide that the question here could be called a "what could" question. Then we pair off and look at the rest of the poem, naming the types of questions Blake uses. This takes a few minutes, and when most of the class is finished we direct our attention forward again and finish our discussion. One group begins. They've noticed that nearly all the questions are "what" questions—some are "in what," some are "on what," some are "what what," but nearly all use "what" to ask the question. We know from earlier discussions that "what" is only one way a poet can ask a question, and we talk briefly about why Blake might have stuck with only this. We also notice that in the next to last stanza Blake asks "did" questions twice, but then in the last stanza returns to "what" questions. We talk briefly about how those "did" questions feel, if they seem to change the poem, if they stand out. One pair says that the "did" questions feel more direct, as if Blake might actually know the answer to these questions. Before the students leave the group and return to their desks, some of us decide to try rewriting one entry from our notebooks, using mostly one type of question, as we noticed Blake did.

ASK A STRANGE OR FANTASTICAL QUESTION

On another day we choose to look at something else in Blake's poem, this time not so much how he asks his questions but the nature of those questions. In our discussion of them we decide that they are, for the most part, strange and fantastical. What does it mean to "twist the sinews of thy heart"? Why is the "brain" in a "furnace"? Why does it seem that the tiger is being constructed out of metal? We decide that Blake's imagination has allowed him to ask questions that one might not normally ask. We turn to our notebooks to see if we can find an entry where we might ask a strange or fantastical question. We locate several. One boy reads, "Is my brother as strong as a lion or as weak as a dog?" A girl finds this: "Does the sun ever dream of darkness?" Before returning to our writing today, several students decide that the entry they are working on could be made more compelling by asking this type of question of it.

ASK A QUESTION OF SOMETHING THAT CAN'T ANSWER

On another day we notice how Blake seems to be asking his questions of something that cannot necessarily answer him. We decide that he perhaps doesn't expect answers, but that doesn't stop him from asking. Again we return to our writing, to consider if there is something in our notebooks (a river? a dream?), something we would like to ask a question of, something that cannot necessarily answer.

OTHER WAYS TO ASK QUESTIONS

We ask if anyone has found examples of poems that ask a question or questions in ways different than those asked in "The Tyger." We give our students a chance to glance through their folders and have another look at some of the poems they have gathered. In a few minutes several hands go up, and we listen to the poems our students think pose questions differently. The first example is this untitled poem by Pablo Neruda, which a student discovered in Naomi Shihab Nye's anthology *This Same Sky:*

What is it that upsets the volcanoes
that spit fire, cold and rage?

Why wasn't Christopher Columbus
able to discover Spain?

How many questions does a cat have?

Do tears not yet spilled
wait in small lakes?

Or are they invisible rivers
that run toward sadness?

Beyond being moved by Neruda's imagery and language, the student specifically notices that this poem raises a question in each stanza, a question that
isn't answered, but instead seems to open the poem outward into the larger
world. This changes with the last stanza, which seems to answer the one that
comes before it, though not directly. We notice also that Neruda's poem, like
Blake's, is built, line by line, out of questions.

Another student has noticed that some poems ask a question in only the last
line, some of these seem to send us back out into the world to look for the answer ourselves. She found an example in Wang Wei's brief four-line poem
"News of Home." This poem is addressed to someone recently returned from
the poet's hometown, and in the last line he asks longingly whether the fruit
tree outside his window was blooming yet. This example, unlike some of the
others, seems to send us back into the poem to look for the answer. We give
names to what we've noticed, for example, "asks a question in the last line," and
write these names out on a chart, to begin gathering in one place what we're
learning (see the following mini-lessons).

ᑕᕈ *Extending Our Thinking*
LOOKING FOR QUESTIONS IN OUR WRITING

As we gather this morning with our notebooks, the first direction I give the students is to look for entries where they have asked questions, and mark them, either with a Post-it or a colored pencil (or however they've decided to best mark
their entries). We then practice taking some of these questions we have found
and writing them out at the top of a clean page, then writing long (see Chapter
2) off the questions. As the teacher, I have already done this myself in my own
notebook, and I show the class the questions I have written at the top of one of

my clean pages. We end the mini-lesson with a brief discussion of what we've found, listening to a few entries, and then return to our desks to continue writing off our questions.

ASKING QUESTIONS OF OUR ENTRIES

On another day, we ask our students to take an entry from their notebooks, not one that already has a question in it, and come up with some questions to ask. To do this they will need to allow the questions within the entry to naturally arise, and then to practice writing them out. As teachers it is always helpful to model our own writing, to show how we choose an entry in our notebooks, and how we ask questions of it. For example, if I decide to model the entry of the man playing the violin in the subway, some of the questions I might ask include What does the man do when he's not in the subway? Has he ever dreamed of playing with an orchestra? Would I miss him if he were gone?

BEGINNING A CHART

After a few days of searching for poems with questions, as a group we decide to look at five or six examples of poems that ask questions in interesting ways, or that place those questions interestingly within the poem. We begin a chart of what we notice, staying with specific examples from poems in order to hold ourselves accountable, and try to name what the author has done, e.g., an "if" question; a "big wondering"; an "impossible" question.

FILLING OUT THE CHART

We've discovered and named through our reading the different ways poets and writers can ask questions, adding two or three each week to our chart. We decide it is time to look at the chart and maybe try one or two of the strategies in our notebooks. Following is a more complete chart than the one we imagine generated by each class, which should be much shorter so that the students will not be overwhelmed, perhaps simply adding one or two each week for the length of the inquiry. At the top of our chart we put a definition—We are looking for questions we don't know the answer to, or that have more than one answer.

Ways a Poet Might Use Questions and Wonderings

- Use a comparison to ask a question (Is my brother as strong as a lion or as weak as a dog?).

- Ask an "if" question to imagine another possibility (If kids ruled the world . . .?).
- Ask the opposite of what exists (If I didn't have a sister, would I . . .?).
- Ask strange or fantastical questions (If there were no sun . . .? Does the sun ever dream of darkness?).
- Address your subject directly (Can you . . .? Why did you . . .?).
- Ask a question of something that can't answer (a pet, the ocean, a grandmother who has passed on, and so on).
- Ask something big you wonder about (Who named things?).
- Ask something small you wonder about (What else is blue?).
- Ask a question about the future, about the past.
- Ask an obvious question.
- Ask a question the reader knows the answer to.
- Ask the same question in five different ways.
- Start with "Does . . .?"
- Start with "I wonder . . .?"
- Start with "What would happen if . . .?"
- Start with "Without . . .?"
- Start with what you don't know, what you don't remember.
- Start the poem with a question.
- End the poem with a question, circle back.
- Write a poem of all questions (Blake's "The Tyger").
- Write a poem for two voices, where one asks the questions and the other answers (Margolis [1984], "Questions").
- Write a poem that doesn't have a question in it but suggests a question or something you are wondering about.
- Find something you wonder about and turn it into a metaphor (A seeing-eye dog is a blind man's hand).
- Start with a "burning question" you have, and explore it.

WRITING OFF THE CHART

We gather and read over the ways we've charted poets asking questions and articulating wonderings, and ask if there's any item on the list anyone doesn't understand, realizing that they may need a little reminding to refresh their memories. Then we ask them to look in their notebooks at the drafts of the poem they are working on. Are there any items on the list they have already tried? any they think might be good to try? Before returning to their seats today each student commits to trying their draft in another way, to using one of the ways they haven't yet tried.

WRITING LONG OFF ONE ITEM ON THE CHART

Since we don't want our students to simply write out one question and assume they have internalized that strategy, I decide to model how I would attempt to write long off one item. I choose the last item on our chart, "Start with a burning question and explore it." I show them my notebook, within which I have been exploring the image of the man playing the violin in the subway. I tell them I am going to write a new entry on the chart in front of them, starting with a burning question. I write,

> *I wonder where the man goes when he isn't playing his violin?*

I tell them I could end my entry here, but as a writer I know it is better if I push myself to say more. I continue writing:

> *I wonder if he puts the violin back in his case and steps into the open train? Does he ride the train all the way to the end, all the way to Canarsie? Does he then walk down a dark street to his home, which is filled with violins? Does he take out the violin he was playing today and set it gently beside the others? Or does he leave it in his case until tomorrow?*

I write slowly, trying to tell them what I am thinking as I write, what decisions I am making, pointing out that I am trying to stay with this image of the violin player and where he goes when he leaves the subway platform, and trying to explore it by asking one question after another. I ask if there are any questions, then we go back to our desks and make a commitment to push ourselves to write long using one strategy from our chart.

৩৩ *Mini-Inquiry*

GETTING THERE IN PRIMARY GRADES

All of our writing is a process. What this mini-inquiry proposes is that we need to find those students in our primary classrooms who can do what Anika has done (Figure 6.1), that is, stayed with her seed idea long enough for a question to naturally arise from it. The point of this, and any inquiry, isn't merely to test whether our students can name and write questions, but whether they have found a way to naturally integrate wondering and questioning into their writing.

Part 4
How come the seagulls
eat crabs and why can't
crabs eat seagulls

FIGURE 6.1   Anika's poem, asking a question.

PART 4

How come the seagulls
eat crabs and why can't
crabs eat seagulls?

—*Anika, grade 1*

Anika, as we can assume from the heading on her entry, came to this question as part of a process, by going at her seed idea in many different ways. Her first entry was an observation, which she tried to write so that we could see it:

Birds were flying in the air and landing on buildings and birds landing on the ground. Little birds in the park, birds on trees.

In her second entry she added details:

Birds flying in groups, birds eating bread and worms, birds in their nests feeding their baby birds.

In her third entry Anika tells a story of when she saw birds:

When I went to the beach I went with my aunt, and we were watching birds near the sea, birds eating crabs, fighting seagulls flying in groups.

Her fourth entry is the question that begins this mini-inquiry, and she goes on to try two more entries, one a list of where she has seen birds ("birds in trees, birds in the sky, birds in buildings, birds on top of buildings"), and the last another moment when she saw birds ("in Central Park").

This inquiry took place late in the year, and Anika was an exceptional first grader in that she was really able to develop an idea over time. We used her writing to model to the class what was possible, knowing that many of the students would not be able to fill four sheets in their folders staying on one topic as Anika did. During this inquiry we also made sure to celebrate the moves our struggling writers were making, those who went back to their sketches and simply added a question mark.

WONDERINGS

Khaliq, a struggling writer, was big for his age, or at least for his grade. On a spring afternoon I was in the assistant principal's office, preparing for an after-school meeting, and Khaliq was in the office as well, for an unspecified purpose. Khaliq, I must point out, was also unendingly sweet, and gentle, the type of boy you want in your class. He could diffuse trouble, for despite his size his smile was even larger. Khaliq asked me what I was doing, and I asked him how his writing was going. Fine, he said, though he'd lost his writer's notebook, again. I found some paper for him and suggested he write an entry while I did my work, and then he could read it to me. I reminded him he could write something about a moment from his life and that he could write it in a way that we, his readers, could see. We had been working on this in his class already. While I prepared for my meeting, he wrote,

> *Somedays I'm so alone in my house I wonder if my sister will ever come home. I wait in the dark wondering what I should do. Sometimes my mother wonders what I am thinking about, sometimes she asks me what I'm thinking about and I always tell her nothing. I go outside and wonder if I will die or if I will stay alive. I wonder if there are any other people like me.*

He wrote quickly, with his head bent to the desk, on a piece of paper I had found for him. I noticed that he had included several "wonderings" in this entry, which pleased me no end, as this was what we'd been discussing and noticing all week in his class. We had more time in the period, so I suggested he mark a line he thought he could say more about, that he could go into with detail. He picked the line "I wait in the dark wondering what I should do." I gave him another piece of paper and told him to begin his next entry with that line. I watched as he copied it word for word onto the top of the fresh sheet. Again he bent his head to the desk, and wrote,

> *I wait in the dark wondering what I should do. The dark is scary but you get used to it. You start to see things like there is a light in the room. Sometimes I can hear a glass fall but I get used to the sound. I could read a book in the darkness.*

Again he wrote quickly, and showed it to me, and smiled his contagious smile. I read it and shook my head, said, "This is really good writing," and suggested he try it again, that he find another line he could say more about, and that he keep using the wonderings to help him move the writing forward. This time he chose the line "I go outside and wonder."

> *I go outside and wonder if I will see the cops pass by here three times. I wonder if they ever stop. I see a little girl fall off her bike and me careless to pick her up. I hear fire trucks speeding by. I even see ambulances come by and I always wonder if it is for someone in my family, and sometimes I even cry. But I still wonder why did I come outside.*

The period was almost over. I asked Khaliq what he was going to do to write more. He decided to try "lifting a line" one more time, which I agreed was a good idea for him, as this was the most I'd seen him write in one sitting. He chose the line about the girl falling off her bike, because, he said, he could "see it clearly," and wrote,

> *I saw the girl lying there and wondered what I should do. I still ask myself why I didn't do anything. Now I try to tell her I'm sorry but she won't accept my apology. But I know what I'll do if anything like that happens again.*

Khaliq handed me what he'd written in this short period, and I made copies of it all. I told him briefly what I noticed he'd done, how he'd used the tool of wondering and asking questions to push his thinking, and how by the end he'd written something surprising and honest. He nodded and smiled and promised to work on it more.

☙❧

I can imagine the chapter titles Khaliq would write for his edition of *Tell Me Why:* "Where are the ambulances going?" or "Does it hurt to fall off a bike?" or "What happens if you fail to help someone in need?" Maybe if he read the book he would be drawn to the chapter on why people walk in circles when they're lost, or the one about why night follows day. Maybe a book like that could help him with some answers, or maybe he just has to keep writing out the questions for now, and wondering.

We include this example of one student's wonderings in order to show how, as teachers, we shouldn't settle for the first thing a student writes, when he hands us half a page and says, *done.* Khaliq found his subjects through the act of writing, by pushing himself, by allowing his mind to keep wondering.

7

Just Being Enough
WRITING OFF PHOTOGRAPHS

Shirley McPhillips

‿

*In the picture Grandma sat in the
garden swing, looking straight at the
camera with a great smile on her face. . . .
"You look happy," I said.
Grandma nodded and looked at the picture.
"The camera knows," she said.
"The camera knows what?"*

PATRICIA MACLACHLAN,

Journey

PHOTOGRAPH
Cynthia Rylant

He washed his feet for the picture,
even his knees,
and wondered about that man
who cared enough to want him to sit there
for a photograph
even though he didn't have
nothing good to hold in his hands,
nor even a dog to sit by his chair.
It gave him, briefly,
some sort of feeling
of just being
enough.

Growing up along old waterways in the rural South, where winters kept things close to home and summers stretched out in languid heat, anything witnessed, anything overheard, anything enacted, could take narrative flight, usually gaining a plush plumage along the way. These stories were appreciated and re-created at Aunt Ruth's Sunday dinner, at oyster suppers at the Baptist church, at Nelson Fig's general store, on Mom's front porch with a glass of sweet iced tea.

At our family gatherings and ritual events, an impromptu snap of a camera might catch the wisdom in the smile of a matriarch, a pensive longing in the eyes of a child, a shock of surprise in an otherwise stoical face. *Staging* a photograph encouraged expressions of uncharacteristic seriousness or of exaggerated mirth as when someone would call out, "Say 'Robert Redford.'" Whatever the circumstances, photographs freeze-framed our moments, notching them on the memory stick of our family history.

Until my mom passed away three years ago, my sisters, Eve and Phyllis, and I continued to go home to Virginia with our families every holiday, as we had since college. Invariably, on some nostalgic night around the kitchen table, when the story bug would outbite the mosquitoes and the black coffee flowed (strong enough to walk, people said, the way the Powells always like it), one of us would run to the downstairs bedroom closet and bring out the photographs. We kept our family pictures in old shoe boxes. Willy-nilly, all ajumble. Eras and ages bumped up against each other in familiarity and surprise. No attempts at organizing them ever met with anyone's success or satisfaction. No album could contain their number or shape their themes. The best part of storytelling with pictures, after all, is the passing around, studying the backs for blurred names, and sorting out dates; putting heads together around one and pressing each other for the story behind the pose; wondering whatever happened to what's-his-name. The best part is sifting through the pile and slipping out the one that always embarrassed you and you don't want anybody to see ever again; or the contrary, picking out the one that still holds you, that captures that distinctive moment; coming to terms with, yes, you did, once, poof up your hair into an unshakable helmet and, shockingly, the paisley pattern on that too-short dress was once high chic.

The best part about storytelling, both oral and written, but not always the obvious part, is gaining access to ourselves, noticing, as Annie Dillard (in Zinsser 1987) says about a child's growing awareness, that you've been "set down here, mysteriously, in a going world." To the extent that photographs frame fragments of our memory, they can give us access to the stories and subtexts of our lives. They can help a poet take what Virginia Woolf called that "loose drifting material of life" and find another arrangement for it.

In the 1930s renowned photographer Walker Evans documented the effects of the Great Depression. His amazing collection of photographs, now at the Library of Congress, tells the stories of ordinary people during those extraordinary times. In her book *Something Permanent,* Cynthia Rylant adds another dimension to these stories by giving voice to the people living in such severe circumstances. We admire all of Cynthia Rylant's poems in this collection—her straightforward, unsentimental way of taking a handful of words and aiming them straight at our hearts. Several here would fit our purposes for studying poems written off photos. But after reading several together, we choose "Photograph" because we feel connected to the photo of the little boy. There's a sense of intimacy between the poem's narrator and the boy that the teacher and I think will help open up possibilities for students to think about their own lives as they write.

We want to say at the outset that, clearly, many of this chapter's mini-lessons hinge on students bringing in photographs from home. We are often in classrooms, however, where a number of students live in shelters for the homeless or in circumstances in which cameras and photographs are not available. If this is the case, you will want to think about how you will handle this. Naturally, we would want every student to feel as invested as possible in the inquiry.

In classes where Nick and I have worked on writing off photographs, teachers keep a folder or basket on hand of black-and-white and color pictures, postcards, and collections of newspapers and magazines, for students without their own photos to peruse and select from. Often a newspaper or magazine picture can strike an emotional chord, provoke a response, or remind us of something in our own lives. *We talk about the fact that Cynthia Rylant's poems in* Something Permanent, *including the mentor poem, were written off someone else's photos;* she used them to interpret and bring life to, in her own way, a particular time in the past.

We notice, too, that even in stark circumstances, it is possible that a family will have saved and cherished photographs. Some will not. Some may have postcard pictures they can use from friends and relatives in another country. (Appendix C lists A Short Photography Bookshelf of books of photos with poems or books with photos as a focus.)

ᇰ&ᓹ *Getting Started*

ORIENTING OURSELVES TO THE MENTOR POEM

Gathered in the meeting area, we begin by looking through *Something Permanent* and talking about what we notice, getting a visual sense of the territory that has intrigued Cynthia Rylant. Since this is a collection of pieces meant to capture the life and concerns of people in a certain time, we don't want to go straight to the mentor poem as if it stood alone. We talk about the Great Depression. I read aloud a few carefully chosen poems from the collection, the mentor poem among them. We listen to the poet-as-narrator giving voice to the people. Reading several poems gives us more of a sense of Cynthia Rylant's way of writing, her style, as well as how she uses that narrator voice to "get inside" her characters.

This seems to be enough for today. The class is not studying the Great Depression, and it's not our goal to spend a lot of time on that. Today, we just want to give students a context around the photo that accompanies our mentor poem, a sense of the larger story of which these poems are a part.

If we didn't have a copy of the book, we could still talk about the Great Depression and how Cynthia Rylant, as poets sometimes do, became fascinated with a particular time or with what it evoked within her as she looked at Walker Evans's photographs—how perhaps, as a poet, she felt that urge to "give voice" to the people in the photographs. And then we would move closer to the mentor poem.

HEARING THE VOICE OF THE POEM

The teacher has printed the poem "Photograph" on a chart, so students have read it over and talked informally about it during the week. Nick and I always read over a poem several times in preparation for talking to the children. Each time we do, and each time we talk with them thereafter, we make new connections, have new insights, as we hope students will when they reread. After hearing some of what they're thinking about the poem, I read it aloud, slowly but naturally, giving the lines their due. I tell the students that I have to read a poem more than once in order to take it in, to savor it and get started thinking about it. "I'll slow it down now," I might say. Or, "I need to hear this again. I'm getting a picture in my mind." Or, "Let's listen again. . . . What do we notice? What do we think?"

We see, for example, that "Photograph," like all the poems in Rylant's book, is told in the third person, seemingly from the point of view of someone in a position to imagine and understand the boy's thoughts and feelings. "We know that Cynthia Rylant wrote this poem," Scott says. "It sounds like she knew all these people." We notice that the narrator uses words and phrases in the style we imagine people from that region (the mountains of West Virginia) and time might use: "He didn't have nothing good to hold in his hands."

Students are intrigued by the voice of the poem, the idea of a "person" looking on, so the teacher suggests the students look through some other mentor poems to notice whose voice they hear (see Chapter 9). Someone suggests they look back at Cynthia Rylant's book *Appalachia: The Voices of Sleeping Birds* to see if the people in that book speak like the narrator in this poem, or if the music of the lines sounds "regional." They will also look at drafts of their own poems for voice.

ORIENTING OURSELVES TO THE PHOTO

As the students talk about the poem, they can't help but look at the photograph accompanying it—a small, barefoot boy sitting rather casually on the edge of a straight-backed chair, staring straight-faced at the camera with a hint of wistfulness in his expression. Even in this stark room, a combination of rough wood and pasteboard-box walls and advertisement wallpaper—Armour's Cloverbloom Butter, a smiling model in a silky slim dress, Santa Claus—there are brave attempts at beauty: a white crocheted table runner, Mason jars on the table, a rectangular mirror hanging from a nail, a cow figurine. The title Walker Evans gives this photo is "Inside a miner's shack: Morgantown, West Virginia."

We wonder what a little country boy, living in such simple circumstances, must make of this stranger who has come to his home and asked him to sit for the photograph. In the poem, the man wanted a picture of *him* even though he "didn't have nothing" but himself to offer. We talk about how the poet's words, in capturing this personal moment up close, also capture, for us, a more universal feeling of everyone's need for recognition; for a sense of worth, of identity, of being "set down here . . . in a going world," however briefly.

SPECULATING ON
CYNTHIA RYLANT'S PHOTO CHOICES

Before asking the students to start bringing in their own photos, we want them to think about why someone would choose one over another—what a photo might represent that would inspire us to write off it. So we speculate about Cynthia Rylant's choices. She must have looked at dozens of Walker Evans's photographs of the Great Depression. There are hundreds in the collection housed at the Library of Congress. Why did certain ones stand out to her? How did she connect herself to a photo in such a way that she could write off it? We imagine that to want to write off the photos, Rylant would have to feel a strong connection to the times, an empathy and admiration for the people.

Together, we look between the poem "Photograph" and the photo. Mark says he thinks Ms. Rylant feels respect and caring for this little boy who is living and surviving in hard times. Stephanie says maybe she sees something of herself in the little boy: "In *But I'll Be Back Again,* we read that when she was four her mother left her at her grandmother's in West Virginia. That's where these pictures were taken. It probably reminds her of how she felt."

We turn to the Author's Note at the back of the book, where Rylant indicates that she knows and admires Evans's work. Perhaps she even read his book *Let Us Now Praise Famous Men,* in which he collaborated with writer James Agee to document rural tenant families. So this research and perhaps her personal experiences growing up in Appalachia, we think, give her a sensibility out of which to work, a desire to give voice to the people in the photographs.

CHOOSING OUR OWN PHOTOS

Every time I
looked at the
picture I
thought how I
should have
kissed her, so
finally I hid it
in the attic
& I wonder
if it's still there
with us both so
young & her
waiting to be kissed

—Brian Andreas, "Waiting to Be Kissed," in *Story People*

Next day, we continue our discussion about choosing photos, our own. We read Brian Andreas's poem "Waiting to Be Kissed" and talk about how some pictures invite us to look at them again and again. They take us to another time, another place. They make us remember and ask questions. I've brought a photo like this. I show the children a picture of my son, Sean, and husband, Edward, sitting on the piano bench in the living room. In this photo Sean has his arm draped loosely around his dad's neck, their heads drawn tightly together. Unlike their usual offhanded, humorous demeanor together, both have serious, pensive expressions. This picture represents a brief yet treasured moment just before my son left for college. Looking at it brings back the sharp anxiety of waiting for acceptances, as well as the understanding that soon our only child would be gone. Years after that picture was taken, I can still feel the emotional pangs of that moment.

We will want children to feel a connection, for whatever reason, to the pictures or photos they will write off, too. And we will want them talking to each other about what those connections and attachments are. We ask them to look around at home for photos, in frames, or in albums, or like mine, in shoe boxes.

Perhaps they will talk to their parents and other relatives about ones that seem interesting to them. Then they will pick two or three and start thinking about what they know about the time, circumstances, people in them.

Some teachers and students write letters home explaining to parents the nature of our inquiry, assuring them the photos will be well cared for in the classroom. We put our supplemental collection in special bins and baskets so that students who might not be able to bring in their own will feel comfortable in looking through these.

ℰ𝒩 *Keeping It Going*

USING PHOTOGRAPHS TO AWAKEN OUR MEMORIES:
TELLING OUR STORIES IN THE MOMENT

Photographs demand that stories be told around them.

—Georgia Heard, *Writing Toward Home*

In Chapter 2, Nick quotes Toni Morrison: "The image comes first and tells me what the 'memory' is about." While she is referring to mental images, we can help students activate a sense of "remembering" through looking closely at photographic images and telling and writing the stories they hold. These stories, the particulars of them, are material out of which poems can come.

In whatever way we have decided to launch our work with photographs toward poetry (e.g., by reading poems with photos from some of the books we mention in Appendix C, by bringing our own photos and telling stories off them, by a mini-inquiry, by talking about images), we will have gotten the students looking closely at pictures in class and searching at home for photographs.

When I arrive next, I ask the students to join me in the meeting area. Holding my picture of Grandpa and me on the porch swing, I tell the story it makes me think of. First, I look at it quietly, deciding how I will begin, finding my "storyteller's voice," as if it were happening now, in the moment. I might back up a bit and get a running start:

It's a hot summer day. Grandma has just shooed us out of the kitchen so she can finish the cookies in peace. We are sitting on the porch in a swing that Grandpa painted green. It's so shiny and wet-looking, I half expect my legs to stick to it. I am looking up at Grandpa as he looks out across the dry cornfield. I think he is worried that it hasn't rained in so long. I am wondering when he will say we can go in for the pineapple ice cream we made this morning, and Grandma's cookies. He pushes his house slippers against the porch floor to give the swing a gentle back-

and-forth rhythm. His big barn boots sit on the steps; they're not allowed in. A combination of the hot no-breeze day, the rocking of the swing, and Grandpa's silent staring eyes, make me feel like I am dreaming. I love these days that seem to go on forever.

Perhaps instead of, or in addition to, my brief story, I'll ask a student to sit next to me with his photo and try just the beginning of his story, finding his storyteller's voice. This will give everyone a better idea of the stance they'll be taking, how it sounds, when they tell their stories to each other. Students get their selected pictures and go off with partners. (If it's a picture from our class basket or folder, they can let that evoke an image or story.) They're quiet for a bit, thinking how they will begin. The teacher and I circulate, noticing who is slowing the story down, thinking along the way, looking around in the story, rather than glossing over the surface quickly. For many students, storytelling does not come easily at first. It requires practice. We ask one or two storytellers to demonstrate at sharing time or to be part of tomorrow's mini-lesson.

For homework and for a few days to come, students will continue to tell stories off their pictures and do some jotting of these "in the moment" stories in their notebooks.

THE REAL STORY

I think of the invisible pictures between the pictures, and under them. . . . Where are all those days no one took a picture of?

—Naomi Shihab Nye, *Words Under the Words*

Naomi Nye's question gets us thinking about the fact that the *real story* is not necessarily what we see in the photo. When we read over "Photograph," a little boy is having his picture taken. But Cynthia Rylant alludes to his living conditions, what he wondered about, how he felt. So much life, so many pictures invisible to us. People often pose for photos; colors are heightened; or right outside the frame another part of the story is happening that can be very different from what we might think as we look at the photo. Sometimes the photographer acts as a "director," telling people how to stand or group themselves or even who to look at and when to smile. If the picture is impromptu, not arranged, the image can be more natural, but even then the photographer has chosen what to snap, at what moment, at what angle, with what focus, thereby naturally editorializing the image. The lens can catch a sense of something intangible—a touch of sadness, stark terror, dreaminess, solitude, celebration—and with the sensitivities the viewer brings to it, can suggest a powerful story.

I show the writers a black-and-white photo from an ongoing series in the *New York Times Magazine* called What They Were Thinking (Figure 7.1).

FIGURE 7.1   The story behind the photograph. Sam Nixon and his
grandfather Fred Brown (*New York Times Magazine,* May 9,
1999).

Nicholas Nixon took the photograph of his son and father. Here, we see a young
boy, Sam Nixon, and his grandfather fiercely hugging each other, their arms so
wrapped you can only tell whose arms are whose by the dark and light colors of
their sweaters. The boy is bigger than the old man, and only his face is visible,
the man's being pressed into the folds of the boy's baggy sweater. We can see the
tip of his grandfather's hand, white with pressing hard into Sam's back. The
boy's eyes are dreamily slanted, almost closed, and he is smiling. When we first
look at the picture, students say things like, "They aren't afraid to show their
feelings to each other." "I think they love each other and like doing things together a lot." "They're very close." In the margin, Sam's words:

Opa was alone. He's getting old and lonely and stuff, so my father and I went to stay for three days. There's not a lot of things I feel like I have in common with my grandparents, so it's kind of hard. Grandpa's got a real nice house and deer in the yard. They have a club. They're pretty well off, and they do stuff like have cocktails on the patio. We don't really do that. So there's a big difference between our world and his. I don't know if that's good or bad. We don't hug a lot, but it was nice when it happened. I love my grandfather, and I don't get to show it that much.

Over the next several days, students meet in pairs to tell and then write a real story their photos may not show. They try to use a conversational tone, as Sam Nixon does. We mention that even photos without people in them have stories behind them. After all, someone took the picture with something in mind.

TAKING IT LINE BY LINE, LOOKING AT STRUCTURE

We don't want to wait too long before returning to our mentor poem. So as writers are storytelling and beginning to write off their photos during writing workshop, we like to have them go back and take the poem line by line. We reread the poem together and ask such questions as, Where did Cynthia Rylant's eye alight? How does she begin? What is she doing next? What in the photo might have inspired her to write this part? How did she write this? what words? what tone? What image does that give me? How does it end?

We notice that in Evans's photograph, the little boy is in light. Rylant, too, focuses on the boy in her poem. In a handful of words, she gives us a feeling for the boy and something of the conditions and times in which he lives. To do this, her eye is drawn to parts of his body that display his condition—his feet, his knees, the wonderment behind his eyes, his hands—and evoke his attitude, his inner thoughts.

To begin her poem, Rylant backs up a moment to say how he prepared for the sitting: "He washed his feet for the picture." It is a telling detail that what seems so scant a gesture to us might have meant, to him, making a special effort, using precious water to get all spruced up—"his feet . . . even his knees." While we might feel sad that he has no shoes this day, maybe strong, clean feet were worthy of showing. "Maybe he has shoes," Jerome says, "but he has to save them for even more special occasions than this." We think his eyes show a kind of wanting to please, a touch of pride.

Then, it's as if the narrator thinks about what must have been in this boy's mind when, in the middle of all this scarcity and isolation, some nice stranger wants a keepsake of him and his surroundings; he wonders about "that man who cared enough." The boy's hands seem oddly placed to us, one flat on half of the seat next to him in a space big enough for someone or something else to have sat, as if something's missing, the other hand looking uneasily placed in his pocket. He seems self-conscious. Then, the narrator tells us, using the local vernacular here, "He didn't have nothing good to hold in his hands, / nor even a dog," a sad circumstance for a country boy.

In the end, she writes a speculative statement that seems to sum up how the boy feels, that despite having "nothing good" to show or hold onto, he feels that for a brief moment, he is of worth.

The teacher writes up the structure we have articulated so that later, when we begin writing more off our own photos, we can return and try out aspects of it. These are the words we come up with. You and your students can come up with different ones.

How We Name Cynthia Rylant's Poem Structure

- **Backs up a moment**
  Before the camera snaps, says what the character did before the picture was taken.
- **Internal thought**
  Character wonders about the photographer and why he wants a picture of him.
- **Details**
  Two things the character lacks, which makes him wonder why the photographer is interested in him.
- **Speculation**
  Character thinks maybe photographer really finds something interesting about him.

WRITING IN THE THIRD PERSON

We have noticed that Cynthia Rylant writes in the third person. Yet she is clearly invested in what she sees, in the story behind it, in the child. I show the writers how I might look at the photo of Sean and his dad on the piano bench (mentioned earlier). I am outside the photo, I say, but I am not outside their experience, their lives. I stand back but I am involved and invested in them, in their hopes and dreams. Thinking out loud, I choose to write about Sean. Then, on a chart or overhead, I just start listing phrases with the word *he* or *his*. And, using what I know about the circumstances and issues going on in our lives at that time, I write and talk out loud about things as I remember them.

> *I write:* He only has minutes these days to sit still for his parents.
> *I say:* But they caught him running out the door for a snapshot or two before he leaves for college.

I write: It's not that he doesn't want to spend some time with his dad, but right now there are too many big questions.

I say: And getting too close might mean being cornered into having to talk seriously about them.

I write: His arm doesn't hold on tight, he hangs it around Dad's neck.

I say: Not to imply there's nothing deep here between them but just the opposite, we're old buddies, right, Dad? No problem. Hurry, Mom. Gotta go.

Looking at my list, Elijah says, "Sometimes I'm like that. I think of ways not to have to talk to my parents if there's something I'm afraid of or if I think they can't handle it."

With a copy of the mentor poem at hand, and their chosen photograph or picture, students try listing in their notebooks using *he* or *she*. As the teacher and I circulate, we notice that sometimes the lists turn out to be short, sort of isolated or unrelated items. Sometimes, as in my list, the writers find themselves forgetting the list and taking off with an idea, stretching the idea, staying in the thought, exploring it a bit further before moving on. If this kind of extending doesn't happen, I sometimes suggest that the writer pick something from the list and write off just that, staying with it, thinking more about it.

When we share each other's attempts at the end of workshop and next day, the writers notice that already there are hints of ideas to pursue further another time. Benny shares his list of sentences in the third person:

His g. grandfather can't hear.
He is scared to get any closer.
They keep saying to come closer.
He can't think of anything to say.
He tries to smile.
He can see red lines in g.g.'s face.

We learn that writing in the third person can put a certain distance between us and the story, the people, the issues, and open up new possibilities and perspectives. When we confer with Benny, we read his lines out loud. We want to linger, to hear their sound. It's an amazing list, we say. He tells us a bit more of the context around these lines, the story. We ask him which parts of what he has written seem to bubble up, make his heart beat a little faster when we read them, places where he knows there's something big there. He checks the second and fourth lines, identifying the essence of what he is feeling. We tell Benny we get more of a picture, too, when he gets up close in the last line with exactly what he sees. We look back at how Rylant does that. Then we leave him to "zoom in" on his great-grandfather, to give us more of an image of him using some other details, and perhaps to intersperse what he observes with what he, as narrator now, is thinking inside (putting the *external* of what is happening next to the *internal* of what he is thinking at the same time), the way Rylant does.

It's interesting when the writer is the same person as in the photo. Flipping to the third person can result in that distancing we mentioned before. And if the photo is a scene with no person in it, I show students how it's still possible to write off it in the third person by talking about the *he* or *she* who was once there, wishes to be there (or not), or *is* there, just outside the frame, the one who took this picture.

TRYING OUT THE WRITER'S STRUCTURE

Now that we have the feel of what it's like to write in the third person like Cynthia Rylant, I show the writers how I might, with the same photo of Sean and his dad, decide to try out the structure that we thought Cynthia Rylant used when we read her poem line by line. We look back at the chart we made listing the structure (mini-lesson Taking It Line by Line). Beginning with the word *he,* (for Sean or for his dad), I back up and write what was happening just before the photo, the preparation; then what he may have been thinking or wondering, using a few details; then a speculation, what thoughts or feelings I imagine he may have come to in the end.

With the mentor poem next to them and something from their fleshed-out third-person lists or from other writing in their notebooks, some writers try Cynthia Rylant's structure, as we named it. Afterward, we share and post a few examples so that we can see the different ways people adapted her structure to their work.

Benny wants to try the structure loosely, using his list of third-person sentences about his great-grandfather:

- **Benny backs up a moment**
  He put on his Yankee shirt for the party.
- **Benny's internal thoughts**
  But his g. grandfather can't hear. Can't see too well.
  They keep saying to come closer.
  He wonders why g. grandfather pulls him.
- **Benny's details**
  He is scared.
  He can't think of anything to say.
  He smiles in a fake way.
- **Benny's speculation**
  Maybe it's OK to hold his hand.
  He has nice eyes.

We celebrate Benny's wonderful efforts at trying on Rylant's poem structure, as we named it. He has an exciting list. We say that between this and his other work on stretching the image, he has lots of possibilities for a draft.

In another class, working out his own structure, drawing on several entries and attempts in his notebook at first and third person, David first writes as if talking to the character (his grandma). Toward the middle, he shifts his stance to third person, stepping out of the poem as if to speak to us, the readers. Then back to grandma, ending in a combination of the two, alternating. It is an intriguing poem and a deeply moving tribute:

CARDINAL IN THE SKY

I never met you, but I love you.
Whenever we talk about you,
　　you appear as a bird,
　　a red bird of love.

Grandma, is that you?

I never met you, but I see you.
I see you all the time.
My shadow lurks and is always
　　following me.

Grandma, is that you?

I never met you, but I wish I did.
I wish that you could kiss me with your
　　smooth lips just once more.

She believed that after she died she would
be reborn like a flower.
It dies in the winter,
then is reborn in the spring,
so that she could always watch over me.

I know that you'll never leave me.
You'll always be flying over me,
　　free.

I met you, but I don't remember you.
I don't remember your blue eyes or red, red hair.
I've seen you, but I can't picture you,
　　all alone waiting.

When I follow the path of my life
back through time there is
　　one moment I remember.

An aged lady in a wheelchair holding a baby.
She looks so happy and I know who she is,
   my grandmother.

She'll never leave me.
When we lost you,
we lost part of our souls.

See Appendix B for a transcript of a writing conference with Sara Scott that looks at structure to study how former U.S. Poet Laureate Rita Dove meshes observations and feelings in her poem "Fifth Grade Autobiography," from *Grace Notes.*

ଚ୨ *Extending Our Thinking*
OTHER WAYS TO AWAKEN OUR MEMORIES

There are many ways to begin activating memories and starting to write off photographs or other pictures, toward poetry. Teachers can't do them all. Certainly we cannot use them all in any one classroom. Here, we talk about some other ways we've found helpful to get students generating and thinking more deeply off their photos. Some of them (e.g., Writing Word Sketches, Zooming in Close) can work well for any picture that triggers a response or connection for a student. A teacher's time frame, consistency of writing workshop time, the enthusiasm and needs of both the students and the teacher will help dictate which mini-lessons might work best.

I REMEMBER . . .

*What did we ever plant?" my father asks, forty springs later, staring
hard at the photograph.
"Tomatoes," I say. "We must have
planted tomatoes too. Let's ask Mom. She'll remember."*

—Naomi Shihab Nye, *Words Under the Words*

We talk to the class about the fact that photographs don't just hold one story. Looking at my photo, I start with "I remember," stretching my mind to recall, quickly, another story, three stories, five stories:

  I remember how Grandpa wore his big barn boots everywhere, except in
    Grandma's house.

I remember that Grandpa didn't talk much around people, but he did to his
   dog, Sally.
I remember how I looked forward to sitting on the porch with them after
   supper, playing "I spy," way after dark, and how they didn't keep telling
   me it was time for bed like my mom always did back home.
I remember Grandma teaching me to make chocolate chip cookies early in
   the morning while it was cool, and how she let me serve them with
   lemonade, as if I had done it all.
I remember that Grandma smelled like lavender flowers she grew in her
   herb garden and Grandpa smelled like the barn at lunchtime and Old
   Spice aftershave on Sundays.

I list some of these memories in short phrases on the flip-chart or overhead pro-
jector, then put a star beside one I want to tell to someone.

During writing workshop, students do the same thing, studying their photo
to find other memories hidden within it, making lists of these in their notebooks. We come back to the meeting area to share our lists with each other.

WRITING WORD SKETCHES

Another way to get up close to a photo and get some early short writing going is
to take a *tour of the photo.* I show the writers how I might start someplace in the
picture and work my way around it (or I jump around the picture in any direction) writing short *word sketches* (a three-to-six-word image) on the chart of what
I see:

   Stiff white neck
   Arm dangling carefree
   Bony twigs reaching
   Blurred raft of chrysanthemums
   Rough bench where Rusty usually sits

Writing word sketches can help us observe and write what we see in more particular and surprising ways.

After watching me at the chart, writers try their hand at writing word
sketches off their photos. At sharing time, students can read out some phrases
from their notebooks that they especially like. We might jot some on the chart
and talk about such things as how the words sit next to each other, or what that
sketch reveals to us about the person or the memory.

WRITING OFF PHOTOGRAPHS TO ELABORATE
OR EXTEND OUR IDEAS

Once we have awakened some of our memories, we need to dig a little deeper, to find other avenues of possibility. The following mini-lessons are suggestions for helping writers use photographs to elaborate or extend their ideas. Often these are the kinds of tryouts that can result in edging away from writing just the *happenings* to more particular writing, to a narrowing of the focus, to a deeper meaning. We can get students trying one or two and then let these serve as options for the work they are doing in writing workshop.

THEN AND NOW

Another way we can get students to move away from considering just what's in the photo, to dig a little deeper, is to ask them to think about it across time. In one class, we talk about how a photograph focuses our attention on a moment *back then.* I start by drawing a line down the middle of the chart paper to make a split page and asking a student to come up with his/her photo and help me teach. Or I can use my own photo. In the first column we list what we notice, what we think about the people, place, or event *then.* In the other column, we write what we think is true *now.* If it seems appropriate, we can talk about the in-between, milestones on the journey from then to now.

When the writers try this out, some of them find words that suit them better, such as, "I used to . . . but now . . ." or "Once I . . . but today . . ." Some writers don't use those time words at all, preferring to take the column jottings and mesh them in different ways. We want this inventiveness, this attitude of playfulness that just may, at some point, take a leap into a poem.

These are not just "cute" imaginative lessons. When students stretch their memory across time or find the "story behind the story," it allows them to explore not just what they see, but feelings or issues that may lie under the surface. They can make personal connections, and possibly begin to find a voice of their own.

ZOOMING IN CLOSE

Students join us in the meeting area with one of their photos or pictures. We look again at Walker Evans's photograph. Of all the things in this simple room, we are drawn to the little boy in the chair—his hands, his feet, his face in light, his eyes, his slight smile. Cynthia Rylant has *zoomed in* on him, too, in her poem, coming up close to him in one moment, charging us with the poignancy of his part in this story. We ask the students to zoom in close on some part of their photograph that seems interesting or calls to them in some way. Maybe it's a *fa-*

cial feature—the hands, the eyes. Maybe it's an *object*—the ring, the chair. Maybe it's a *point of action* or an *attitude*—the drape of the arm, the reflection in the pond, the blur of the landing bird. I remind them of how I am drawn to Grandpa's tall barn boots, for example. I can picture him in them. They symbolize so much about his life, about my feeling for him.

As a matter of fact, Cynthia Rylant has a poem in this collection called "Shoes," which could be another example. All the poems in *Something Permanent* have one-word titles: "Utensils," "Walls," "Signs," "Grave." Walker Evans gets up close in his photographs, finding the most significant part of a situation, a scene, for him. Within that, Cynthia Rylant finds her most significant places. Sometimes we tell the writers to make a small circle using their thumb and forefinger, or we give them a small square paper frame, and ask them to bring it in close to the photo on a part they want to focus on. Framing can help them shut out surrounding bits and focus their attention.

During the week, writers try their hand at staying with the focus, giving as many particular details as they can. To start, they ask themselves, What do I notice? What is this making me think, wonder about? What surprises me here? To write, they can try some of the same strategies we've used in other mini-lessons (e.g., Writing Word Sketches, Then and Now), except now they're being applied to the close-up.

EXPLORING THE CONTRASTS

I used to dream of having a loose-leaf life (as opposed to a spiral notebook kind of life) and guessed those old black-and-white photographs must have heard me.

—Naomi Shihab Nye, *Words Under the Words*

By now the students have noticed that the photo inspiring our mentor poem in *Something Permanent,* and some of our own photographs and pictures, are *black-and-white.* One day, we look at the black-and-whites more closely and talk about our reactions to them, how they are different from color photos or pictures. We study one together, a magazine picture showing a collection of old bottles on a windowsill, the early light of morning touching tiled French rooftops in the distance. We notice that without color, the contrasts seem sharpened—vivid light, deep dark, multiple shades of gray in between. If we keep looking, we can begin to forget that we are looking at bottles and look for the interesting effects, the abstract shapes of shadow and light. I tell the students the story about my oil painting teacher who, in trying to show me how to "read" the folds of a white tablecloth that I was trying to paint, said, "You will notice that white in shadow can be darker than black in light." My brain found it almost impossible to release the grip of primitive notions about black and white until I saw the shades as they were, as if I weren't looking at folds of material. I forced myself to paint what I saw, as dark or as light as it appeared, as each sat next to the other, not what I was accustomed to seeing in my mind's eye. The result was an illusion of folded cloth.

Naomi Nye says she likes to, on occasion, write off a black-and-white photo. Her husband, Michael, is a photographer and takes pictures in black-and-white, as he did for their anthology *What Have You Lost?* She says they seem "more real" to her somehow and at the same time more abstract. The teacher and I can remember some films that seem so right in black-and-white: *Citizen Kane, Schindler's List.* We mention the contrast of the black-and-white flashbacks in films like *JFK.* Students remember a book in their classroom library called *When I Was Little,* by Toyomi Igus, about a boy and his granddad fishing. The granddad's past stories about "how it used to be" become black-and-white flashback illustrations within the present-day colored ones. It's an effective technique for contrasting the times.

Some of the writers want to dig back into the family "archives" for a black-and-white photo or find one that interests them in a newspaper, magazine, or in our basket of pictures. How is it different to look at? What in it seems most "real?" What is the reality? Where is the drama? They can try some of the same strategies on this picture that we used to write off a color picture.

ENTERING THE PHOTOGRAPH

In his book *Crafting a Life in Essay, Story, Poem,* Donald Murray talks about entering into a subject and going "as far and deep as you have the courage to go." He is looking at photographs from a book about World War I. As he does this, he feels himself "entering a photograph." Here are a few excerpted lines:

> I am 19-years-old when I join the line of soldiers
> in the photograph. We are quiet. No songs
> just the muffled clatter of guns, mess kits,
> grenades, bayonets; the sucking sound
> boots lifting up from muck. . . . The village is larger
> than I remember. The fields stretch longer
> to the horizon. A horse circles in a field,
> dragging a one-man plow. The clouds are dark,
> still boiling, but it is not thunder we hear . . .

During workshop, I work with a small group of students who want to look closely at their photographs (and maybe put together a small collection of photographs around the same time, event, interest). I ask them to imagine, as did Murray, themselves entering the photo, becoming part of the environment, the mood, the energy of what's happening. What's going on? What do I see, feel?

What does this make me think, wonder, ask? What does this make me want to say? After I give them six minutes or so just to get started, some of us read aloud our early attempts. As one reads, the rest of us try to conjure up the image in our minds, to see if we can see, feel, imagine what it's like, along with the writer. We tell the writer what we see and feel. We ask each writer what it was like to "enter" the photo. The writers continue for homework and during writing time for a day or two.

ᎶᏅ *Mini-Inquiry*

What role do photographs play in our lives? In some classes, the teacher and I decide to edge into the photo work with a short class mini-inquiry. We gather the students and say that while we are rereading and looking more closely at our mentor poem, it might be fascinating to get us all noticing the role that photographs play in our lives. We will do this mini-inquiry over a few days, gathering photographs and beginning to talk about how they safeguard moments across time. Getting conversation and enthusiasm going around the photographs also prepares us to select some we will want to work with more closely.

For homework, we decide to look around the house. What photos do we surround ourselves with? Where are they placed? Which ones are framed, and how? Are there albums? big ones? small showcases around themes? shoe boxes? Are there few photos? none?

Over the next few days, we share our findings and stories connected with them. I tell the class that in my house some photos are of family members and friends, framed and sitting around on tables and shelves. Most are in drawers and boxes. When I was growing up, my mom had gold-framed photos of family members on every available surface—on the piano top, young and old mingled in various stages of growth. You could trace the eras through hairstyles, jewelry, makeup, clothing, and types of poses and expressions. People visiting our house stood before the piano as if in a gallery. My mom's photo arrangements were quite unlike those of a friend who devotes his entire basement to baseball memorabilia—his passion, the New York Yankees. Walls, cases, albums are carefully organized with photographs of the team through the years—favorite players, memorable plays, famous managers, himself at the games posing with his idols. Mine is a casual continuation of the shoe box legacy; his is a systematic, organized display about a deep passion.

We continue our inquiry over several days, the students interviewing their parents and relatives about the role of photos in their lives. What photos do we keep near us, on the bedside stand, in our pocketbook, or in a special drawer? I tell them my husband keeps a much-sat-upon photograph of a very young me, with 1970s juice-can-straightened hair, in his wallet. I found out recently, much to my quiet alarm, that he actually shows it to people when they ask (or don't ask) about his family. I think there are several stories here!

Some students and the teacher bring in photos or albums. We ask questions such as, Who took most of the photos? Why? Which ones did *we* take? Who's in the pictures? Who is hardly ever to be found? I tell the story about my sister Eve, who studied photography and has a fancy Leica camera with telephoto lens, but won't be caught in a picture herself. When she sees one in the old shoe box or a sneaked one of her in the pile from Christmas that she doesn't like, she slips it out and rips it up without compunction. It's her image and she'll display it, or not, her way! The rest of us sigh at the loss; we want to keep her image, no matter what she thinks it reveals.

My brother, George, liked taking pictures of panoramic scenes—long-range mountain peaks, color-splashed hillsides, shoals and inlets along the Rappahannock River that he knew as a boy. People looking at his photos, however, sometimes complained that it was just too much sustained beauty, that they couldn't tell what the point was without people in them. For him, a keepsake view of his significant places was enough. He could remember or imagine the rest.

Recently my nephew called to ask for some of our photographs from the old shoe box: his dad growing up. He wants to study the images of the boy he never knew as a man, now lost to him. Photographs set us down in a going world. We pause, to gaze again, from time to time, and catch sight of what we have found, what we have lost, what will outlive us.

8

A Story That Could Be True

TIME

Nick Flynn

"Eternity," Blake said, "is in love with the productions of time."
Perhaps, in fact, eternity inheres in the things that time makes;
perhaps that's all of eternity we'll know: the wave, the flower,
the repeated endless glimmerings and departures of tides.

MARK DOTY,

Heaven's Coast

A STORY THAT COULD BE TRUE
William Stafford

If you were exchanged in the cradle and
your real mother died
without ever telling the story
then no one knows your name,
and somewhere in the world
your father is lost and needs you
but you are far away.

He can never find
how true you are, how ready.
When the great wind comes
and the robberies of the rain
you stand on the corner shivering.
The people who go by—
you wonder at their calm.

They miss the whisper that runs
any day in your mind,
"Who are you really, wanderer?"
and the answer you have to give
no matter how dark and cold
the world around you is:
"Maybe I'm a king."

Think of those few minutes when you first arrive at the movie theater, before the previews have begun, and you're chatting with whomever you came with, and at a certain point the lights begin to dim, almost imperceptibly at first, and it seems to take a long time; your friend may be in the middle of telling you about her hard day and you can't tell if she's noticed, you don't want to interrupt her and you can't tell yet if it's really happening, if the light is really leaving the room, or if it's just your eyes playing tricks; you glance around and no one else seems to notice, and then, yes, the room is definitely growing dimmer and the whole theater slowly comes to a hush and turns as one toward the plush red curtains that are meant to suggest that the movie has been going on behind them all this time, just awaiting the right moment to open. As the curtains part and the screen brightens you can almost convince yourself that you're looking into the future, even though you know that the light comes from behind your head, even though you know that the movie exists in the past, was created in the past, as an event that has already happened. By now the room is definitely dark. The movie is Hitchcock's *Vertigo,* which you've seen before, but never on the big screen, so it doesn't feel so much like you're repeating something.

I know there are situations when time moves at different rates, that is, when our *perception* is that time moves at different rates, because time, it seems, is fixed (or is it relative, and our perceptions fixed?). I think of swimming in the public pool near my apartment in Brooklyn, that time moves very differently there than when I am teaching, water being a different medium than the medium of a classroom. In the classroom we have so much information we want to impart, and so many things we'd like to try, that often we're surprised when the period is over. Time moves too fast, at times, during the school day. But when I'm doing laps back and forth in the pool, when I can finally tell myself that I have nothing to do but breathe, five minutes can feel like a week. Swimming for me is what I think of as meditative, as a time to step outside the pace of New York, and meditation has something to do with time. The Buddhists say that time is like our breath: the more we try to hold onto it, the more quickly it is lost.

And yet we cannot step out of time, even for an instant, even in sleep. We say, "I don't have time for that," or, "I've run out of time," yet we exist only in time. Each day an hour is the same length, relatively. We daydream for ten minutes, and that ten minutes is gone. This is not an argument against daydreaming, at times a perfectly productive way to spend an afternoon, especially for a poet. In Samuel Beckett's *Waiting for Godot,* one of the characters, after another long, fruitless exchange, notes that it "passed the time." The other character answers, "It would have passed anyway," which always seemed an essential, if brutal, truth: that this thing we call time does not care about us, that it is the medium we exist in and yet it is going to go on, with us or without us. Even the Rolling Stones, who will be singing "Satisfaction" long after I'm in my grave, began with "Time Is on My Side" and quickly sobered up to "Time Waits for

No One." The poet Mark Doty, in *Heaven's Coast,* his beautiful, harrowing memoir, writes,

> *The more one tries to live in the present, it seems, the more one learns the inseparability of time, the artifice of our construction of the trinity of experience; yesterday, today, tomorrow meld into one another, blur in and out. We move between them at the speed of memory or of anticipation. Trying to remain in the moment is like living in three dimensions, in sheerly physical space; the mind doesn't seem to be whole unless it also occupies the dimension of time, which grants to things their depth and complexity, the inherent dignity and drama of their histories, the tragedy of their possibilities. What then can it mean to "be here now"? That discipline of paying attention to things-as-they-are in the present seems simply to reveal the way the nature of each thing is anchored to time's passage, cannot exist outside of time.*

I notice this same difficulty that Doty talks about in day-to-day living when it comes to writing. For me it's nearly impossible to describe anything well without making associations with where that thing has been or what has come before. I would go even further to say that it is impossible to write anything in English that means just one thing. Everything is connected to everything else, and often that connection is manifest in time.

In the early 1970s, tucked away in a side hallway in Boston's Museum of Science, a cross-section of a giant redwood was mounted to the wall, tiny lights embedded in its age rings. This was a favorite exhibit of mine from about age ten on. When you pressed a button next to a blacked-out sentence on the wall the sentence would light up, corresponding to one of the embedded lights, which also lit: "*Sputnik* launched"; "Columbus discovers what he believes to be India"; "Jesus born." Each tiny light was dated, so history appeared as a sequence of events, contained. My eyes moved from the lit sentence to the tree and back: right there, "The Civil War begins": over two thousand years radiating out in concentric circles from the unlikely sapling. I could reach out and touch it, touch time, if the guard wasn't looking. The closer I got to the center, to the beginning of time, the easier life seemed. The Russians had to invent a whole spaceship; all Jesus had to do was be born.

I don't know if this exhibit it still on view. At some point it probably became an embarrassment for the museum, an anachronism—dated, like the egg-hatching display I read about in the paper recently: it didn't really extend our knowledge of the world, yet people came to the museum expecting to see it. They'd hold their children up to see the egg's first shiver, then the beak poking through, the spherical thing become the thing with wings, a known wonder. I imagine, with time, my redwood cross-section was relegated to the basement or to storage, along with The Visible Woman and The Sand Mandala. Today, it's all dinosaurs and holograms, artificial intelligence and rain forests. Science and poetry have moved into questions of the future and how to represent it. To marvel at a tiny lightbulb embedded in a tree ring, meant to represent a significant historical fact, is perhaps naive now, quaint. For what can this tell us about time? that events happen once? that they can be located, frozen? that there is much behind us? The redwood was, even then, no longer prominently displayed, hard to find; more likely you'd simply come upon it than seek it out. Still, I stood before it and pressed the buttons, the cross-section a great clock, its hands removed, all the minutes made real, etched in. Each storm was there, in the swallowed layers, layer swallowing layer, each axe that had tried over the years to fell it and failed. Press a button: "Napoléon defeated at Waterloo." This felled tree had become a metaphor for time, and it excited me, strangely, made me understand something about the world, about time, in a way I could return to, could imagine. Press a button: "The *Titanic* sinks"; time made real, tangible, named.

Perhaps this, this illusion of cohesion, of time being made solid, of everything happening at once, is what led me to become a poet. Poetry, I found, was able to move through time quicker than most fiction; it had legs that were able to leap. Robert Bly has a book entitled *Leaping Poetry* in which he explores this ability. And this ability attracted me as a writer, early on, because it mirrored my own experience with time. While washing the dishes, say, my mind would be reliving a moment ten years earlier, perhaps as I helped my mother with the dishes, and then I'd remember a movie I'd seen the month before, and then the phone would ring and a long-lost friend would have tracked me down, and I was still washing the dishes while we spoke, while we caught each other up on those ten years. Even looking back at the last two paragraphs I notice how I have tried to use my writing to move through time. For better or worse, several thousand years are covered in a few lines. I could have just as well slowed time down, lingered for an entire paragraph on, say, the *Titanic,* if I was qualified to do that. Or I could have speculated on whether the summers really were longer when I was younger, or whether it's because my mass was less and therefore I was moving through the light at a different speed. Time then, it seems, is another rich field for us to dig into, a "place" for us to put our attention.

As teachers we can decide to do an inquiry with our students on how writers, how poets, use time in their work. All writers deal with time in some respect, whether consciously or unconsciously. William Faulkner, to paraphrase loosely, claimed that time was the subject of all literature. His body of work can be read, in one sense, as the effect of time on families and on a specific culture. It could be argued that even the writings of the Bible deal primarily with time, beginning as they do with "In the beginning," with the six days it took the Lord to create the world, with endless genealogies of who begat whom. This intersects in the twentieth century with Einstein and his theory of relativity, which leads to Stephen Hawking and his question, "Why do we remember the past but not the future?" In his book *A Brief History of Time,* Hawking ends up going back in time to the writings of St. Augustine, agreeing that "time did not exist before the beginning of the universe." Or think of watching a movie, arguably the art form of the twentieth century, where we've come to accept that a year can pass in an instant, before our eyes, time's essential fluidity revealed.

ᎯᎧ *Getting Started*

It's just after the New Year, and as a class we have begun a discussion of what it means to look at time in literature: what we notice, how it is used, why an author might "play" with time, what effect it has on our reading. We have been looking for examples in literature where we notice the issue of time being addressed. We have read Stafford's "A Story That Could Be True," from *The Way It Is,* and are considering it for one of our touchstones, for a mentor poem. It is on a chart in a prominent place in the room, and it has been read several times aloud to the class.

ON CHOOSING STAFFORD'S POEM AS A MENTOR POEM

I am pleased that this class has decided upon Stafford's poem as a mentor, for I have read this particular poem many times and in many classrooms, always with good result. There is something archetypal about the dead mother and lost father that makes even reluctant would-be poets pay attention, as it seems to deal with something "real." Also, it is a clear poem, presenting us with clear images, even if it takes place mostly in the mind of the poet. Third, it is not a poem where the shifts in time are too wild, too extreme, which, if they were, could perhaps be akin to riding a roller coaster: exciting, but hard to pay attention. The time shifts in this poem are simple; it begins in one place (the past), and ends in another (the present). It is perhaps good to start an inquiry such as this one simply, especially as it is a subject that occupied much of Einstein's thinking. For this inquiry we could have gone to, say, Frank O'Hara's "The Day Lady Died," a poem about Billie Holiday, which begins, "It is 12:20 in New York a Friday / three days after Bastille day, yes / it is 1959 and I go get a shoeshine / because I will get off the 4:19 in Easthampton / at 7:15 and then go straight to dinner / and I don't know the people who will feed me." This, clearly, is a poem that situates us in time, and it is a poem that I love, but I worry about the poems that would result from my students' trying to imitate it too closely ("This class ends in three minutes / at 11:23 and yes / lunch comes after that . . .") and therefore think it is not an ideal choice as a mentor poem. But, finally, to reiterate, the main reason to choose any poem for a mentor poem is that it be a poem we love.

NOTICING TIME IN THE MENTOR POEM

After a week of thinking informally about time and writing, we gather to talk specifically about our mentor poem. The first thing we notice about Stafford's "A Story That Could Be True" is that it doesn't deal directly with the issue of time. It never tells us what time of day it is, or how long ago any of it happened.

If we try to picture the person, the "you," standing on the corner shivering, some of us think it is in the middle of the day, some of us think it is at night. But we know that nearly every piece of writing deals with time, in some way: if something is happening, it must be happening in time. For this mini-lesson, my intention is for us to begin to understand this, to notice where in the mentor poem we know where we are in time, and to notice where we don't.

NOTICING VERBS IN THE MENTOR POEM

During our next meeting, Stafford's poem is on the chart beside us. I begin this mini-lesson by pointing out that we have been thinking for a few days now about how authors use time in their writing, and the effect it has on us as readers. The students have already noticed various uses of time, and today we would like them to look at Stafford's poem in this context. We read the poem again to them, asking them if they notice where the time shifts. Several raise their hands, and one girl notices that the poem begins "sort of" in the past and is then in the present for the rest. I ask her to stand up and point to where she thinks it changes from the past to the present, and she points to the second line of the first stanza. I ask her how she knows it is in the past, and she points to the word *died* and says that if it was now it would say *die.* I tell her, yes, the verbs are a really good place to look to tell when something is taking place. We look at the rest of the verbs in the poem and see that after *died* the rest are all in the present tense. This is the discussion I wanted to get started for today, and will follow up on in subsequent mini-lessons.

An inquiry into the uses of verbs could be a much longer discussion. The tenses used in "A Story That Could Be True" are more complex than simply present and past (the first line, for example, is in the conditional past), but for the purposes of this inquiry, which will cover other ways to look at time besides verb usage, it seems best to keep it simple at this point. Grammar, we all know, can scare many away, and it is perhaps enough to get them to simply notice and identify the verbs to start off.

NOTICING VERBS IN OUR WRITING

We gather this morning with our notebooks in front of us. I ask the students to find an entry they've written and then to mark the verbs in it, to see if they move through time at all in that entry, if time shifts, as in Stafford's poem. After five minutes they finish marking one entry and show their neighbor what they've noticed. The teacher and I eavesdrop on a few of the conversations to see how they discuss it, and then ask a few of the students to share their discussions with the class. When they head off to write today we ask them to think about time as they write, and about how the verbs shift in the entry they write today, if at all. During our sharing time we continue this discussion.

After a few days of gathering to talk about verbs, and what we notice and are trying in our writer's notebooks, it feels like time to move on with our inquiry. Besides, we are starting to notice other ways to express this thing called time.

∽ *Keeping It Going*
SLOWING DOWN TIME

In his book *The Child's Conception of Time,* Jean Piaget writes that "memory is a reconstruction of the past, a 'narrative.'" In one chapter he demonstrates the trouble a six-year-old has in arranging a series of photographs to show a sequence of events. The example he gives is a cup falling from a table: at six the child does not yet know that the cup must be on the table before it can end up broken on the floor. This point in our inquiry seems like a good place to work on the idea of slowing time down with our students, to get them to focus on a specific, small event (such as a cup falling to the floor), rather than trying to sequence even so much as an hour of their lives, let alone an entire day, or their summer. For today's mini-lesson I tell my students that we are hoping for them to focus on one small event, reminding them that we are not looking to know everything they did at the amusement park; rather, we hope they will focus on the one thing they did at the park that they really remember. In order to do this we could first make a quick list of the things we did at the park: the rides, the food, our friends. I let them know that if a writer chooses to focus on the rides, she must slow time down and tell us everything she can remember about just one ride. Or if she is focusing on the junk food she ate, we have her slow the time down that it takes to buy and eat a single hot dog, or to make a mess of a wad of cotton candy.

Maisha, a bilingual second grader, went through this process of slowing time down to achieve the following poem, also shown in Figure 8.1.

Me, my friend and her big sister
played a game
where you try to find gold
but it takes a lot of days.

The days pass in seconds
like if one second passed
one day passed. You have
till November to find
the most gold you can.

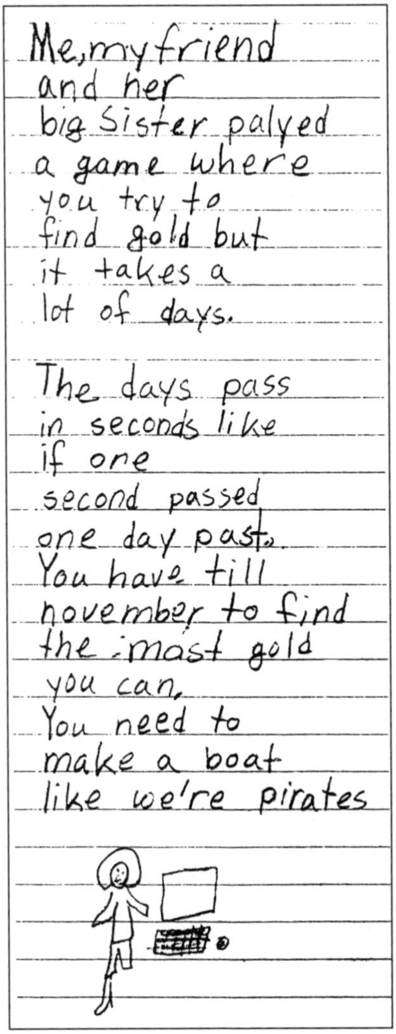

> Me, my friend
> and her
> big Sister palyed
> a game where
> you try to
> find gold but
> it takes a
> lot of days.
>
> The days pass
> in seconds like
> if one
> second passed
> one day past.
> You have till
> november to find
> the most gold
> you can.
> You need to
> make a boat
> like we're pirates

FIGURE 8.1   Final poem from the process of slowing time down.

You need to make a boat
like we're pirates.

TIME LINE OF THE MENTOR POEM

It is time to look back at our mentor poem. Although we have already noted that the verbs shift from the past to the present only in the first stanza, in each stanza the sense of time feels different. We need to look more closely at each stanza. I propose we make a time line of this poem, in order to chart what we notice. I draw a line on the chart and divide it into three sections, to represent the three stanzas:

_____ / _____ / _____

In some classes I find it helpful to sketch out what is happening in each stanza. In this class we decide to use words. The first stanza, we notice, begins with a birth, which seems to be looked back on from the present, though it could all be taking place in the past. The mother has died and the father is separated from the child. So on the time line for the first stanza we write

birth, mom dies, father and child separated /

In the second stanza, we notice, it feels like we have moved away from birth and early childhood, that the "you" in the poem is older, because now he or she is standing on a corner in the rain. The father has still not found the child. To the second part of our time line we add

/ child older, looking for father /

Now the third stanza. Again, the sense of time feels a little different to us from the first two stanzas. Both the first and second stanzas gave us an image (see Chapter 2), whereas the third stanza seems to take place mainly in the narrator's mind. It is a thought more than an image. And it is a thought the narrator has often, "any day," so we decide to call it a continuous thought:

/ continuous thought ("Maybe I'm a king")

Once we have done this, the students are directed to go back into their notebooks and make a time line of one or more of their entries. It is understood that the first couple of tries will be practice until they get the hang of it.

DEVELOPING A LONGER PIECE

As with any writing cycle, by the second or third week we should have chosen an entry and begun developing it into a longer piece. We do this by writing other entries that are connected to the first entry in some way, using strategies we have been noticing other writers use, and practicing those strategies in our writing. Since the inquiry for this cycle is time, we will return to that in our mini-lessons, while keeping track of other lessons with which our students clearly need help. For example, while we are thinking about time, we may notice that many students are still struggling with writing long on a topic, with going deeper into their seed idea. Their entries are either very short or they seem to bounce from one idea to another. Some more attention will have to be given to developing this skill (see Chapter 2 to review writing long).

❧ *Extending Our Thinking*

MARKING THE PASSAGE OF TIME
IN THE MENTOR POEM

Robert Hass, a former U.S. Poet Laureate, has written, "Poems imitate life in time. They move and accumulate, ripen; some things fall away and other things come up." We think about this as we look back on our mentor poem. Although Hass's statement doesn't apply to all poems (he doesn't intend it to), it seems a fair assessment of what is going on in Stafford's poem. As a class we have already noticed how it moves through time; now we can go back and notice how his images accumulate and ripen. We gather again, and take the poem stanza by stanza. First, we see that the lost father in the opening stanza is replaced by the lost son (or daughter) of the second stanza, and by the third the concern shifts into the interior life of the lost child. While we are still gathered we go back to the entries we have been developing and mark those places where we have shown the effects of time on our subject, where something has changed, however slightly.

MARKING TIME THROUGH THE USE OF AN OBJECT

The Red Violin, a recent movie, follows a certain rare and perfectly pitched violin through a few centuries. This is one example of a way that an object can be used to illuminate historical epochs and the passing of time. In our writing, too, we can use objects to mark time, drafting a piece of writing around the "life" of an object. There are many examples of this in literature (one favorite is *Wilfrid Gordon McDonald Partridge,* by Mem Fox, where the title character ends up quite sensibly confusing the word *memory* with objects). A poem that uses an object to evoke an entire life beautifully is "What Came to Me," from *Otherwise,* by Jane Kenyon:

WHAT CAME TO ME

I took the last
dusty piece of china
out of the barrel.

It was your gravy boat,
with a hard, brown
drop of gravy still
on the porcelain lip.
I grieved for you then
as I never had before.

The students have already been asked to bring in an object from home. We have pointed out to them that toys will often contain less "time," and therefore less "story," than will something from the natural world, and may prove harder to write off. Those who were not able to bring in an object from home are told they can find a place in their writing where an object plays a significant role, or could be expanded to play a significant role. We also direct them to the science section of the classroom, where there are many objects whose lifespans are long (seashells, rocks, crystals, etc). (See Chapter 10 for more on writing off objects.)

STRETCHING AND SHRINKING TIME

On another day we try a few quick writing exercises: one, to see how long we can stretch out a minute of our lives; another, to try to cram our whole life into three sentences. We then return to what we have been working on and see if either of these exercises could be fit into our ongoing work in any way.

∾ Mini-Inquiry
MEMORIES AND MOMENTS

Apollinaire wrote, "When I speak of time that's because it's already no longer there." Much of what we write is from memory; many of those memories are made up of moments. A moment is a discrete unit of time, and usually the moments that stay with us, that become part of our own memories after we read them, are, as we have seen, those that create an image for us. One way we can define the word *moment* is as something that occurs or occurred over a very short span of time. This mini-inquiry is meant to offer a few of the types of moments we can write from.

MOMENTS IN THE MENTOR POEM

We gather to look back over our mentor poem, and to mark the different moments we notice in it. The infant being exchanged in the cradle is one; the son (or daughter) standing in the rain is another; the question being asked and the answer given are both one. Perhaps we could name more, but for today this feels like enough to get started. I then direct the students to try writing a moment or two from their lives in their notebooks, first turning to a neighbor and saying out loud what they plan to write. Some grasp the idea of writing out a moment from their lives right away, and some are initially confused. The best way, I've found, to tell who gets it and who is confused is by looking at their writing. Ideally, the moments they chose will contain some imagery (see Chapter 2), and thereby be able to be sketched out.

A SHORT LIST OF POSSIBLE MOMENTS

When we next gather it is time to list on a flip-chart three or four types of moments we could try, along with brief examples of each. Here are some possibilities:

- An everyday moment
- A moment that happened only once
- An observed moment
- A remembered moment

This short list seems enough to get started. The students now look at the moment they've tried writing out and name how they wrote it: Was it an everyday moment? an observed moment? Then they can write one they haven't yet tried. Examples of two of these moments are discussed in the following mini-lesson.

SKETCHING OUT A MOMENT

As we learned in Chapter 2, it is good practice for a writer to sketch out his or her moments. To follow up on our last mini-lesson I want to give students an example of an everyday moment, and show them ways I could sketch it out. After we gather, I first tell them the story of my cat, who waits patiently every morning at my closed door until I wake up. As soon as I open the door she runs to her bowl and cries for milk. I point out to the students that this is something that happens every morning, that I know exactly how it will go, and as I'm telling the story I sketch some part of it out on a chart—maybe the cat at the door waiting, or the cat at her bowl looking back at me (Figure 8.2). As I sketch ei-

FIGURE 8.2　Sketch of Nick's cat waiting for breakfast.

ther scene out I remind them that I am making a choice as to what to sketch, that even within this small moment there are still choices I have to make as a writer as to what I will focus on. I mention that the difference between this moment and an observed moment is that the moment with my cat happens every day, whereas an observed moment happened to someone else and I simply watched it unfold. On another day perhaps I would give them an example of an observed moment. For this I could use the man I saw playing the violin on the subway platform (see Chapter 2), and again as I sketch it I point out the choices I am making as to what to focus on. I could focus on the people passing him in the tunnel, or on what the man looks like, his eyes closed and the violin tucked under his chin, or I could focus on his open violin case, where he is hoping people will toss some change if they like the song.

From this mini-inquiry, we hope that our students get a chance to understand and apply the idea that a moment is measured in time, yet is made real by the images we use to capture it, as in a movie.

Which leads us back to the dim movie theater. The few previous paragraphs could have been thought out in an instant, during the title sequence of a movie, say, which in *Vertigo* is stunning, with the body falling into an endless spiral. As the plot unfolds, at some point Kim Novak flees from Jimmy Stewart through a redwood forest: he finds her at an exhibit of a cross-section of a redwood. In trying to convince him she is crazy, she points out two of the tree's age rings and says, "Here's where I was born, here's where I died." Which leads us full-circle back thirty years to the Museum of Science and my redwood tree. To update that redwood there would need to be another ring, one that represented the present, that would light up along with the sentence "Boy presses button in the Museum of Science" or "Boy first feels the weight of the past pushing down on him" or "Boy learns that both Napoléon and Jesus weigh the same," pinpoints of light in a fallen tree.

9

Sitting Close to the Center
A SENSE OF PLACE

Shirley McPhillips

*This was the house for the self that stood a little apart
and at an angle, the self that thought a good place
to spend the day was between two walls of books
in front of a big window overlooking life.*

MICHAEL POLLAN,

A Place of My Own

THE COPPER BEECH
Marie Howe

Immense, entirely itself,
it wore that yard like a dress,

with limbs low enough for me to enter it
and climb the crooked ladder to where

I could lean against the trunk and practice being alone.

One day, I heard the sound before I saw it, rain fell
darkening the sidewalk.

Sitting close to the center, not very high in the branches,
I heard it hitting the high leaves, and I was happy,

watching it happen without it happening to me.

laces exist. They have shaped themselves according to some inherent law. Or, as Winston Churchill said of buildings, we shape them, and are thereafter shaped by them. Place is the experience we have there, how we live, the projects we pursue, the personal and intellectual terrain we cultivate, the textures we weave with other people. Poet Gary Snyder (1990) says that native people everywhere have a "home place" no matter where they wander, and they can "prove it at any campfire or party by singing their own songs."

In *Writing Toward Home,* poet Georgia Heard says, "Home is a blueprint of memory." When I remember my deepest experience of place, I feel again some concentrated stirring inside me—a flavor, a fragrance, its essential oil. Reading through one of the notebooks I kept when my husband, Edward, and I "dropped out of society" in the 1970s and went to live on a hilltop farm (The Hill) in upstate New York, I feel again the hunger for the realness of things that took us there. I enter the place, as William Stafford said, that summoned for me the quiet of my own spirit:

> *June 21, 1975. The deep murmurs of the cattle answering one another across the hills, borne on a late spring breeze which sweeps across the back pasture. It is at the grassy edge of the garden where I meet each day, from now until the first killer frost. . . . The arrangement of the rows, the textures and staggered heights of the plants, promising mounds of hidden hope fill me with continual expectation. The tomato leaves are new and tender and in the coolness of this morning the whipping wind is teaching them a harsh lesson. Tonight we will cover them with baskets. . . . Each day is one of inspection—for a sign of change, for curious creatures, for any slight failure, for something to celebrate.*

Eight years later, when I was ambivalent about the move back to suburban New York City, my friend Thelma Plender said not to worry, that I would never leave The Hill because The Hill, like all our deepest places, was in me, that everything thereafter would resonate with hillsound. Sometimes now, when the Manhattan skyline blurs in an early morning haze and I see the purple foothills behind the silo tower; when in a night clearing of elusive sleep, I hear the silence of snow falling on the pond; when the last sconeful of red currant jelly stings my taste for things homemade, I know she's right.

We can find our poetic material in this deep kind of connectedness to place, to the things that represent place in our lives, that, as Donald Murray says, "surround us, that spark memories and imaginings." We have chosen Marie Howe's poem "The Copper Beech," from *What the Living Do,* for the centerpiece of our inquiry into writing out of a sense of place. The poems in her book seem to be rooted in places in and around a childhood home. This poem brings us into an intimate moment, turning us inward and outward in the same space of time.

๑ ๑ *Getting Started*

NOTICING HOW OBJECTS REPRESENT PLACE

During one of our first readings of Marie Howe's poem, Daryl says it reminds him of how he likes to fasten blankets around the lower bunk bed, his sleeping place, and make a dark cave. He switches on a clip-on light and draws, reads, or sets up imaginary confrontations with toy creatures. He leaves a peephole of thin sheet so he can vaguely see out. From this small warm refuge he can look out at the world and dream in his own way.

In light of what Daryl has said, we look back at the poem. The narrator's image of the copper beech tree seems to recall a sense of self, something deeply experienced when she, or he, goes to the tree to "practice being alone." "That's *his* tree," Jason says. "That's where he can see out and hear the rain, but he's protected from it. Sort of like an invisible wall is around it."

We ask Daryl to give us more of a picture of what it was like when he was inside his bunk bed "cave." He tells how his mom would call; he would hear her voice "out there" but not answer. His brother would pass by, going in or out of the room; he would see the shadow but imagine it was an alien, not part of his world now. "It's like I was in power," he says. Jason thinks that, like the character in Howe's poem, Daryl was happy in the bunk bed place he had created for himself. "In there, he controlled things."

This conversation, and Howe's title, has gotten us thinking about how poets let objects represent place. Before we go off to work on our writing, we decide together that during the week, students will look back over other poems we've read or collected to find examples of this. And we'll be thinking about our own places connected with objects.

WHO'S THE "I" IN THE POEM?

We notice that some students are saying "she" and some are saying "he" with respect to the narrator in Howe's poem. Talima feels strongly, for example, that the narrator is a girl "because the author is talking about her life and wrote this poem." Jason pictures a boy, like himself, when he reads the poem. Usually, it wouldn't matter in our discussion. We could say "he" or "she," and let it go at that. But as this seems to be an issue with them, sometimes arresting the flow of conversation about the poem at hand, we decide it will be instructive for future reading and thinking about poems to take a moment or two to talk with them about the voice in poems.

We flash back to the earlier conversation when Jason, Talima, and others got sidetracked about who "I" was in "The Copper Beech." This is a good question, and we wanted to come back to it. It has implications for all our poetry conversations. In the spirit of inquiry, we check Howe's book *What the Living Do* for clues, for any clarifying information. Since I hold the only copy of the book, I read a few blurbs of praise from the inside and back-of-the-book notes. Students notice that reviewers say Howe is a fearless "truthteller," and the dedication mentions names of people who also appear in some of the poems. All this Talima thinks bolsters her case. Jason makes the point that if "The Copper Beech" weren't in this book, "If it was a poem in another book of different poems [an anthology], we wouldn't know all this and we would just picture ourselves in it." His point seems reasonable, too. So we decide that this question is one we can keep open in our minds as we read poetry and perhaps talk about again if we like.

I say, though, that while we believe the material and the fuel for poems come out of a poet's experiences, a poem itself comes from one's imagination. It is created. I don't think we can assume the person speaking in every poem is the author. And so the voice speaking the poem, the "I" in this case, is a narrator. We'll just say "the narrator" for now. If someone forgets in conversation, we'll all understand that they are imagining the poem their way.

SKETCHING IMAGES OF PLACE

We've noticed that Marie Howe's poem begins with an image of the copper beech tree, "immense," with strong, low limbs. Students have already done some work sketching and writing images (see Chapter 2), so now we want to draw on that to get our own images of place. First, we ask them to make a quick sketch of what they see in their mind's eye as I read aloud again the first three stanzas of "The Copper Beech." Quick sharing of two or three sketches leads to discussion of the line "it wore that yard like a dress." This line, with others, brings everything from trees shaped vaguely like human forms with great waving frilly arms, shaggy with flowing leaves, taking up the whole expanse of yard, to stately, almost leafless trees, the sketches emphasizing massive and strong-looking boughs ascending into the sky. Most sketches contain a person. One shows the small face of a figure framed in leaves, another the tip of a sneakered foot dangling just below a limb. Some students, anticipating the rest of the poem, fill in various types of rain connecting with the tree, some driving rain, some misty and gentle.

We talk about what in our sketches gives us the feeling we think the character in our mentor poem has "leaning against the trunk," practicing being alone.

During workshop and tonight for homework, students read through their notebooks, or cast their minds back to remember places they connect with for some reason, then make a sketch or two, trying to let an object represent that place. We suggest that it might help to label the sketch the way some poets have titled their poems: The Copper Beech, Under the Porch, The Overstuffed Chair, The Clubhouse. Tomorrow, we will tell the stories of our places to each other from our sketches.

❧ *Keeping It Going*
LOOKING FOR OTHER POEMS OF PLACE

The class wants to get a better feeling for poems that seem rooted in place and in which poets let objects represent place. They've been looking through their folders and a few poetry books from the class collection. In just one book, Paul Janeczko's anthology *The Place My Words Are Looking For,* we find "Enchantment" by Joanne Ryder, about summer nights on the porch; "Deserted Farm" by Mark Vinz, an image of a dilapidated barn; and Valerie Worth's "Haunted House," how it looks and what it reminds the characters of. William has found "a gold mine," he says, on the poetry bookshelf—*Home,* edited by Michael Rosen. The mother lode. "All the places people call home." He thumbs through it. "A kitchen table, under the back porch, in the elevator!" "Under the Bed" by Jon Scieszka reminds them of Daryl's bunk bed hideaway because it was a place to imagine new worlds. And Myra Cohn Livingston's "Closet" was the same kind of place: an ordinary place made secret, where imagination flies in surprising ways. They've been reading some of these poems all week long, alongside the mentor poem, and the teacher and I are delighted at how easily they refer to them. Not only are they making amazing connections, they're going deeper into what the poets are doing as regards a sense of place. Talking across texts, putting poems next to each other in their minds as they read are habits we want to nurture.

WRITING WITH DETAIL ABOUT OUR IMAGES

After our discussion of Marie Howe's image in "The Copper Beech," and sketching our own images, we gather today to look at how we might talk about them in order to bring more detail to the surface. Having conferred with William and heard some of the context around his image, I ask him to help us teach the mini-lesson. William has sketched the beanbag chair his brother left him when he went away to college last year. We want William to tell us about the beanbag-chair-as-place, not in a general way ("It reminds me of him"; "I sit in it"; "I miss my brother"), but in particular ways. We know if we can get him to *say* these particulars, then he and the others will have a better sense of how they might write them. In years past, we've exhorted young writers to "use details" or "put in some more details here." But we've learned that that doesn't mean all students know how a detail differs from anything else they are writing. Sometimes they think each thing they write is a detail. Also, a student may "add" details because we say so, and wind up listing more, but not necessarily *write with detail.*

William says he misses his brother and he sits in the beanbag chair every day like his brother used to do. From what he tells us, he feels a curious mix of idolatry and loss, intimacy and release. What does he miss? He misses not having to dive for the chair and wrestle with his brother in order to claim it for himself. Just sitting down there without a tussle seems odd. Somehow it still seems like his brother's chair and he's just sneaked a seat. I ask William what makes him say this. It still has the deep hole in it from all the times his brother flopped his considerable weight in it. "He pumps iron." And when he leans back, he can smell a whiff of some kind of lotion or shampoo.

He likes to do things his brother did in the chair. Like what? someone asks. When he sits there, doing his homework or watching TV, he fingers the little white peas of stuffing leaking out of the hole his brother tried to patch with duct tape, aims one at the guitarist's belt buckle on the back-of-the-door poster and yells "bull's eye," the way his brother used to do. We tell William that he is beginning to give us a wonderfully vivid sense of how he is in that place. The teacher writes a couple of his statements on the chart now. From her notes, she will write the details later so we can examine them further and refer to them.

I miss my brother when I look at the beanbag chair.
Details:
Sneaking into room after dinner
Diving for beanbag chair
Colliding on top, wrestling
Showing muscles, leaning back, Aaahh
Like pushing scrap of paper off chair
I like to do things there like my brother used to do
Details:
Finger white peas/stuffing, leaking from hole brother patched with
   duct tape
Aim at guitarist's belt buckle
Yell "bull's eye"

As they go off to write, we ask students to look back at how Marie Howe writes in particular ways and note some examples. And whatever our images representing our places, we will use our mentor poem and what we learned from William to help us explore these places and write with detail. We will add other examples to the chart as our inquiry continues.

Joshua stands at the classroom window and turns what he sees upside down. "Sky" (Figure 9.1) is rich with imagery and metaphorical detail. And Patricia's

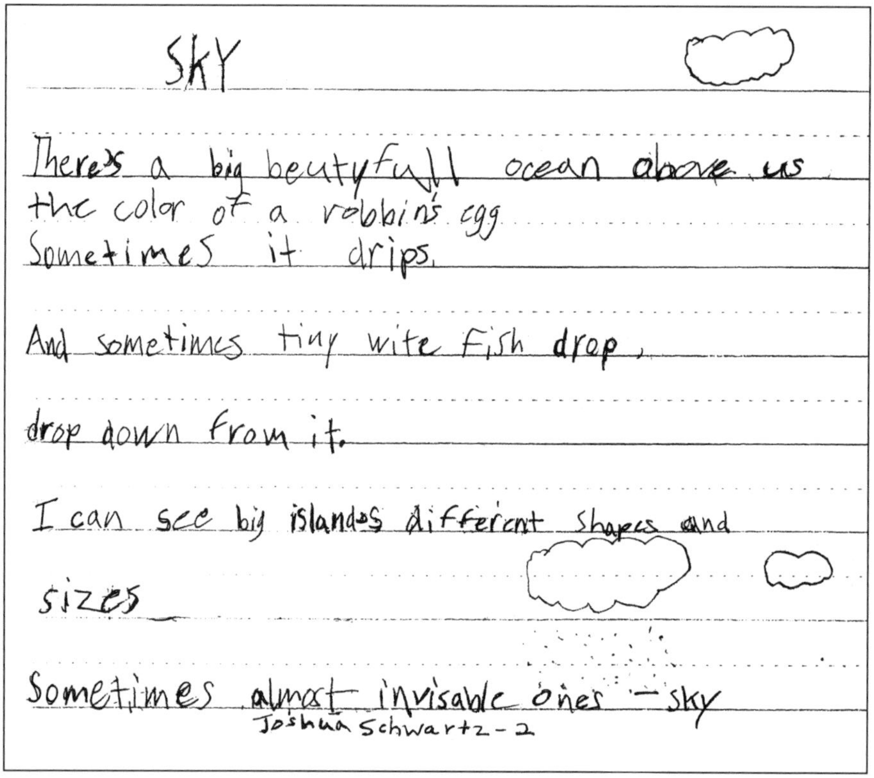

FIGURE 9.1   Joshua's poem with metaphorical detail.

crafted poem shows a writer using specific details to bring us into a poet's room at the moment frustration turns to creation:

A SPARK OF IMAGINATION

Crumpled, torn
pages of an unwanted poem
litter the floor
like paper popcorn balls.

The trash can
overflows
with rejected ideas.
The writer mumbles, frustrated.

The room is musty and dark.
The shades are drawn

and the light curtains
that should cheer up the room
lay motionless at the window's edge.
The glass
that stands near the computer
holds ancient water.
Suddenly,
a streak of light
hits the glass
with a brilliant spark

finding its way
to the imagination
of the writer.

The room bursts
with a magic light
and the steady hum
of a machine.

JOTTING THE INSTANT

One day Sarah said, "I wonder if Marie Howe ever took her notebook into the copper beech with her." It amuses and delights us that the writers imagine everyone doing the same kinds of things they are doing. Sometimes they're right. When we ask what makes her wonder this, she says, "It's like she's not just telling about a person sitting there, in a tree, for nothing. She's noticing things. She's having all these thoughts about herself. Even if she doesn't tell them all. That's what a notebook's for." (It's still hard for the writers to think of the narrator's voice in a poem as being different from the author's. Often, we let it go.)

This makes us think about how we might use our notebooks to do what Mary Oliver describes in *Blue Pastures* as writing down something "extremely exact in terms of phrasing and of cadence" while in a certain place. Small snippets, meant, she says, not to fill us in on all we saw or thought in that place, but to capture the essence of something seen, heard, thought, felt. I read them two or three examples from her book, then from Nick's notebook, and from mine:

Beginning is a kind of music

Murmurs of heartcry

yellowing up
    the over-wintered
    landscape

Who wished this rosebush would roar?

Funny how weather moves through us

I can imagine us spreading out about the room to try writing in this way, but today we decide just to sit in the meeting area and try "catching the instant," right here. After a few minutes, Richard reads,

What big bang
will explode
from so many minds?

And Luis:

Pencils scratching a mile a minute.

Elizabeth:

I hope my wish is louder than these words.

The students decide that during the week, they will take a walk outside several times with their notebooks, lingering in places, trying to "jot the instant" with exact phrases. They will also take their own walks, sit in their self-chosen places outside of school, and do the same. Later, we will reread our poem drafts to see if any of these lines can fit in or help us rethink our poems. We'll also see if we can use some of these lines as seeds for new poems.

NOTICING THINGS UNFOLDING IN PLACE, PAST AND PRESENT

We have noticed that "The Copper Beech" is written in the past tense, as a story or memory would be. After the initial image, starting with "One day," Howe tells us the scene of what happened, story-like, but in particular phrases, as if she is remembering the details of how it unfolded: "I heard the sound . . . rain fell / darkening the sidewalk. . . . / I heard it hitting the high leaves . . . / watching it happen. . . ."

We decide to look at Gary Snyder's poem "Late October Camping in the Sawtooths," from *Left Out in the Rain,* next to "The Copper Beech." Here, Snyder seems to be noting precisely what is happening at a campsite, but in the present tense, almost as it is unfolding. We read each line, picturing it step by step as if we are in that place ourselves, as if we are having the experience, right now:

Sunlight climbs the snowpeak
    glowing pale red
Cold sinks into the gorge
    shadows merge.
Building a fire of pine twigs
    at the foot of a cliff,
Drinking hot tea from a tin cup
    in the chill air—

On another day, we look at how the character in Archibald MacLeish's poem "Eleven," tired of the strictures of adult demands at the house, takes respite in the gardener's shed. (The poem is excerpted here and given in full in Appendix A.)

Push back the shed door and upon the sill
Stand pressing out the sunlight from his eyes
And enter and with outstretched fingers feel
The grindstone and behind it the bare wall . . .
. . . .
. . . And sit there, quiet, breathing
The harsh dry smell of withered bulbs, the faint
Odor of dung, the silence. And outside
Beyond the half-shut door the blind leaves
And the corn moving. . . .

Again, the poet gives us the feeling that he has his notebook out and is fixing what he sees and does at that very moment. We know that this is not how these poems took their final shape, but we can practice making this kind of move in order to achieve a sense of place and perhaps to explore the significance of it.

Today, during writing workshop, tonight and during the week, we can situate ourselves in a certain place and try writing a scene unfolding, as if we are there with our notebooks, jotting down what we see and do, right now. And we can go back through our notebooks and find a moment (or think of a new one), enter it again in our mind's eye, and try the same thing.

❧ *Extending Our Thinking*

PUTTING A CHARACTER IN PLACE

Studying "The Copper Beech," writing in place, being "present" in our places (as well as our work, for example, with photos, the image, or eavesdropping) have resulted in many of the students' poems having a narrator's voice using "I." Like a friend, we think, telling us a secret. Michael says that in our mentor poem he pictures a person in the tree. But, he says, in Stafford's poem "Being a Person," from *Even in Quiet Places,* there doesn't seem to be a character. There's no "I" or "we" or even "he" or "they." But, he says, we hear "a voice, like an old person who's had experience. Telling us things to do there. Like advice." The narrator. (Appendix A gives "Being a Person" in full.)

This same work has led some students to become interested in the character in poems. So we all get into the conversation. We begin to search through our poetry collections for poems with characters in them and to ask some character-related questions: Where in the poem does the character come in? Is there scant reference to the character, or a few references? Is the character, or some feature of the character, the central focus of the poem? Is the character referred to, or does the character speak? What does the character have to do with the big ideas or connections or truths the poet might be pondering? that we, the readers, might be pondering?

Over a few days, we look specifically for examples of how poets write characters into their poems. In Paul Janeczko's "Section 7, Row 1, Seat 3" we notice that an old lady is the central image: how she looks, her habits, how she measures her life through the game of baseball. In the end, she speaks to us, revealing the lifeline that, to her, is baseball. In "Finger Print" (Booth 1989), Harry Thurston writes about "My grandmother," the narrator focusing on her hands as they work side by side through the rituals of the kitchen, the "fingerprint" becoming a metaphor for this kind of apprenticeship. Carole Boston Weatherford's "The Farmer" (Steptoe 1997) tells us who the central character is in her poem. She gives a strong image of "papa," of his lifetime working in the hot fields of Georgia. Blake's character, the "tyger," a source of mystery and intrigue, leads the narrator to ponder some bigger, philosophical questions (see Chapter 6). And so on.

We ask ourselves, What is the writer doing specifically? with reference to the character in each poem. We make notes about what we notice. Then, keeping our mentors close by, we look back at our own drafts. If we've written memories in our notebooks, for example, we'll draft a poem, including a character, trying out some of the techniques we've identified. If we have written images off objects or sketches that don't contain a character, we can now try putting a character into the image. As we revise, we can notice such things as where the character comes in; the character's voice if she speaks; the role and stance of the character; whether the narrator seems to be meditating or identifying a larger issue or big idea through the character.

Michael, a fourth grader using an earlier description from his notebook about the moon outside his bedroom window, explored and crafted "Year of the Moon," this time with a character in mind:

YEAR OF THE MOON

Every night before I sleep
my dad comes in my room
to say, "Michael, look at the moon."
He says my grandparents
are running around like children
up there. They died when he was
my age. Then tears come out of his eyes.
I say I feel sorry I never got a chance
to meet them. He says the memory
doesn't end.

BRINGING IN OBJECTS TO REPRESENT PLACE

Along with sketching objects that represent place, we encourage writers to bring in objects that could get us thinking more about the places of our lives. I show the class a list in my notebook, for example, of some things in my small office at home, things that make this room a place to work in, to think in, to dream in:

- A quote on the wall from Natalie Goldberg, "There is a quiet place in us . . . that is connected to our breath, our words . . ."
- A large brass apple given to me by some teachers I once worked with
- A square oak clock with huge numbers
- A small Andrew Wyeth watercolor of white snowdrops
- A brown woven basket that holds CDs
- A Calvin Klein teacup
- A flowerpot of purple pens

I tell them how each and all of these things are part of a mosaic that makes up what my room is to me. Each one holds a story of its own. Together they make this place mine.

I show one object from my list, the Wyeth watercolor, which I've brought to class today, and tell what I see in it; what I remember about getting it; what it evokes when I look closely at it; why I put it in my room, at eye level, so that it meets my glance and often my gaze when I swivel in my chair from one part of my desk to the other.

We ask the students to look around in their own places, perhaps to make lists of things around them, then bring in an object that represents that place for them. Those who do will tell their partners the stories, as they saw me do. Eventually, we will write off them. Students who do not bring an object can use their sketches for this purpose.

SAVING PLACES

And that is where that little piece of my prairie is today; my place, my past, my landscape; in a glass on my windowsill.

—Patricia MacLachlan, *Bringing the Prairie Home* (Durrell et al. 1993)

In *What You Know First,* Patricia MacLachlan writes about a little girl who loves the place she is leaving and dreams about what she will take with her of what she knew first. In Howe's "The Copper Beech," we think the narrator remembers sitting close, not very high, safe inside the beech's branches, watching the rain happen out there, in very much the same way—a remembered place, where she can still recall that feeling, where she found something of herself. We half expect her, like MacLachlan's character, to steal away a leaf or a piece of bark to take with her. She's taken the memory: the kind of person she was in that place; how she saw the world from there.

We think back to places we feel connected to, past or present, and jot some phrases in our notebooks, trying to be as specific as we can:

The corner store on my old street where Mr. Martinez always gave us
    jawbreakers
The tree in the park across the street where my dad used to come meet me
    on Saturdays
In Santo Domingo, sitting next to Grandmama at her dining room table
    always with flowers and cakes

We pick a place and walk there in our minds, focusing on an image of us, or others, in that place. We linger in the place, perhaps making a quick sketch. We ask ourselves: What do I see? How am I in this place? What happens here? What part of it am I saving? What am I taking with me?

Students go off with their writing partners to tell each other their images, to give each other a sense of their places and the answers to some of these questions. Then they write.

ALL THE PLACES WE KNOW BY NAME

Whenever I go on a trip, I
think about all the homes I've
had and I remember how little has changed
about what comforts me.

—Brian Andreas, "Comfort," in *Story People*

The students and I are talking one day about the power of place names to evoke images, and memories and feelings. "The Copper Beech" seems like such a place name. We can imagine the poet saying that name, *The Copper Beech,* and savoring, or not, the memories it brings back. We talk about some place names that summon images and feelings we remember for the things we don't savor. And poets write about those, too.

Some place names evoke our own small and intimate moments, while others carry memories through story, through time. I tell the students about "Doc Worthington's place," the long-deserted home of a revered country doctor in the county where I grew up. The mere mention of his homestead in the community set stories swirling, like the time Sister Carrie Didlake, on the way home from a tent revival meeting, almost had her baby in the carriage when it pulled up to Doc Worthington's house in the worst fireworks of a thunderstorm anybody had seen since the capture of Richmond and her husband, Jasper, couldn't get the horses to stop rearing every time the lightning bolted.

The teacher tells about a place she still remembers from childhood called Pearl Drop, where she and her brother used to fish the stream for minnows. They looked for pearls, to no avail.

The next day, continuing this conversation, we read Naomi Nye's poem "Little Blanco River." The little river, with all its fresh sounds and delicate way of life, is not deep enough for someone to "make a state park out of you," and for that she is glad. How she seems to celebrate that small stream. Also, the teacher reads Cynthia Rylant's "Beaver," from *Waiting to Waltz,* about a small country place a girl feels glad to grow up in.

We ask the writers to take a few minutes to jot one or two place names in their notebooks that seem interesting. Then we start saying them out just to get a sense of what people are thinking—Black Forest, Mama's Cafe, Wild Kingdom, Skate World, Froggy Park. They move off with writing partners to talk a bit about these place names and what they conjure up. We will be finding more poems with place names and using them as mentors for our own poems. Someone suggests they interview parents, grandparents, and adults in school to find out stories around memorable place names from their experience.

◌◌ *Mini-Inquiry*

FINDING OUR QUIET PLACES

*I am talking about the quiet place that stands for a departed friend,
or the sweet trance inside a book you love, or some old tree, some
riverbend that summons for you the quiet of your own spirit.*

—Kim Stafford (quoting his father, William Stafford),
"Afterword," in *Even in Quiet Places*

Students say they think the copper beech is a place where the character goes to
feel safe, liking how it feels to be alone, watching things happen, not being
afraid of things on the outside, finding a sense of peace. The way she "lean[s]
against the trunk." The way she listens, hearing "the sound before I saw it," and
hearing it "hitting the high leaves." The way she notices, seeing the rain "darkening the sidewalk." Feeling contented there, for a time.

"The Copper Beech" and the preceding quotation from William Stafford
help us to talk more about this kind of physical place that nurtures a place inside us. We decide to read Stafford's poem "Being a Person" and talk about it
next to our mentor poem.

I share excerpts from Kim Stafford's "Afterword" in *Even in Quiet Places*.
Here, he speaks of the Methow project, for which his father wrote a series of
road sign poems to be placed along the Methow River in the Cascade mountains, "in a very quiet place," where wanderers can stop and read, "I like to live
in the sound of water. . . ." In "Being a Person," William Stafford begins, "Be a
person here. Stand by the river, invoke / the owls. . . ." Lila thinks the poet
would have "spent time there, getting personal with the places, letting the
sounds run through him, as in 'Copper Beech.'" Derek says you can't get the
feeling of a place by just stopping by. "You have to stay there long enough to
stir something up." We wonder if that might be what Stafford meant by "invoke the owls." That we stand and listen in such a way that we begin to sense
the eternal nature of things, or until something stirs within us when we're quiet
enough to hear it: a longing, a question, a connection, a truth. Marie Howe does
that, we think. She could have stopped with "and I was happy." Instead, she
adds that one line at the end, separated from the others, which seems to say, this
is the part about being here—back up against the trunk of this sturdy tree,
alone, looking out—that makes it a safe place.

During workshop and at night, we make a list of quiet places where we
might try our hand at writing, taking lessons from Howe "to enter it" and
"practice being alone," finding our reasons for being there. And lessons from
Stafford, to accept what the place offers us, just being part of things, to "invoke

the owls," to "listen for the next things to happen." We get started with this over the next day or two.

Wendy's sense of self, the quiet of her own spirit, is palpable in her final version of "Skating":

SKATING

Standing still
on an
ice covered creek

Open
to almost nothing
at all

The sound of a blade
rushing
across the creek

Reminds me
that somewhere
underneath
my frozen toes

Lay
tons and
tons
of memories

And Lee (Figure 9.2), looking at flowers with notebook in hand, is metaphorically transformed.

WRITING IN PLACE, FINDING OUR OWN IDEAS

After he was quiet
a long time, words
began to come to
him in dreams &
told him their
secret names & this
was the way he learned
the true nature of
the world.

—Brian Andreas, "Secret Names," in *Story People*

Lee

Rainbow

I m stuck in a place
where all the flowers look
like a rainbow.
All the flowers grow
and look like frut , the purpl
flowers grapes, the
tulips apples, the
dandelins lemons

FIGURE 9.2   Lee, entering his quiet place.

We meet to hear one or two students' entries written in quiet places. Megan, always early to awaken, has written in her bed in the quiet of morning before anyone else is up. Christopher sat next to a fountain in the park across from his apartment building. Both their entries consist mainly of sensory images. We are delighted that the particulars they have written allow us to imagine their places, and we say out a few that seem especially vivid.

But we are also reminded of how the writers of our mentor poems not only give us a physical sense of place but let it help them find a truth or question or idea. I say I've been thinking about what Lila said last time. I read her quote from my notebook about staying in a place, "letting the sounds run through us." We talk about how when we forget ourselves, open up to what a place, or an experience in that place, can reveal to us, we think we are *being a person there*. It's funny to think of losing ourselves in a place in order to be present. Michael thinks fly-fishing at the lake is like that. Chris thinks reading *Harry Potter* (J. K. Rowling) is like that. I think digging in the garden is like that, or sitting at the edge of it.

We decide to return to one of the places we feel connected to (and to writing we've done so far in a quiet place) and see if we can practice what Lila and our mentor poets are telling us: "Come back and hear the little sound again"; let the sound run through us; perhaps dream there. Amir, a fifth grader, has caught the sound and spirit of a quiet place:

THE JETTY

Whispering wind
telling a long lost myth.

Shadowy creatures
wandering in the whirlpools
waves rippling
through the jetty.

High tide
damps the sun-baked sand
as the flickering moon
cools the lost voices
of happy children.

In Appendix A, see "Caught on a Strong Wind" and "The Walk," crafted poems with an intimate sense of place containing personal insight.

The idea of putting our stamp on places, of places putting their indelible stamp on us, shaping who we are, is one of continual fascination to students in classrooms where we work. Once into the inquiry, as with any deep investigation, we can begin to find the connectedness of things, and possibly with that, a little of our own "essential oil." In some classrooms, students initiate their own investigations, quests arising from work already being done: What about looking at places that comfort us? What if we think about the secrets a place might hold? What about the idea of "changing" places? How does light or time or weather affect a sense of place? And, as usual, the search for poems to help us explore these questions begins again.

10

Hiding Inside the Black Granite

LOOKING INTO

Shirley McPhillips

*You can keep a beautiful snakeskin in a poem, and you
can keep the look of the sun shining through it.*

PATRICIA HUBBELL,

in *The Place My Words Are Looking For* (Janeczko 1990)

FACING IT
Yusef Komunyakaa

My black face fades,
hiding inside the black granite.
I said I wouldn't,
dammit: No tears.
I'm stone. I'm flesh.
My clouded reflection eyes me
like a bird of prey, the profile of night
slanted against morning. I turn
this way—the stone lets me go.
I turn that way—I'm inside
the Vietnam Veterans Memorial
again, depending on the light
to make a difference.
I go down the 58,022 names,
half-expecting to find
my own in letters like smoke.
I touch the name Andrew Johnson;
I see the booby trap's white flash.
Names shimmer on a woman's blouse
but when she walks away
the names stay on the wall.
Brushstrokes flash, a red bird's
wings cutting across my stare.
The sky. A plane in the sky.
A white vet's image floats
closer to me, then his pale eyes
look through mine. I'm a window.
He's lost his right arm
inside the stone. In the black mirror
a woman's trying to erase names:
No, she's brushing a boy's hair.

I once stayed up all night waiting for the night-blooming cereus to blossom and transform the darkness. My Aunt Ada said that it bloomed only once and that even if you weren't looking at it, you'd know its flowers had opened by the heavy drift of vanilla that they exhaled into the night air. These magical flowers would expand in the dew of evening, spread themselves out to eight white inches, and breathe for six hours, then gasp and wither away. But Ada said that wasn't bad because the secrets they unleashed into the atmosphere were of such portent that six hours of their breath would be all the world could take. Six hours to celebrate a lifetime journey. What if I missed its brief display of splendor, never had a chance to share its secrets? I wanted to pull up a seat in front of the night-blooming cereus, to watch it in repose, then see its flowers spring forth like the tears the miracle watchers witnessed rolling down the statue of the Madonna's cheek. But Ada said, no, the cereus had its own time and would want to unfold in its own way, without a lot of eyes staring at it. She said it was too late, that we should go upstairs and she would read me a Perry Mason mystery, until tomorrow when we might catch the distinctive balm, which she could recognize from years of breathing the same air as plants.

Long before Perry had found a clue, Ada was asleep. But I, tempting all the roosters and chickens out of their fox dreams, sneaked out the side screen door, into the torpid summer night, to stare at the cereus, in case in its brief-blooming life, it hadn't learned to tell time. Like Ada, it didn't stir. Two twilights later, walking up the bank from the river, Ada caught the signal. "The night-blooming cereus," she announced, like the majordomo at a royal party, "has arrived!" Racing to the side of the porch steps, we saw it. Proud, I thought, like a new mother. Clusters of small spines radiating outward and terminating in glorious white trumpets, still and new in the rising moonlight.

Ada had a startling knowledge about plants, I thought, for an ordinary person living alone along the rural banks of the Rappahannock River. Only she, in these parts, lived within the shadow of an Osage orange. She alone knew just when we could climb up the clay banks and expect to pluck the red-ripe fruit from the prickly pear cactus. After her suppers we would taste the alien nectar of the figs she had willed to ripen from her exotic fig bush, she said, just for us. She could remember the fancy names of plants as well as their pet names and peculiarities. But more than that, they responded to each other's signals like seeing-eye dogs and the blind. She had a kinship with them; an understanding along sap lines.

Thinking back on it, I see that her stretches of curiosity and devotion to her environment, born of long-limbed days and solitary spaces, allowed Aunt Ada to develop a sensibility for *looking into* plants, not just *at* them. She knew intimately what others knew only casually. She knew what artist and writer Hannah Hinchman (1991) knows, that there are "many degrees of spring." That until we "strip away the tendency to generalize," to see things only in broad strokes, "we can't see the stunning complexity and drama" of our surroundings, of our lives.

Poems invite us to look *into* things, not just *at* them. Naomi Nye has written this, she says, on boards across the land. Poems ask us to look long enough to discover something and perhaps to transform it. "Discovery," says poet James Dickey. "Everything is *in* that. Everything *is* that. We can't create those trees or that water," he tells us. "But we can recreate it. We are secondary creators. The difference lies . . . in the slant, that we individually put on it, that only we can put on it. That is where our value lies" (Dickey 1998).

Poems ask us even to *stare* into things, to twist them this way and that, to be surprised. Some things amaze us and we can't explain why. Like the night-blooming cereus, they are mysteries, coming from our deep places. "We have a hunger deeper than the headline news," says Naomi Nye. We have a hunger, not just to stand by, but to stand inside; we hunger to find a place to affect something, to be affected by.

Komunyakaa's poem "Facing It," from *Dien Cai Dau,* touches our hearts in deep ways. It is a powerful example of looking long, of looking into and trying to make sense of things for ourselves. In reading and rereading it, we can experience a common sharing of life's mysteries, and find the courage to explore our own.

ᕫᕬ *Getting Started*

ORIENTING OURSELVES TO THE MENTOR POEM

"Facing It" is longer than many poems we've read, so we want to give students ample time to reread it and talk with each other about it, to feel familiar with it. I read it through once, aloud. Then, since the poem is centered on an experience at the Vietnam Veterans Memorial, a place that no one in this class has visited or knows much about, I feel I want to say something to orient the students before I read it again. I tell them I have stood at this wall, in the morning light, among tourists and veterans, and I have wept with them, though I have not stood at the wall the way the character in "Facing It" stands. I tell them that Komunyakaa served in Vietnam and has written other poems as well as this one out of his experience.

Today, the mentor poem has inspired an eagerness for information that the teacher and I decide to let play out. We believe this curiosity will anchor an interest in the poem that will allow us to stay with it longer. Fernando, for example, is amazed at 58,022 names. So many dead. How could they carve so many names into the stone? Sal believes his Uncle John went to Vietnam. Carmel wonders at the stone itself; she reads from her copy, "It says, '*In the black mirror a woman's trying to erase names.*'" Students will read the poem again and continue having discussions with their writing partners over the next couple of days.

REVISITING THE MENTOR POEM

Several days later, we gather the class to read Eve Bunting's *The Wall*, a picture storybook about a father and his young son searching the Vietnam Veterans Memorial for the name of the grandfather the boy never knew. A quiet and sensitive account, it gives one a feeling, like our mentor poem, of being there, of being affected by the wall in deep ways. We believe that by reading and discussing this book, students will have a better understanding about what the wall signifies in the lives of so many people. It will give them another way to revisit the poem.

Their first inclination is to compare the two. Carmel says the story feels sad, like the poem. In the poem, he is holding back the tears. In the book, too, people are solemn, pensive, some crying. Ron notices that in both accounts someone scans the names, actually touching them. Zack says that people in both, as they face the wall, see something behind them reflected in the wall. Students search both accounts for examples of what is reflected: themselves, and trees, and "dark, flying clouds," in the book; and in the poem, "a red bird's wings," "a plane in the sky," a woman "brushing a boy's hair." Edwin notices that, in the book, a veteran at the wall has lost his legs, and in the poem, an arm.

We think this is a good place to stop. Students are rereading the poem with purpose, locating exact lines and reading them out. They are beginning, from what we hear them say, to get a sense of the power of the wall to affect people in similar yet individual ways. This will be a helpful concept to refer to as they later *look into* their own objects.

LOOKING INTO OBJECTS FROM OUR LIVES

Say it, no ideas but in things.

—William Carlos Williams, *Paterson*

During the initial mini-lessons around the mentor poem, the teacher and I have asked students to bring in an object that holds some interest or value for them. Interest, we say, meaning it seems intriguing and you can see yourselves spending some time observing and thinking about it, and value, not in terms of money or medals, but maybe something small that you hold dear for a particular personal reason. The teacher has already shown them an old book of essays sent to him in college by his grandfather. Inside is a note written in the kind of watery purple ink we don't see anymore. This was the first and last such correspondence between them. He keeps the book on his desk at home, a reminder of the bonds and bridges formed by words. To demonstrate that the object doesn't necessarily have to come with heavy emotional ties, he shows a banded stone he picked up on a walk in the fall, now a paperweight on his desk.

By the time I arrive today, most students have brought in an object from home. Still the teacher has quite a few interesting things about the room—natural objects in the science center, art objects—which, though not personal, students can observe if they haven't brought something. And some students have entries of observations they've been working on. Today, Julian has agreed to co-teach the mini-lesson. He unwraps the tissue paper from around a small pinkish slipper shell. We ask him to make a quick sketch on the chart paper of an image that comes to mind. He sketches a square with little shells lined up inside, then tells us the story of walking the beach with his cousin Peter. How Peter found this one and put it in his, Julian's, bucket. As he sketches, Julian tells how they spread out rows of slipper shells on the beach towel, picking them up, saying what hid inside, what they could hear when they put each one to their ears. "Pretending, of course."

Often, when we don't want them to focus on the drawing, we ask students to open up their notebooks and, on the spot, make a quick sketch. Today, we feel it will be better if they have their objects in front of them, close to them, to get their ideas going. For that, writers will need more space. As students settle to sketch, we circulate, helping some to look closely, to verbalize if they need to in order to find an image. Then they spread out about the room with their objects and sketches to tell their partners the story from the sketch.

We do this all together today because we believe students will be invested in each other's stories and have a way to proceed when making other observations on their own. We think the sketches have stimulated a good beginning dialogue, opening up possibilities for further inquiry. They will serve as seeds for conversations to come as students revisit the mentor poem and think about what they're looking into. Tonight and tomorrow, they will write these images in their notebooks (see Chapter 2).

The students put their objects on a special observation table, accessible to them when they are working on their writing. In one class, See Woo, having observed outside the school and looked closely at a leaf, crafts this poem:

LEAF

Winter
Shiny thin ice
Trapping beauty
Like a jewel hidden
inside a drawer.

Lost
A leaf,
only a memory.

❧ *Keeping It Going*

LOOKING INTO "RIGHT NOW," WRITING SKETCHES

Sketching and writing about an image have been helpful in getting started looking into an object. Now we want to find other ways to explore our object, so we turn again to our mentor poem. What do we notice about where the poet put the character in relation to the Vietnam Veterans Memorial? I read the first ten or so lines. Edwin says, "It's like he's there, right up close to the wall. Staring into it. He doesn't really look anywhere else." Tasha notices that the character is there *now*. We look for evidence of that: "face fades . . . reflection eyes me . . . I turn . . . I go down the . . . names . . . I touch . . . I see . . . names shimmer." As we talk, the teacher writes these phrases on the chart so we can examine them. (If students have a copy of the poem, they can find and underline examples.)

We talk about writing in the present tense and how that gives a sense of "right now," as Tasha has said. The students reread an image they've written off their object (or any writing off something they've observed, or that they can picture in their minds now). We ask them to write a few word sketches—quick, short, list-like phrases of words—to give us that "right now" feeling (see also Chapter 7). Julian writes,

> I pick up the pink slipper shell
> I stare into the small hole
> I try to fit my pinky into it
> I watch Pete put it to his ear. I copy him.

One or two others read out their word sketches. We feel this is a good start toward helping the writers focus their thinking and get themselves into a closer relationship with the object. They will work more on these phrases during the week, with the mentor poem next to them.

William crafts a poem, "Goldfish." His word sketches are detailed, giving us a sense of things happening before our eyes. Toward the end, the poet reaches out to touch the goldfish, as Komunyakaa does the wall:

GOLDFISH

Orange shiny scales
Golden fish with fat tiny bodies,

Small black eyes, looking at me.
Their mouths opening into "O"s,
Long smooth tails,
Trapped in a copy of their real world.
Swimming back and forth.

I put my finger inside their home,
They snap at my finger—

Swimming,
Slowly away.

LOOKING FOR THE MYSTERY IN OUR OBJECTS

*Celebrate the ordinary, the obvious, the things that
surround us that spark memories, and imaginings.*

—Donald Murray, *Crafting a Life in Essay, Story, Poem*

In W. S. Merwin's *The Unwritten* (see Appendix A for complete poem), the character looks deeply inside an ordinary object, a pencil, and finds all the stories waiting to be told, all the poems waiting to be written, words waiting for the right call from the writer. In one class the teacher and I want students to put Merwin's poem alongside Komunyakaa's "Facing It." The character in our mentor poem stays a long time at the wall, looking deeply into it, letting it make him think about his experiences connected with it. Some of his images and reactions seem almost surreal, mysterious, as he tries to sort out his feelings.

Merwin's character, too, looks long inside a pencil. After some conversation about the poem, we think he's not looking into the pencil at all, that the pencil is a vehicle for looking into the condition of a writer. What he sees seems to be a mystery, and throughout the poem he's pondering the matter, ending with a meditation about what might be happening here.

We ask the writers, as they go back to work on their own poems, to look back at their objects, their writing, and ask, What's the mystery here? They study how Merwin and Komunyakaa stretch their images and ask questions of them; how they ponder long. Students try asking questions and meditating a bit in the poems they're working on (see Chapter 6).

Charles, a second grader, fascinated with the sun shining through his magnifying glass, lifts a line from another entry in his notebook, writes it at the top of the page, and searches for the mystery of "light" (Figure 10.1). Some writers make a split page, the images on one side and questions and meditations on the other. Later they can try meshing the two.

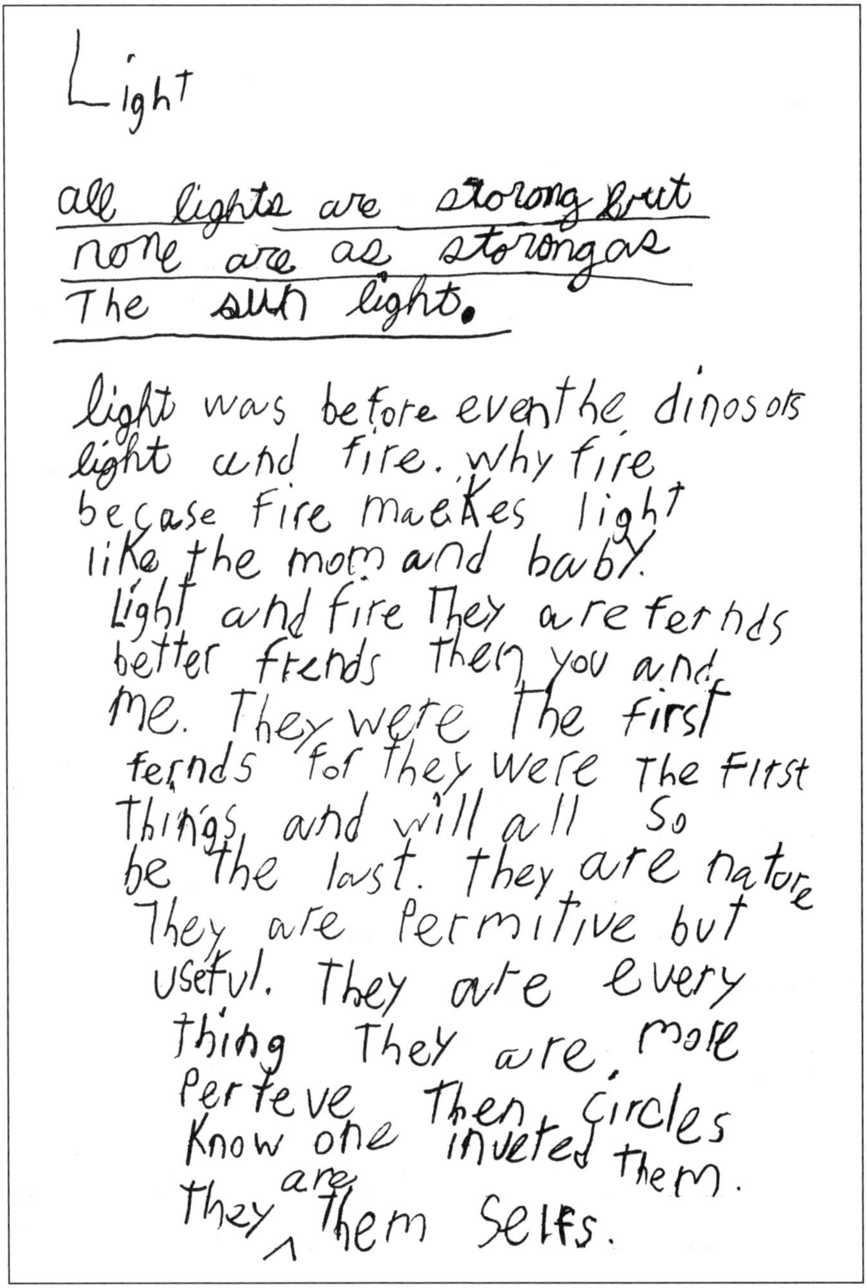

Light

all lights are storong but none are as storong as The sun lights.

light was before even the dinosos light and fire. why fire becase fire maekes light like the mom and baby. Light and fire They are fernds better frends then you and me. They were the first fernds for they were the first things, and will all So be the last. they are nature They are permitive but useful. They are every thing They are more perteve Then circles Know one inveted them. They are Them Selfs.

FIGURE 10.1   Charles, writing off a line, probes the mystery of light.

LOOKING AT STRUCTURE TO EXTEND OUR IMAGES

We want to look more closely at our mentor poem in order to see how we might extend the word sketches we have written. We notice that the poet extends some of his images after an action, so students begin to pull out from the mentor poem the places where the character specifically does something: *I turn, I go down, I touch, I see.* Julian and others point out that they, too, have written actions like this. Identifying actions helps us chunk the poem so that we can select smaller sections to explore. Fernando, fascinated earlier with the number of names, suggests we take the part starting with "I go down." We read through to see how much of a chunk we will examine—from "I go down" to "white flash," five lines related to looking closely at the names. We try to articulate the structure of just this part. The character

- Looks down the list of names (an action)
- Half-expects something (an inner thought)
- Touches a name (another action, closer)
- Remembers something (a memory of an image, a flashback)

This seems like something we could try. We simplify our list:

- An action
- An inner thought
- A closer action
- A flashback image (or memory)

Students experiment with this structure using their own word sketches and images written off objects. They can try this out using any other poems they're working on as well. The teacher puts some on the overhead in a few days, the writers leading a discussion about how they approached using the structure and what they notice.

Julian sticks rather closely to the structure we have named, and he feels free to pick up a word of two from Komunyakaa:

I stare into the pink pocket of my shell
half-expecting to see
a small wave.
I put it close to my ear
I hear the splash of you laughing.

Over time, the class can return to the mentor poem, taking other sections of it, naming what the poet is doing, how he stretches the line or the image.

Appendix B shows a transcript of a conference with Jonah to help him notice how he might stretch out his poem's actions, move between action and observation, and slow down his poem.

ᕼᕽ *Extending Our Thinking*
LOOKING INTO THE TEXTURE OF THE MENTOR POEM

Our mentor poem is richly textured, the poet using various kinds of details and poetic devices, including simile and metaphor, to pull us into the character's external and internal experience at the wall. We can focus more on simile and metaphor at some point. For today, we want our writers just to be generative in picking out whatever specific examples they see of the poet's details and to try to articulate what the writer is doing and how that affects our reading of the poem.

We don't just see a bird, for example, we see "brushstrokes flash" (a metaphor, something standing for the movement of the bird), then "a red bird's wings cutting across my stare" (wings doing something).

We also notice an extended line such as, "My black face fades, / hiding inside the black granite." We imagine a surface so dark and shiny that the whole face cannot be seen, giving the illusion of hiding. This image, appearing at the outset, prepares us for accepting all the other half-illusory images to come.

We see not just any kind of face but the "clouded reflection" staring back (reflection doing something) like a "bird of prey" (specific comparison), piercing, still.

We see not just a woman, or the names on the reflection of her blouse, but a shimmer of names, moving as she walks away. One student sees a movie in her mind of the woman turning to walk away, blurred black letters shining, twisting.

Instead of the wall, we see a "black mirror." In it, the action of the woman trying to erase names, then a change of thought: no, she's "brushing a boy's hair." These last two contrasting details make one student actually picture an arm moving up and down in an erasing attitude, then himself turning away from the wall, in his mind, to see an ordinary brushing of hair.

We write some of these lines up on the chart as we talk about them. And, right here, the writers take a few minutes to find part of something they're working on in their notebooks and to try, briefly, giving it more *texture*. Not everyone is successful at doing this quickly. But a few students share their attempts with all of us before we move off to continue working. Those who need it will have more time to try this now in their own poetry.

Jennifer catches the mystery, the enchantment, in a pool of water near her house as she tosses stones into it. In her crafted piece, "Water," she builds texture, making surprising comparisons, stretching them out, using active, energized words. She acts, reacts, building an intimate relationship with the water, at times speaking to it. She draws us into her experience:

WATER

You hold my reflection
Pure,
crystalline smooth like a mirror,
reflecting myself
in another dimension,
in another world.

       l
     p o
   x   d
You e   e
like thunder.
Thrusting a million erupting pearls
of liquid
into space.

I catch
one of your pearls
I am enchanted.

When sleeping
It is still,
silent,
quiet
Until a pebble is thrown
and ripples waver
on your crystal surface,
Like ribbons
skating across the ice.

LOOKING CLOSELY AND SEEING BIG THINGS

She saw herself
reflected in the
store window &
then the sun
changed & she
disappeared &

> *all she could*
> *see was her eyes*
> *& she remembered*
> *thinking, I make*
> *a very nice floor*
> *lamp & that was*
> *the day she decided*
> *to quit her job.*

—Brian Andreas, "Epiphany," in *Story People*

When the character in "Facing It" touches the name of Andrew Johnson, he sees an image, "the booby trap's white flash," in his mind's eye—a flashback memory, not something literally there. Julian has put the shell up to his ear and heard, not what he actually may have heard, but the memory of the laughter of his friend as they played on the beach that day.

Today, we want to talk further about poems in which the character looks closely and sees, not just something literally there, but something metaphorical. We feel it's important to give students time to speculate about the abstract, to pose possibilities for what the poet might mean. It's not a question of "getting the right meaning" because we don't know what the writer may have meant, and we don't believe there is a "right" meaning. But what we're doing is to put ourselves in a position to begin to understand how one or two poets use metaphor so that, as writers, we can learn from it.

From a collection we're making of examples of poets looking closely into things, I read aloud Sonia Sanchez's "My Father's Eyes" (Steptoe 1997):

MY FATHER'S EYES

I have looked into
    my father's eyes and seen an
        african sunset.

The narrator has looked into her father's eyes and seen—*an african sunset.* Why a sunset, we wonder? Someone says sunset is at the close of the day. A peaceful time. A boy wonders if the father is very old. If he is dying. The teacher wonders if maybe he loves his life now; he accepts it, like a sunset that streaks the sky with brilliant colors just before it goes dark. We agree that we can only imagine what Sanchez's narrator has seen and how that connects with what she feels and understands, that we would have to talk with her to find out. But we know that her words have touched us. And when we read her poem again we feel uplifted, investing our voices with a prideful energy as we make the turn around the corner from the second to the third line.

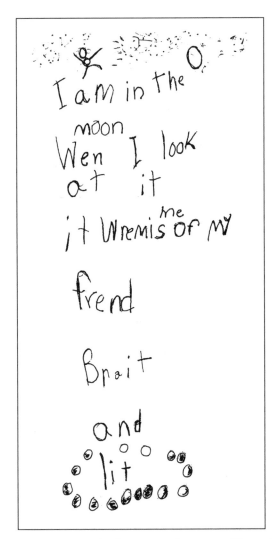

FIGURE 10.2   Daniel's poem looking into the moon. ("I am in the moon. When I look at it, it reminds me of my friend. Bright and light.")

We notice that in the narrowed focus, the clarity of her father's eye, the narrator is able to see something large in the landscape, and we talk about how *sometimes when we look carefully at something small, we can think big things.* The teacher asks students to write this line in their notebooks to remind them as they write.

Before they head off, students find something in their notebooks that they're already looking into and mark a couple of places where they think they can try making a turn from "looking into" to seeing something that's not literally there. If they're thinking of something new, they can jot that down. Some students make a list in their notebooks of possible things—not the usual—they can look into: a new baby's smile; the corner of a secret; the bounce of a basketball; the heart of a violin. We agree that our purpose is to practice looking closely and stretching our thinking here, so we are not necessarily using a haiku structure. As students work on their poetry over time, looking at and looking into, some will keep these beginnings, revising them slightly. Others will extend their images, their metaphors, into longer poems.

Daniel, a first grader, writes of looking into the moon and seeing a friendship (Figure 10.2). Casey, in another class, writes, "I look into a sidewalk of stone and see the homeless tread of old men." His teacher writes,

> *I look into someone else's story and hear a world of strangers singing in mysterious incantations, wave after wave of what came first and who came second to this alien land of dreams. I dig into someone else's story and pull up the loose end of a thread of my own.*

೮৩ *Mini-Inquiry*

JOURNEYING TO DEEP PLACES

A teacher told us when I was in school: The things that cause you friction are the things from which you might make art.

—Naomi Shihab Nye, *What Have You Lost?*

As members of our classroom community build up a trust and respect for one another, as well as an openness to reading and discussing different kinds of poems, we want our students to see that poetry is also a journey to places of deep feeling—sadness and disappointment, mystery and misunderstanding, joy and enchantment. We learn from poets like Julia Cunningham, who says that her journey to these places turned into poems that "healed and helped and made of me a very grateful writer" (Janeczko 1990). We want to include, in our reading, poems that take us to the very heart of things, so that we might learn to write poems from our own deep places.

We wonder about the title of our mentor poem, "Facing It." Obviously the character is facing the wall, but what else do we make of the title? Thinking about what Cunningham said, Anthony thinks it must have been hard for the poet to write about the wall considering his experiences in Vietnam. "He would have to think about all the bad times in the war. Then when he stands in front of the wall, it's like all the pictures of the people he knew, what happened to them, all come back at him." Taylor wonders why he writes about the wall since it's so painful. That's a good question. We're not sure, but we think the poet probably writes about a lot of things out of his experience. Like the novelist John Cheever, who said he wrote to make sense of his life, maybe Komunyakaa is trying to make some sense of the war as regards his own life now. Nicole thinks maybe the images we see reflected in the wall are all things the poet is "facing," all the things that stay with him. "A lot of it seems like a dream." Anthony refers to the names section, how the character half-expects to find his own. "He touches Andrew Johnson. 'J' is right before 'Komunyakaa.' Maybe he's facing that he didn't die the way they did. He would be glad. But it would be hard to lose all your friends."

We keep the conversation focused on the mentor poem, always turning back to it for examples, always with the idea of being instructed by it. As teachers we try to demonstrate the tentative nature of talking about a writer's work, that the point of the discussion is not to find "the answer," as if we knew it, but to imagine possibilities that can fuel our own thinking about our own lives and work.

USING OTHER POEMS TO FIND
SOMETHING OF OURSELVES

To find the essential grain of oneself—everything else is incidental to that quest.

—Stanley Kunitz, in a talk paraphrasing Gerard Manley Hopkins

In "Facing It," the poet shows us how sights and sounds at the wall can trigger memories. He has put his character in a position to remember, to face something in his life ("I said I wouldn't, / dammit: No tears. / I'm stone. I'm flesh."). As we read our mentor poem and others, as we write off our memories, we are positioning ourselves to let our memories speak to us, to speak back.

We read Cynthia Rylant's poem "Forgotten," in *Waiting to Waltz: A Childhood,* about a girl's reaction to hearing of her father's death. The teacher remembers Rylant's saying in *The Place My Words Are Looking For* (Janeczko 1990) that she thought a boy she knew was a real poet because he saw things and tried to make sense of them with his heart. He let little things matter.

Students reread their notebook entries and mark places where they've noticed the small things around them, where memories and images are strong. We will in the next few days be noticing, writing down what we observe, what we remember, trying to write about things in ways that show they matter to us.

USING OTHER POEMS TO HELP US
EXPLORE THINGS THAT MATTER

One day we read the poem "Locked In" by Ingemar Leckius, from *This Same Sky* (Nye, ed. 1992), in which a boy says he has all his life lived in a coconut. After discussing and rereading the poem, some students try writing about the places where they live, where they hide (see Chapter 9).

At another time, we read Julia Cunningham's poem "Carousel" (Janeczko 1990) and talk about how this writer, caught by the music and magic of the carousel, is transported back in time to an image of her lost father.

Students jot in their notebooks some "mysterious places" of their own where they think they can, as Cunningham invites us to do, "walk with our words." Rafael, a fourth grader, speaks about his "dark" place in an untitled poem:

Dark is outside.
It is very quiet and wakes up the owls.
Dark makes me scared and shakes me.
Dark is blind and makes me blind
as I feel my way around
in its blackness.

And Jessica, a fifth grader, takes us deep into the world of the hearing impaired:

DEAFNESS

Hands twisting,
hands saying words,
ears sleeping,
the hand has a mind of its own,
as my eyes are traveling
through a maze of movements,
mouth moves while I can't hear myself.

I have to live with sleepy ears.

LETTING WORDS TAKE US TO DEEP PLACES

As we've said, the character at the wall in "Facing It" touches a word, a name, and an image flashes in his mind. We want to explore ways in which we can look into words, turn them, unlock them, bounce them, let them take us where they will.

One day I introduce "The Woman Cleaning Lentils," written by an unidentified poet in Zahrad, Armenia, and translated by scholar and poet Diana Der-Hovanessian.

THE WOMAN CLEANING LENTILS

A lentil, a lentil, a lentil, a stone.
A lentil, a lentil, a lentil, a stone.
A green one, a black one, a green one, a black. A stone.
A lentil, a lentil, a stone, a lentil, a lentil, a word.
Suddenly a word. A lentil.
A lentil, a word, a word next to another word. A sentence.
A word, a word, a word, a nonsense speech.
Then an old song.
Then an old dream.
A life, another life, a hard life. A lentil. A life.
An easy life. A hard life. Why easy? Why hard?
Lives next to each other. A life. A word. A lentil.
A green one, a black one, a green one, a black one, pain.
A green song, a green lentil, a black one, a stone.
A lentil, a stone, a stone, a lentil.

This poem exemplifies what can happen when we trust words, when we let them take us places. We've noticed that sometimes when we first read this poem aloud students titter at the repetition of a word like *lentil*. But quickly they are intrigued as larger themes sneak in around the words.

After we talk some about what we notice, we reread the poem, looking specifically at what happens to the words. "A lentil, a lentil, a lentil, a stone / A green one, a black one, a green one, a black. . . ." Liquid-sounding words bouncing along in a regular rhythm, seeming to imitate the way we can imagine the act of cleaning lentils would be. Then,

. . . a word.
Suddenly a word. A lentil.

Words stopping each other, shocking each other in proximity:

. . . a word next to another word. A sentence.

Words adding up, stringing out into phrases:

Then an old song.
Then an old dream.

An allusion to a memory, to another life:

Lives next to each other. . . .

Allusions to hard times, challenges. Almost-images, questions, spiraling in and out of a life:

Why easy? Why hard?

An allusion to pain. Then the promise of "a green song." The word *lentil* is sporadic by the end, sharing space with *stone.* And we're back to one-word repetition, as in the beginning.

Even though the poem is composed only of single words and bare snatches of words, no complete sentences or thoughts, we have the impression of having been on a journey, a flashback of memory and emotion. As we read, it's as if *we* complete the thoughts, fill in between the lines, with images and memories of our own. And we are moved.

The students have been collecting words in their notebooks since the beginning of the year: surprising words, intriguing words, words that conjure up memories, questions. They have also underlined words on occasion and written off them: free-flowing entries, images, moments. Now we ask students to look through these words, or through their notebook entries, and pick one (or jot down a new one), and over the next couple of days to play with it, bounce it around. What happens if we bounce it into something else? What reverberates? What echoes? What backfires? What chimes?

During writing workshop this week, some start copying the word over and over, letting things come. Some jot images they get when they think of the word, to help them get started. Jeremy looks back at his entry on wishing for a dog. Then, with "The Woman Cleaning Lentils" next to him, glancing back and forth between the poem and his notebook, he writes:

A boy, a boy, a boy, a wish, a wish,
a wish, a wish, a boy, a dream. A boy,
a deep wish, a dog dream. A force, a boy,
a longing, a begging, a no-dog force.
Why deep? Why a dog dream? A boy, a force, a boy.
Dog forces crossing each other out.

In another class, Jonathan, a third grader (Figure 10.3), seems almost frantic about figuring out words in general. He bounces the word *word* and puts emphasis on knowing this word, on needing *help,* by repeating those words. Stretching out the words at the end, the whole of it results in a plea that tugs at our very core. ("A Woman Cleaning Lentils," and the students' poems here also

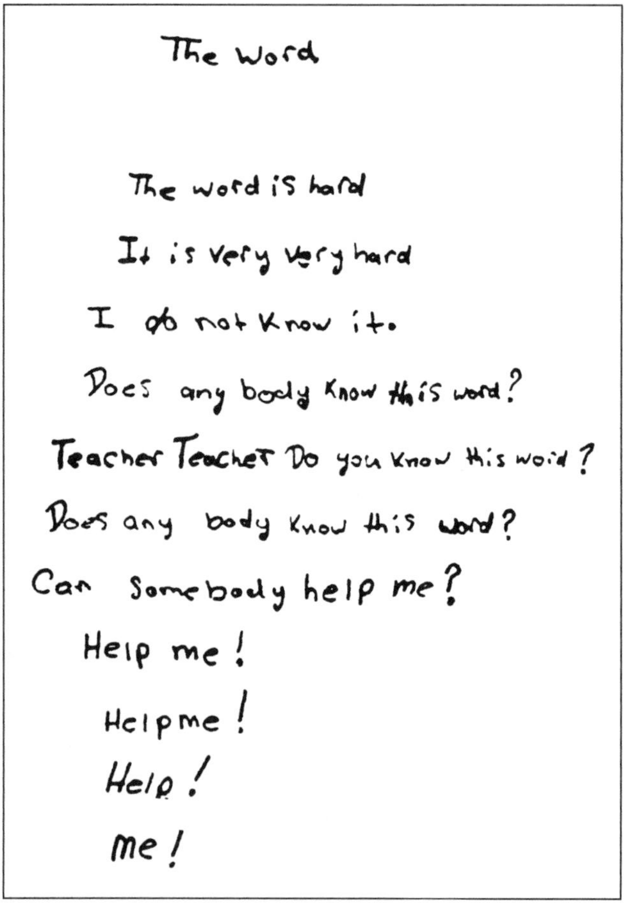

The Word

The word is hard
It is very very hard
I do not know it.
Does any body know this word?
Teacher Teacher Do you know his word?
Does any body know this word?
Can Somebody help me?
Help me!
Help me!
Help!
me!

FIGURE 10.3   Jonathan's poem looking into words.

would have served us well in Chapter 5 on sounds of language. This multi-functionality is true with many other poems we mention throughout the book.)

GROUPS LOOKING BETWEEN THE LINES

Our friend Naomi Shihab Nye sometimes gets writers, as a group, to look between the lines and into them. She says this might be a way to stretch our minds and open up new territory, to get a sense of abundance and variety. The teacher and I decide we should all try it first at the chart. We have searched for lines we feel are open and provocative by looking through first lines in our own poetry books: "Behind the dead wall of winter"; "Every night I lie awake";

"When I turn to say goodbye"; "At night the air relaxes"; "A stranger came in from . . ." I decide on a line I heard Naomi Nye read at a workshop: "I spill from a . . ." One by one, volunteers come to the chart to write the next line and the next. We remind ourselves to reread carefully before we write, to try to keep within whatever image is coming to our minds, to keep within the spirit and voice of the emerging poem. Today they write,

> I spill from a
> basket of books
> all the pages
> I never read
> and ride away with Harry Potter
> on a broomstick
> to magic time

No one has spoken during the writing. So when the last writer finishes, voices erupt in a burst of pent-up laughter and amazement. We read it through aloud to catch the sound, and we talk with the writers about how they decided what to write when it was their turn.

Now, in groups of about four or five, the students follow the same procedure as at the chart. The first student reads the line the teacher has written at the top of the paper (today each group has a different line), tries to form an image or connect a thought to something in memory, and writes another line, then passes it to the next writer, who writes a line and passes it on, until everyone has written. The last few people have to be aware that they will be bringing the poem to a close. One student reads the entire poem through to her group and they talk about how it sounds and what they notice. Then they write their work on chart paper and put it up for all to read. Students like to look across the charted poems to talk about the lines and marvel at how much they wrote. They notice, for example, which poems seem to hang together around a central image; which look inside and go deep; which ones hold metaphors; where the places, the words are that moved them, and so on.

At the end, it's fun, and instructive, to show students the poem from which the line was excerpted. Writers can see the different ways people read and connect with ideas; the different images and lines of thought that emerge from words sitting together in a certain way. We encourage the students to search for their own open-ended lines and contribute those to the class chart.

We like it, too, when each group is writing off the same line so we can see the poems move in different directions; and sometimes, if the group is small, we pass the paper around twice to try to extend the poems. Sometimes we start with a question.

Deep inside a poem are all the things we feel. Here is where we find camaraderie with others in the world just like us, and discover, at the same time, our own uniqueness. When my Aunt Ada looked into her plants, she touched something of the very essence of them, and they her. And though she never wrote a poem, that's the way she taught us what poets know. In a sense, many chapters in this book are really about "looking into" things, getting off the known and traveled trail and onto the footpath that leads off into more unclaimed territory, perhaps to claim it for ourselves. Discovering, turning things, looking in back of them and underneath. Putting our individual slant on things, finding what is deeply true. But maybe focusing on "looking into" as we do in this inquiry can help us understand the ways in which it's *all* about that.

11

Kingdoms with Love
SPIRITUALITY AND SOCIAL JUSTICE

*I dream of an art so transparent that you
can look through and see the world.*

STANLEY KUNITZ,

in *Interviews and Encounters with Stanley Kunitz*

BROTHERS AND SISTERS

Brothers and sisters,
where do we come from?
A pool or a book? Or from outerspace?
Where ever we come from it must be safe.
There are some of us might die.
Brother, sister, even twin.

—*Christley Jones, grade 3*

A s the poems of this world find their way to us, in our final chapter we find ourselves coming back into the world. We want to end by briefly addressing the idea of writing about larger issues, whether spirituality, social justice, or simply what it means to be a human being as one millennium gives over to the next. Poems begin with the experience of being, Charles Simic (1994) says, as "a voice in solitude for which the present moment is everything." And this found voice can lift our awareness of ourselves and our place in the world, until we realize the world is speaking to us and we're speaking back. We also want to use some young people's poems as mentors here because, ideally, that is what each will become—a mentor to someone else, if not through their poetry then through whatever it is they choose to pursue in their lives.

We Come to the World Spiritually

In *The Spiritual Life of Children,* Robert Coles defines spirituality as the struggle to make sense of the larger questions: Where do we come from? Why are we here? What happens when we die? Cassandra draws a coffin with her father inside. His speech bubble is empty. Chanel writes, "When I close my eyes to see my mother I see thunder." Ozairez is in kindergarten but already he knows that when people die they "turn black." Shaneal writes, "the Devil told this man to kill my uncle and my uncle died." By Coles's definition, the poem by Shawndell that begins this book (see Chapter 1 mentor poem), the poem by Christley that begins this chapter, and the following poem by Carlos, are all spiritual poems.

THE AFTERLIFE

They put you on a line
    & they ask you
for your name,
    & if your name
is in the book you go up
    the elevator
& they put you on a test,
    put you
in front of a door.
    If you enter
you go to Hell.
    If you knock
a wise man will come
    & let you in

& you will see
   your mom & dad
& your ancestors.

—*Carlos, grade 6*

These writers, then, all children in New York City public schools, are in some sense spiritual writers—they are pushing against the unanswerable, understanding that the act of writing can be like the idea of God: a lingering in mystery. Understanding that writing can also be a means to move toward a "concrete mysticism," in which the devil speaks and mothers are thunder, where everyone's home is a kingdom, where even the dead are given speech bubbles, just in case.

In the poems by Shawndell, Christley, and Carlos, each writer uses strategies we have already looked at, the only difference being that what they choose to write about deals more directly with issues of spirituality. Inevitably, these issues will emerge when teaching poetry—it's one of its prime functions and pleasures. We hope our classrooms will be safe places to explore these deeper questions—that a necessary level of trust and community will have been established early on.

Christley (pronounced *Christ-ly*) starts his poem with a question, one he likely overheard in church or on television. His poem embodies the sound of a sermon, *brothers and sisters,* possibly one he sat through more than once, and its cadences and syntax stayed with him. But how did he know his question (*the* question) could remain unanswered, something not always taught in school (especially when we must teach more and more toward multiple-choice tests)? How did he know that having the answer before you ask is not always useful? How did he know a sermon could also be a poem? His question is followed by a list, rangy yet precise: *a pool? a book? outerspace?* What is religion but speculation? In the beginning was the word, and these are the words that have found a place inside him. And asking questions and making lists are some of the strategies that he has been able to internalize and apply gracefully in his writing.

Carlos had also been moved, not by a question, but by a single word. He noticed an advertisement for a movie in train stations and on the sides of buses that suggested that one should "get an afterlife." The movie concerned the "life" of a ghost (not the *holy* ghost, but the *friendly* ghost), "ghost" being a semi-concrete way to explain the phenomenon of loss mingling with presence. For Carlos, the word *afterlife* was resonant enough for him to construct an entire poem from it. That he was able to craft a poem from this one word suggests that he has internalized, among others, the strategies of both eavesdropping and listening to the sounds of language. Aside from these strategies, Carlos has also been able to imagine a place (heaven) and to write about it in such a way as to give his readers an image of that place. Another student, Jason, a second grader, also looked to cartoons with his questions, much as Carlos did. After Jason's father was shot and killed, he wrote, "I am the Hulk / and I rule the sky / I live in the clouds / and wait for people to die." Often it is necessary to take what is at hand, whether it is comic books or poetry, to make sense of the world.

Like Shawndell's poem in Chapter 1, which can be considered spiritual in that it asks serious questions about what could be called *social justice,* Othiamba's poem dares to ask provocative questions about where his character, and others like him, stands in a troubled world:

THE GUARDIAN

High in the sky lives the one who has lived
for years.
The one who has guarded our world,
the one who calls himself the guardian.
Why is it that he who calls himself the
guardian has not seen the trouble,
the trouble that has taken over our world.
He who calls himself the guardian
does not know why I call him.
He who says he sees all does not see me
    alone,
    trapped,
    lifeless.
He does not see me running away from this world.
    Does not know why,
    why I call him,
    or why he is the guardian.

Poet Marge Piercy says, "We can hear what we hope for and what we most fear in the release of a cadence's utterance." In this Othiamba has prevailed. He has nurtured his inner voice for sound, and he mesmerizes us. The way he picks up the last words in a line and uses them to start the next line keeps the sound moving, layering the feeling. We can feel the voice of the poem move us, move in us.

We Come to the World Socially and Politically

Stanley Kunitz says, "Poetry wants to communicate what it feels like to be alive," and so in that sense, "There is no way you can separate poetry from history. History—the experience of the race—is the subject matter of poetry." A poem, written from the passion of what is deeply true for that writer, can have the effect of stirring things up in the larger world, of challenging experience and long-held beliefs. W. B. Yeats wrote poems in support of Ireland's Easter Uprising. The Turkish poet Nazim Hikmet, imprisoned in his own country for twenty-seven years for the act of writing poems, continued to write while in prison. Lucille Clifton, an American poet of African descent, writes out of her experiences in a way that could be termed political in that many of them serve to point out persistent social inequities. It's not that poets purposely set out, always, to change how things are done socially or politically, or to influence people's thinking about issues or events. It's just that as poets make poems out of their experience, inevitably the political will, at times, filter in.

To return again to Shawndell's poem by way of example: this poem presents, in a nonjudgmental way, the class disparities in our culture, disparities that a third grader living in Harlem in the 1990s would come face-to-face with daily. We were fortunate enough to work in his school for six years, during which time we walked from the subway past countless burned-out shells of buildings, a neighborhood that had been given up on. The last year we were there, the last year of the twentieth century, things showed signs of change, slowly: some buildings were being renovated, people were moving back in. Inside, though, the school always felt like a refuge, a safe place away from the harshness of the streets. Shawndell was able to write his poem in this refuge, using strategies he seems to have internalized, including comparisons and a strong use of imagery. We have used this poem to good effect in many other classrooms, often beginning by having the students sketch out the images that Shawndell has given us. Nearly each line, we discover, generates a new image, any one of which he could have lingered with for a while longer, and perhaps he did, in his notebook. The sketch that has often come from these discussions is of what Shawndell might have seen from the window of his apartment—the New York City skyline, a doghouse behind his building, a homeless man looking through a Dumpster. He then applies the same metaphor to each thing he sees, that of a *kingdom,* and this is what holds all he sees together, in his imagination, and ours.

Another, more direct, example of how poetry can come to involve issues of social justice comes from the following poem by LeRoi Johnson. LeRoi challenges us to consider certain oft-quoted words, exploring the tendency of overused words to lose their power, words "that get said so much, what do they mean? Who believes them?" From some of his mentors he's acquired a deceivingly simple conversational tone, one that makes us want to read the poem again and again, for all it says, for all it doesn't say.

WHAT YOU CAN'T SAY

You can't say freedom
and walk on down the street

as if you just said
have a nice day,
'cause nobody will believe you.

You can't say words
like "dream" as if you
slept in a feather bed
with a lot of warm covers
pulled up to your chin,

'cause dreams don't come out
while you sleep.

In LeRoi's class, the students had read Dr. King's "Letter from a Birmingham Jail" and then had begun an inquiry into the Civil Rights era, comparing what they found to today's world, to their own neighborhood. Through integrated studies of this kind students can engage the issues of the world, which can lead them to discovering, and then grappling with, various "burning questions." In LeRoi's class they did this by writing speeches, editorials, and essays, and by building arguments. Rereading their notebooks and writing again, they then transformed some of their passion into poems. (See Appendix A for other students' poems around big questions in their lives.)

In an inquiry into these "big ideas," it is important at some point to sit with the students and ask them what purpose they feel writing serves, for them individually. In Shawndell's school, when we asked this, Lourdes said, "When I write [about a difficult subject] in my writer's notebook it starts to go away. When I wake up it is gone." For Charles, writing "takes it out of my head." Irma, on the other hand, feels "if I write about it, I think it will happen." Writing as cure, writing as curse. Each of these grade-school writers came upon a one-to-one relationship with spirituality: if I do this, this will happen; when someone dies, this happens. Words themselves are imbued with a spiritual presence, with transformative powers. Through the act of writing, they begin to become more aware of the world around them, and to take responsibility for their part in it.

Erica Jong, in an introduction to *In Their Own Voices: A Century of Recorded Poetry*, writes,

> *People think they can do without poetry. And they can. At least until they fall in love, lose a friend, lose a child, or a parent, or lose their way in the dark woods of life. People think they can live without poetry. At least until they become fatally ill, have a baby, or fall desperately, madly, in love.*

One thing we can learn through reading and living with poetry is that bad days will pass, and that this may be a reason for not, say, pouring battery acid into a stream, or even saying something hurtful to a stranger, for tomorrow we may want to fish in that stream, or we may find ourselves lost and needing to ask directions of that same stranger.

The poems in this book, slipped under your door, have come a great distance to find you. Bring them inside. Let them nurture you. Then pass them on.

APPENDIX A

Poems

Chapter 3

A year later, Samantha's crafted poem, "Right Before My Eyes" from an eaves-dropped line.

RIGHT BEFORE MY EYES

Once and only once did it take
for me to realize it all,
It came like lightning hitting a rock.
Her hands, guarding her face from fright.
Closed in like a dark shadow.
Then out it came
like a busted soda machine in rapid flows.

*Right before my eyes it happened. I felt so
enclosed, so powerless. Jason and I
sat with him all night, Jason kept telling
me go talk to him, kiss him.*

*I said as the doctor came forward with a shrieking look,
whatever you have to say, say it gently.
He said there is no gentle way to say it. He's gone.*

Silence filled the room. Only the
sound of the clock. Tick. Tick. Tick.
That feeling in the dark. The one you
don't want to have.
What's death? Words. These words.
Words that eat away at my heart.
Too many. Too harsh.

Her fingers scrambled as she tried to open
a box of cookies. Her nail struck the tape.
With deep conclusion as if her hand
was distributing all her anger.
She seemed lost.
You could see it in her eyes.

All I wanted to do was just give her a hug
and when I did I felt a warm, loving, comforting hug.
Like there was a monster and
she was the woman of armor
and I was the queen.

—*Samantha Weinberg, grade 6*

ONE BOY TOLD ME
Naomi Shihab Nye

Music lives inside my legs.
It's coming out when I talk.

I'm going to send my valentines
to people you don't even know.

Oatmeal cookies make my throat gallop.

Grown-ups keep their feet on the ground
when they swing. I hate that.

Look at those 2 o's with a smash in the middle—
that spells good-bye.

Don't ever say "purpose" again,
let's throw the word out.

Don't talk big to me.
I'm carrying my box of faces.
If I want to change faces I will.

Yesterday faded
but tomorrow's in **BOLDFACE.**

When I grow up my old names
will live in the house
where we live now.
I'll come and visit them.

Only one of my eyes is tired.
The other eye and my body aren't.

Is it true all metal was liquid first?
Does that mean if we bought our car earlier
they could have served it
in a cup?

There's a stopper in my arm
that's not going to let me grow any bigger.
I'll be like this always, small.

And I will be deep water too.
Wait. Just wait. How deep is the river?
Would it cover the tallest man with his hands in the air?

Your head is a souvenir.

When you were in New York I could see you
in real life walking in my mind.

I'll invite a bee to live in your shoe.
What if you found your shoe
full of honey?

What if the clock said 6:92
instead of 6:30? Would you be scared?

My tongue is the car wash
for the spoon.

Can noodles swim?

My toes are dictionaries.
Do you need any words?

From now on I'll only drink white milk
on January 26.

What does minus mean?
I never want to minus you.

Just think—no one has ever seen
inside this peanut before!

It is hard being a person.

I do and don't love you—
isn't that happiness?

Chapter 5

Reina's "over-and-overness" builds feeling.

My Club

We gather up hands
together.
Chantelle is
in
Shanyd is
in
Megan is
in
Corren is
in
Shamilia is
in
Then we go . . .
Power!

Reina Rodriguez, Grade 1

Vanessa repeats the ends of lines for a spiraling rhythm.

TREES

    Trees remind me
that it is Spring
    Spring reminds
me of flowers
    flowers remind
me of Mom
    Mom reminds me
of stars
    stars remind me
of Dad
    Dad reminds me
of clouds
    clouds remind me of
me

—*Vanessa Graves, grade 2*

Influenced by Byrd Baylor, Emily gives us that "over and over" feeling by repeating phrases.

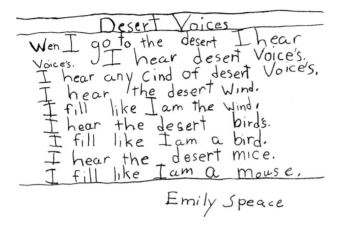

```
            Desert Voices
Wen I go to the desert I hear
Voice's. J I hear desert Voice's.
I hear any cind of desert Voice's.
I hear the desert Wind.
I fill like I am the Wind.
I hear the desert birds.
I fill like I am a bird.
I hear the desert mice.
I fill like I am a mouse.
```

Emily Speace

Chapter 9

Suzanne and Katie bring us into intimate spaces with their own personal insights.

THE WALK

We stroll together
up a mountain trail.
Fishermen and birds
sing their own songs.
The mountain waters
Cold and fresh
against my fingers.
Nature reaching out at me

And here am I
finding new feelings.

—*Suzanne Cardonas, grade 4*

CAUGHT ON A STRONG WIND

I slam the door
in the face of the wind.
It calls to me to play
but I am too busy.

Each sacrifice,
each stroke,
brings me closer to
what I have been working toward.
I will not weaken
and I will not give up.
I am ready.
When I pull my arms out of the water
they feel like the wings of a bird
caught on a strong wind,
gulping for air,
every stroke brings me closer to the medal.
I can hear my swimmer's clock from deep inside of me,
telling me I have beat my time.

—*Katie Barzelatto, grade 4*

BEING A PERSON
William Stafford

Be a person here. Stand by the river, invoke
the owls. Invoke winter, then spring.
Let any season that wants to come here make its own
call. After that sound goes away, wait.

A slow bubble rises through the earth
and begins to include sky, stars, all space,
even the outracing, expanding thought.
Come back and hear the little sound again.

Suddenly this dream you are having matches
everyone's dream, and the result is the world.
If a different call came there wouldn't be any
world, or you, or the river, or the owls calling.

How you stand here is important. How you
listen for the next things to happen. How you breathe.

ELEVEN
Archibald MacLeish

And summer mornings the mute child, rebellious,
Stupid, hating the words, the meanings, hating
The Think now, Think, the Oh but Think! would leave
On tiptoe the three chairs on the verandah
And crossing tree by tree the empty lawn

Push back the shed door and upon the sill
Stand pressing out the sunlight from his eyes
And enter and with outstretched fingers feel
The grindstone and behind it the bare wall
And turn and in the corner on the cool
Hard earth sit listening. And one by one,
Out of the dazzled shadow in the room,
The shapes would gather, the brown plowshare, spades,
Mattocks, the polished helves of picks, a scythe
Hung from the rafters, shovels, slender tines
Glinting cross the curve of sickles—shapes
Older than men were, the wise tools, the iron
Friendly with earth. And sit there, quiet, breathing
The harsh dry smell of withered bulbs, the faint
Odor of dung, the silence. And outside
Beyond the half-shut door the blind leaves
And the corn moving. And at noon would come,
Up from the garden, his hard crooked hands
Gentle with earth, his knees still earth-stained, smelling
Of sun, of summer, the old gardener, like
A priest, like an interpreter, and bend
Over his baskets.
    And they would not speak:
They would say nothing. And the child would sit there
Happy as though he had no name, as though
He had been no one: like a leaf, a stem,
Like a root growing—

Chapter 10

THE UNWRITTEN
W. S. Merwin

Inside this pencil
crouch words that have never been written
never been spoken
never been taught

They're hiding

they're awake in there
dark in the dark
hearing us
but they won't come out

not for love not for time not for fire
even when the dark has worn away
they'll still be there
hiding in the air
multitudes in days to come may walk through them
breathe them
be none the wiser
what script can it be
that they won't unroll
in what language
would I recognize it
would I be able to follow it
to make out the real names
of everything

maybe there aren't
many
it could be that there's only one word
and it's all we need
it's here in this pencil
every pencil in the world
is like this

Chapter 11

Brendan looks out at the physical world and finds a larger social
  concern.

The soaring wind chills
    my spine,
as does the world today.
Silver rivers once
    ran swift
in this desolate place.

Golden fields are now
    bare.
Barren deserts
in their place.

Lush green forests,
now a valley
of rotted stumps.

I awaken.
A cold sweat pours
down my back.
    The terrible
thought that this could be,
    reality.

—Brendan T. Sullivan, grade 5

Seunghyun comes to the world with a philosophical question about his life.

WHAT WILL I BE AFTER GROWING UP?
What will I be
After growing up?
Will I become a thin poor man?
    If so,
I won't be happy.

What will I be
 after growing up?
Will I become a fat rich man?
    If so,
I won't be happy.

What will I be
 after growing up?
Will I become a respectable man?
    If so,
I will be happy.

by Seunghyun Lee

Louis asks us to see the world with different eyes.

THE URBAN JUNGLE

The concrete deserts—
    why can't we

look past the plagues
   and the diseases?

Have you ever
   taken a moment
to look, really look
at the eyes of a rat

really peer
into them?
You can see
their black beauty.

   Have you
   ever seen,
   really seen, the
   silky wings of a moth?
   A veil of ivory whiteness.

Have you ever thought
   about the fur
   of the raccoon
in your trash can?
   See how beautiful it is.

   Don't think of them as
pests, but think of them as
pleasures or treasures.

Next time you go to
   the urban jungle,
   Look, really look.
   You'll see.

—*Louis Perez, grade 5*

APPENDIX B

Conferences with Students

Chapter 2

WRITING CONFERENCE WITH SARA VOGEL, GRADE 5

Holly Kim, a colleague and staff developer at the Teachers College Reading and Writing Project, Columbia University, in New York City, generously lent us transcripts of her own teaching conferences as examples for our book.

s: I'm trying to think of other words and other phrases because they don't explain much. I think the new ones explain better. Should I show you what I have first and second?

h: Sure.

s: First I have "You know the way bypassers go / And you know what the people inside are up to." I didn't really like that. It was too plain. Then I wrote, "When I look out of you Window / I can see the snow without getting cold."

h: What do you think you did there?

s: I think I explained more that the window can see things differently.

h: So it gives the reader a different image of the window than we're used to.

s: Yeah, and the way the window is when you look at the window without the feelings. Like here I wrote, "Window you have grace, you stand up tall." I didn't really like that because it doesn't give you a clear picture.

h: So you really wanted to focus on the images and not on the emotion.

s: Yes. And then I wrote, "Window you have a lot of time / You have nothing to do / We are busy bees compared to you." I didn't mean to rhyme.

h: So you want to focus in on the image. Is there a poem that we've read that you feel does that really well? Rather than emotions, it focuses you on images?

s: "The Fish."

h: Okay, let's take a look at that. Can you point to a place in this poem where she does an amazing job of giving you the image without telling you the feeling? 'Cause that's what you're trying to do. Give the reader the image without the feeling so we get the feeling based on the image.

S: Right here. It says parts about age but doesn't say how old it is.

H: Yeah, right there she zooms in on things that represent age and the feelings she as a poet has about the fish's age, but she doesn't tell us her feelings.

S: Yeah, she shows instead of saying.

H: Exactly! So instead of saying the fish looks old, she describes the barnacles and fine rosettes of lime. Now can you find a place in your poem where you can show the reader what you feel instead of stating it?

S: I want to show that it's alone, that it has nothing to do. I wrote that, "You have a lot of time" but that's sort of like a feeling.

H: So how could you give the reader an image that really lets us know that time is passing, it's alone? How would you know if you were to observe a window?

S: Most of the time you see cracks in the glass. You see all this dust on top of the windowsill. So if it was old I could say you have all this dust on you instead of you have nothing to do. But I might want to keep this part, "We are busy bees compared to you."

H: Well, I think that line beautifully contrasts the stillness of the window with our activity. You might want to think more about what kinds of images you can convey to the reader that show what you want them to feel.

S: Like when you said show, not tell.

H: Exactly. Show it to the reader, don't tell the reader. Give the reader something to think about. Give the reader the feeling of age from this window. Think about what an aged window looks like and show the reader.

S: Okay.

Preconference draft of Sara Vogel's poem from her notebook:

> The Window 1st Draft
>
> Window you see in
> Window you see out
> You know the way by passers
> go
> And you know what the people
> inside are up to.
> Window you have grace.
> you stand up tall. You
> see everything but
> do not speak up.

Revised version of Sara's poem after the conference with her teacher about using images to show feelings:

Window you see in
Window you see out
When I look out
of you Window,
I can see the snow without
getting cold.
Window your sills
have gathered dust,
and your wooden planks
have split from age.
Your glass has layers of dirt
from being so still.

Window
You see the world but
    do not speak.

Chapter 3

"SUN" CHART

Holly Kim leads a third-grade class in reading the mentor poem, Valerie Worth's "Sun," from *all the small poems and fourteen more,* noticing specific examples of what the poet is doing, imagining the poet's purposes, and creating a name for that. This process allows students to make thoughtful decisions about which observation or strategy can help them in their own work.

SUN
Valerie Worth

The sun
Is a leaping fire
Too hot
To go near,

But it will still
Lie down
In warm yellow squares
On the floor

Like a flat
Quilt, where
The cat can curl
And purr.

"Sun," by Valerie Worth

What I notice in the poem	Possible reason why poet does that	Our name for it
Poem doesn't rhyme	Wants us to pay attention to words, not beat	Create images without rhyme
Talks about one thing	Wants us to think about one thing, not to distract	Zooming in
Line breaks separate important points or statements	Wants us to notice the important points or statements	Line breaks
Comparing sun to leaping fire, quilt, yellow squares	Wants us to think deep into the words	Similes/metaphors
Writes how she feels about the sun	To express feelings	Feelings
Curl, purr	To flow; captures cat's action, sounds	Specific action words
One sentence	To get our minds focused; each stanza supports another aspect of sun	One-sentence poem
Space after four lines	Different detail about sun	Stanza break

Chapter 7

WRITING CONFERENCE WITH SARA SCOTT, GRADE 5

Holly Kim and Sara Scott study the structure of the mentor poem, Rita Dove's "Fifth Grade Autobiography," from *Grace Notes,* to see how she meshes her observations and feelings.

FIFTH GRADE AUTOBIOGRAPHY
Rita Dove

I was four in this photograph fishing
with my grandparents at a lake in Michigan.
My brother squats in poison ivy.
His Davy Crockett cap
sits squared on his head so the raccoon tail
flounces down the back of his sailor suit.

My grandfather sits to the far right
in a folding chair,
and I know his left hand is on
the tobacco in his pants pocket
because I used to wrap it for him
every Christmas. Grandmother's hips
bulge from the brush, she's leaning
into the ice chest, sun through the trees
printing her dress with soft
luminous paws.

I am staring jealously at my brother;
the day before he rode his first horse, alone.
I was strapped in a basket
behind my grandfather.
He smelled of lemons. He's died—

but I remember his hands.

Sara shows Holly what she's been working on: alliteration; looking at the beginning of the mentor poem, the end; trying some things with her own poem.

H: Since you've learned so much from Rita Dove already, why don't we take another look and see if there's anything else she did that you loved.
S: I love the way she brought up her brother. She's been jealous of her brother all her life. You kind of get that feeling and in the end she says, "But I remember his hands," like she's getting back by saying she remembers but he doesn't.
H: So you like the way she lets the reader know her feelings and emphasizes it at the very end.
S: Yeah.
H: Okay, so let's focus on that part and think about how she does that. She introduces the photo, she makes observations of her brother, her grandmother, her grandfather and then . . . she gives you a hint of her feeling—"I am staring jealously at my brother"—and then more observation about her brother

and herself, so in the end she zooms in on herself, then that powerful ending—"But I remember his hands." It sort of bounces off the jealousy she
brought up earlier. So now let's go back to yours. Is there a place where you
could inject your feeling within all your observations and then connect your
ending with that feeling?

S: (*thinks*)

H: At the end of your poem, you write, "I'm still smiling." Can you give the
reader a sense of foreshadowing? That's when you give the reader a hint of
something to come.

S: Maybe over here when it says, "I'm tickling my cousin because he won't
smile." I could say I'm mad because he won't smile and later on, "But I'm
still smiling."

H: So do you see how that gives the reader a sense of what's to come at the end?

S: Yeah.

H: But we're just trying stuff out. You don't have to keep that in there, but
play with what Rita Dove did by giving the reader a sense of something to
come that gives the ending more power.

S: Okay.

Chapter 10

EXCERPT FROM WRITING CONFERENCE
WITH JONAH BEALY, GRADE 5

The mentor poem is Elizabeth Bishop's "The Fish," from *The Complete Poems,
1927–1979*. Jonah tells Holly what he's been focusing on: rhythm of his poem,
wanting to slow it down, make it mysterious like "The Fish." He has used line
breaks, which he thinks really helped. But perhaps there are other ways in
which Bishop slowed down her poem. They look back at it.

H: Can you point to where you think she slows things down for you, the
reader?

J: "He didn't fight / He hadn't fought at all."

H: So can you name what she does in order to slow it down?

J: I'd say using fight and fought kind of made it two different sentences from
one sentence. She says the same thing but puts it in the past.

H: So it makes you stop and think about why she does that and what she means
by that?

J: Yeah.

H: So can you go back to your poem and find a place where you could play with
the tense so the reader is forced to think about something for longer?

J: I think it was right there.

H: So what would you do to change the tense?

J: I could be like, "You cry and you shout / You shouted real loud."

H: Why don't you jot that down next to that line and then think of other places you could do that. Do you see what you're doing here? You're going back to a poem and noticing what Bishop does to slow things down, and then you can go back to your own writing and try it out. It doesn't mean that you'll keep it in the end, but you should at least try it out. Okay? I think it's a good idea to slow down a poem by using line breaks but you can also slow it down by the words.

J: Okay. I like it.

H: Before you go, can I point out another spot where I think Bishop slowed it down for the reader? Right here she talks about the eyes. [*reads the lines*] She starts with action of the eyes, but what does she do in between the action of the eyes?

J: She extends the subject of the eyes, to keep it going.

H: Right. She really forces the reader to see the eyes, not just what the eyes are doing. Can you also try to find a place in your writing where you can slow it down using that technique?

J: "You blubber your head off . . . You . . ."

H: Don't worry about it sounding great right now. Just play with it.

J: "You blubber your head off / With an ocean of tears."

H: Yeah, do you see how you can slow things down by staying with an image longer, moving from the action of the person or object to your close observations?

J: Yes.

H: So let's go over the three things you can do: line breaks, shifting tense, staying with an image. You can make the changes right on your page or you can use Post-its. What would you prefer?

J: I think I'll add on to the page.

APPENDIX C
Bibliography

A Short Poetry Bookshelf

Adoff, Arnold. 1995a. *OUTside INside Poems.* New York: Lothrop, Lee & Shepard.

———. 1995b. *Street Music: City Poems.* New York: HarperCollins.

Booth, David, ed. 1989. *'Til All the Stars Have Fallen: A Collection of Poems for Children.* New York: Viking.

Carlson, Lori M. 1994. *Cool Salsa: Bilingual Poems on Growing Up Latino in the United States.* New York: Henry Holt.

Dillard, Annie. 1995. *Mornings Like This: Found Poems.* New York: HarperCollins.

Esbensen, Barbara J. 1992. *Who Shrank My Grandmother's House? Poems of Discovery.* New York: HarperCollins.

———. 1996. *Echoes for the Eye: Poems to Celebrate Patterns in Nature.* New York: HarperCollins.

Fletcher, Ralph. 1997a. *Ordinary Things: Poems from a Walk in Early Spring.* New York: Atheneum.

———. 1997b. *Room Enough for Love: The Complete Poems of* I Am Wings *and* Buried Alive. New York: Aladdin.

Greenfield, Eloise. 1978. *Honey I Love, and Other Love Poems.* New York: Harper & Row.

———. 1988. *Nathaniel Talking.* New York: Black Butterfly.

Hoagland, Tony. 1998. *Donkey Gospel.* St. Paul, MN: Graywolf Press.

Hopkins, Lee B. 1995. *Been to Yesterdays.* Honesdale, PA: Boyds Mills Press.

Hughes, Langston. 1960. *The Dreamkeeper and Other Poems.* New York: Knopf.

Janeczko, Paul B. 1998. *That Sweet Diamond: Baseball Poems.* New York: Atheneum.

Janeczko, Paul B., ed. 1990. *The Place My Words Are Looking For: What Poets Say About and Through Their Work.* New York: Simon and Schuster.

Lyne, Sandford, ed. 1996. *Ten-Second Rainshowers.* New York: Simon and Schuster.

Nye, Naomi S., ed. 1992. *This Same Sky: A Collection of Poems from Around the World.* New York: Four Winds Press.

———. 1995. *The Tree Is Older Than You Are: A Bilingual Gathering of Poems and Stories from Mexico with Paintings by Mexican Artists.* New York: Simon and Schuster.

———. 1999. *What Have You Lost?* New York: Greenwillow Books.

———. 2000. *Salting the Ocean: 100 Poems by Young Poets.* New York: HarperCollins.

Rosen, Michael J., ed. 1992. *Home.* New York: HarperCollins.

Rosenberg, Liz, ed. 1996. *The Invisible Ladder: An Anthology of Contemporary Poems for Young Readers.* New York: Henry Holt.

Rylant, Cynthia. 1984. *Waiting to Waltz: A Childhood.* New York: Simon and Schuster.

Soto, Gary. 1992. *Neighborhood Odes.* New York: Harcourt Brace.

———. 1995. *Canto Familiar.* New York: Harcourt Brace.

Steptoe, Javaka, ed. and illus. 1997. *In Daddy's Arms I Am Tall: African Americans Celebrating Fathers.* New York: Lee & Low.

Stevenson, James. 1995. *Sweet Corn: Poems.* New York: Greenwillow Books.

Thomas, Joyce C. 1993. *Brown Honey in Broomwheat Tea.* New York: HarperCollins.

Worth, Valerie. 1994. *all the small poems and fourteen more.* New York: Farrar, Straus, Giroux.

A Short Professional Bookshelf

The Writer's Notebook

Angelillo, Janet. 1999. "Using the Writer's Notebook Across the Day and Beyond the Writing Workshop." *Primary Voices K–6* 8, 1: pp. 30–35.
The writer's notebook as a unit of study in grades 2 and up.

Bomer, Randy. 1995. *Time for Meaning.* Portsmouth, NH: Heinemann.
Time and the art and craft of teaching for literacy in middle and high school. Includes a section on the writer's notebook as a "tool for thinking and living."

Calkins, Lucy, with Shelley Harwayne. 1991. *Living Between the Lines.* Portsmouth, NH: Heinemann.
Focuses on the writer's notebook as an important tool for finding and developing ideas for writing.

Fletcher, Ralph. 1993. *A Writer's Notebook: Unlocking the Writer Within You.* New York: Avon Books.
Shows practical purposes and real ways to use a writer's notebook as a "seedbed" for writing to come.

———. 1996. *Breathing in, Breathing out: Keeping a Writer's Notebook.* Portsmouth, NH: Heinemann.

Hindley, Joanne. 1996. *In the Company of Children.* York, ME: Stenhouse.
Rethinking management and teaching issues in the author's third-grade reading and writing workshops, including use of the notebook as a writer's tool.

Kuusisto, Stephen, et al. 1995. *The Poet's Notebook: Excerpts from the Notebooks of Contemporary American Poets.* New York: W. W. Norton.
A book that gives insight into the process of writing.

Nurturing the Poet Within Us

Behn, Robin, and Chase Twichell, eds. 1992. *The Practice of Poetry: Writing Exercises from Poets Who Teach.* New York: HarperCollins.
Filled with exercises intended to open our minds to possibility.

Hall, Donald. 1993. *Lifework.* Boston: Beacon Press.
A distinguished poet reflects on his life as a writer.

Heaney, Seamus. 1995. *The Redress of Poetry.* New York: Farrar, Straus, Giroux.
Lectures delivered by the Nobel Laureate as Professor of Poetry at Oxford between 1989 and 1994.

Heard, Georgia. 1995. *Writing Toward Home.* Portsmouth, NH: Heinemann.
Inspires us, through wise parables and lessons, to find the sources of our own writing.

Hirsch, Edward. 1999. *How to Read a Poem.* New York: Harcourt Brace.
A distinguished poet and critic speaks to all who yearn for poetry in their lives, about the music of poetry, what it means, and why it matters.

Kozol, Jonathan. 1995. *Amazing Grace: The Lives of Children and the Conscience of a Nation.* New York: Crown.
We include this as a complement to our final chapter.

Kunitz, Stanley. 1993. *Interviews and Encounters with Stanley Kunitz,* ed. Stanley Moss. Riverdale-on-Hudson, NY: Sheep Meadow Press.
Interviews, accounts of conversations, encounters, and memories of other poets awaken us to the life and thought of one of the most influential and inspiring poets and teachers of this century.

Moyers, Bill. 1999. *Fooling with Words: A Celebration of Poets and Their Craft.* New York: Morrow.
Takes us behind the performances at the Geraldine R. Dodge Foundation's Poetry Festival at Waterloo, New Jersey, to talk to major poets and explore the sources of their imagination and creativity.

Murray, Donald. 1996. *Crafting a Life in Essay, Story, Poem.* Portsmouth, NH: Heinemann Boynton/Cook.
Pulitzer prize–winning journalist and Professor Emeritus of English at the University of New Hampshire, the author takes students and teachers into his own writing workshop to demonstrate the discipline and delight of his craft.

Nye, Naomi Shihab. 1996. *Never in a Hurry: Essays on People and Places.* Columbia: University of South Carolina Press.
A journey of encounters, observations, insight, through the eyes of a loved poet.

Oliver, Mary. 1994. *A Poetry Handbook: A Prose Guide to Understanding and Writing Poetry.* New York: Harcourt Brace.
To understand how a poem is put together.

———. 1995. *Blue Pastures.* New York: Harcourt Brace.
Fifteen beautifully crafted prose pieces about her life, her world, her love of nature, and the craft of writing, by a Pulitzer prize–winning poet.

———. 1998. *Rules for the Dance: A Handbook for Writing and Reading Metrical Verse.* Boston: Houghton Mifflin.
Inspiring introduction to rhyme, sound, meter, scansion. Helps us understand what makes metrical poems work.

Phillips, Rodney, et al. 1996. *The Hand of the Poet: Poems and Papers in Manuscript.* New York: Rizzoli International Publishers.
Based on an exhibit at the New York Public Library, this book draws the reader into the world of the poet by inviting us to look at working drafts, diary entries, letters, and photos.

Stafford, William. 1986. *You Must Revise Your Life.* Ann Arbor: University of Michigan Press.
   Part of the "Poets on Poetry" series. Stafford talks about his life as a writer, shares his poems about writing, and speaks about the origins and influences of his art.
Ueland, Brenda. 1987. *If You Want to Write: A Book About Art, Independence and Spirit.* St. Paul, MN: Graywolf Press.
   Carl Sandburg called this "the best book ever written about how to write."

The Art and Craft of Writing

Anderson, Carl. 2000. *How's It Going? A Practical Guide to Conferrig with Student Writers.* Portsmouth, NH: Heinemann.
   Anderson breaks down methods and roles of conversation in this clear, concise book.
Bomer, Randy. 1995. *Time for Meaning.* Portsmouth, NH: Heinemann.
   Through his own experiences and insight as a teacher, Bomer helps us inquire about time and the art and craft of teaching for literacy in middle and high school.
Calkins, Lucy. 1994. *The Art of Teaching Writing.* 2d ed. Portsmouth, NH: Heinemann.
   Deepens our understanding of the writing process and introduces us to additional topics such as genre studies, reading/writing relationships, thematic studies, and assessment.
Dillard, Annie. 1989. *The Writing Life.* New York: Harper & Row.
   Gives us a deep insight into the workaday life of the writer, and "what the actual process of writing feels like . . . inside the mind at work."
Fletcher, Ralph. 1993. *What a Writer Needs.* Portsmouth, NH: Heinemann.
   A look into how teachers of writing might help students improve the quality of their writing.
Graves, Donald. 1994. *A Fresh Look at Writing.* Portsmouth, NH: Heinemann.
   Revisits and expands on the author's earlier work, demonstrating how we might experience the joy and craft of writing alongside our students.
Heard, Georgia. 1989. *For the Good of the Earth and Sun: Teaching Poetry.* Portsmouth, NH: Heinemann.
   Shares the essentials, practically and personally, of both teaching and living like a poet.
———. 1998. *Awakening the Heart.* Portsmouth, NH: Heinemann.
   Sequel to the preceding book, this book celebrates the power of poetry to teach us what we need to know as writers of poetry.
Jordan, June. 1995. *June Jordan's Poetry for the People: A Revolutionary Blueprint,* ed. Lauren Muller. New York: Routledge.
   Based on Jordan's legendary San Francisco workshops.
Murray, Donald. 1968. *A Writer Teaches Writing: A Practical Method of Teaching Composition.* Boston: Houghton Mifflin.
   Shows theory and practice illuminating each other in the writing workshop, with practical ideas for conference and workshop teaching.
Paley, Vivian Gussin. 1992. *You Can't Say You Can't Play.* Cambridge, MA: Harvard University Press.
   An essential glimpse at how Paley created community within her classroom.
Ray, Katie. 1999. *Wondrous Words: Writers and Writing in the Elementary Classroom.* Urbana, IL: National Council of Teachers of English.

A detailed look at how teachers and students might study the craft of writing using loved authors as mentors.

Weaver, Constance. 1996. *Teaching Grammar in Context.* Portsmouth, NH: Heinemann.
   A book that actually makes us realize again how significant grammar is, and how it can be taught.

Zinsser, William. 1990. *On Writing Well: An Informal Guide to Writing Nonfiction.* 4th ed. New York: Harper & Row.
   A writer, editor, and critic reveals, with humor and style, the attitudes toward language and craft he believes are critical to success.

A Short Photography Bookshelf

Because almost any poem can be used to teach many of the elements of poetry that we talk about in this book, a list of books exemplifying them would be too amorphous. An exception is the process of writing off photographs, for which we list several books that could be directly useful.

Daniels, Jim. 1990. "Baseball Cards #1." (Poem) In *The Place My Words Are Looking For,* ed. Paul B. Janeczko. New York: Simon and Schuster.

Dove, Rita. 1989. "Fifth Grade Autobiography." (Poem) In *Grace Notes.* New York: W. W. Norton.

Esbensen, Barbara J. 1992. "Old Photograph Album: Grandfather." (Poem) In *Who Shrank My Grandmother's House?* New York: HarperCollins.

Franklin, Kristine L., and Nancy McGirr, eds. 1995. *Out of the Dump: Writings and Photographs by Children from Guatemala.* (Poems and photos) New York: Lothrop, Lee & Shepard.

Heard, Georgia. 1995. "Visual Archaeology." (Essay) In *Writing Toward Home.* Portsmouth, NH: Heinemann.

MacLachlan, Patricia. 1991. *Journey.* (Novel) New York: Delacorte Press.

Myers, Walter Dean. 1993. *Brown Angels: An Album of Pictures and Verse.* (Poems and photos) New York: HarperCollins.

———. 1995. *Glorious Angels: A Celebration of Children.* (Poems and photos) New York: HarperCollins.

Nye, Naomi Shihab. 1995. "Loose Leaf" (Introduction) and "Passport Photo" (Poem). In *Words Under the Words.* Portland, OR: Eighth Mountain Press.

———. 1998. "Picture" and "Class Pictures." (Poems) In *The Space Between Our Footsteps.* New York: Simon and Schuster.

Nye, Naomi Shihab, ed. 1999. *What Have You Lost?* (Poems and black-and-white photos) New York: Greenwillow Books.

Rodriguez, Aleida. 1996. "My Mother in Two Photographs, Among Other Things." (Creative nonfiction) In Judith Kitchen and Mary Paumier Jones, eds., *In Short.* New York: W. W. Norton.

References

Adoff, Arnold, ed. 1968. *I Am the Darker Brother.* New York: Macmillan. Rev. ed. New York: Aladdin, 1997.

———. 1995. *Street Music: City Poems.* New York: HarperCollins.

Andreas, Brian. 1997. *Story People.* Decorah, IA: StoryPeople Press.

Bachelard, Gaston. 1969. *The Poetics of Space.* Boston: Beacon Press.

Beckett, Samuel. 1954. *Waiting for Godot.* New York: Grove Atlantic Press.

Behn, Robin, and Chase Twichell, eds. 1992. *The Practice of Poetry.* New York: HarperCollins.

Bishop, Elizabeth. 1983. *The Complete Poems, 1927–1979.* New York: Farrar, Straus, Giroux.

Blake, William. 1984. *Songs of Experience.* Mineola, MN: Dover. Originally published ca. 1826.

Bly, Robert, ed. 1975. *Leaping Poetry: An Idea with Poems and Translations.* Boston: Beacon Press.

Booth, David, ed. 1989. *'Til All the Stars Have Fallen.* New York: Viking.

Brooks, Gwendolyn. 1963. *Selected Poems.* New York: Harper & Row.

Bryson, Bill. 1998. *A Walk in the Woods.* New York: Broadway BDD.

Bunting, Eve. 1990. *The Wall.* New York: Clarion Books.

Carson, Jo. 1989. *stories I ain't told nobody yet.* New York: Theatre Communications.

Coles, Robert. 1990. *The Spiritual Life of Children.* Boston: Houghton Mifflin.

Cox, Sidney. 1957. *A Swinger of Birches: A Portrait of Robert Frost.* New York: NYU Press.

Cullinan, Bernice, ed. 1996. *A Jar of Tiny Stars.* Honesdale, PA: Boyds Mills Press.

Der-Hovanessian, Diana, and Marzbed Margossian, eds. 1978. *Anthology of Armenian Poetry.* New York: Columbia University Press.

Dickey, Chris. 1998. *Summer of Deliverance.* New York: Simon and Schuster.

Dillard, Annie. 1989. *The Writing Life.* New York: Harper & Row.

———. 1995. *Mornings Like This.* New York: HarperCollins.

Doty, Mark. 1996. *Heaven's Coast.* New York: HarperCollins.

Dove, Rita. 1989. *Grace Notes.* New York: W. W. Norton.

Durell, Ann, Jean George, and Katherine Paterson, eds. 1993. *The Big Book for Our Planet.* New York: Dutton.

Eliot, T. S. 1920. *The Sacred Wood: Essays on Poetry and Criticism.* London: Methuen.

Elledge, Scott, ed. 1990. *Wider Than the Sky.* New York: HarperCollins.

Epstein, Mark. 1995. *Thoughts Without a Thinker.* New York: Basic Books.

Forché, Carolyn. 1981. *The Country Between Us.* New York: Harper & Row.

Fox, Mem. 1985. *Wilfrid Gordon McDonald Partridge.* New York: Kane/Miller.

———. 1993. *Radical Reflections: Passionate Opinions on Teaching, Learning, and Living.* New York: Harcourt Brace.

Gilbar, Steven, ed. 1989. *The Open Door.* Boston: David R. Godine.

Giovanni, Nikki. 1991. *Spin a Soft Black Song.* New York: Farrar, Straus, Giroux.

Greenfield, Eloise. 1978. *Honey I Love, and Other Love Poems.* New York: Harper & Row.

———. 1988. *Nathaniel Talking.* New York: Black Butterfly.

Gross, Harvey, and R. McDowell. 1996. *Sound and Form in Modern Poetry.* 2d ed. Ann Arbor: University of Michigan Press.

Gutkind, Lee, ed. 1997. *Creative Nonfiction #10.* Pittsburgh: Creative Nonfiction Foundation.

Hall, Donald. 1971. *The Pleasures of Poetry.* New York: HarperCollins.

Hass, Robert. 1984. "Transtromer's Baltics: Making a Form of Time." In *Twentieth-Century Pleasures: Prose on Poetry.* New York: Ecco Press.

Hawking, Stephen W. 1990. *A Brief History of Time: From the Big Bang to Black Holes.* New York: Bantam Books.

Heard, Georgia. 1989. *For the Good of the Earth and Sun: Teaching Poetry.* Portsmouth, NH: Heinemann.

———. 1995. *Writing Toward Home.* Portsmouth, NH: Heinemann.

———. 1999. *Awakening the Heart.* Portsmouth, NH: Heinemann.

Henri, Robert. 1923. *The Art Spirit.* Philadelphia: Lippincott.

Hinchman, Hannah. 1991. *A Life in Hand.* Salt Lake City: Gibbs Smith.

Hirsch, Edward. 1999. *How to Read a Poem.* New York: Harcourt Brace.

Ho, Minfong, trans. 1996. *Maples in the Mist: Children's Poems from the Tang Dynasty.* New York: Lothrop, Lee & Shepard.

Howe, Marie. 1998. *What the Living Do.* New York: W. W. Norton.

Hughes, Langston. 1960. *The Dreamkeeper and Other Poems.* New York: Knopf.

Igus, Toyomi. 1992. *When I Was Little.* Orange, NJ: Just Us Books.

Janeczko, Paul B. 1998. *That Sweet Diamond: Baseball Poems.* New York: Atheneum.

Janeczko, Paul B., ed. 1990. *The Place My Words Are Looking For.* New York: Simon and Schuster.

Jong, Erica M. 1995. "The Necessity for Poetry." In *In Their Own Voices: A Century of Recorded Poetry.* Los Angeles: Rhino Records.

Kenyon, Jane. 1990. *Let Evening Come.* St. Paul: Graywolf Press.

———. 1996. *Otherwise: New and Selected Poems.* St. Paul, MN: Graywolf Press.

King, Martin Luther, Jr. 1992. *I Have a Dream.* San Francisco: HarperSanFrancisco.

Kitchen, Judith, and Mary P. Jones, eds. 1996. *In Short.* New York: W. W. Norton.

Komunyakaa, Yusef 1988. *Dien Cai Dau.* Middletown, CT: Wesleyan University Press.

Kunitz, Stanley, ed. 1993. *Interviews and Encounters with Stanley Kunitz,* ed. Stanley Moss. Riverdale-on-Hudson, NY: Sheep Meadow Press.

Leokum, Arkady. 1967. *More Tell Me Why: Answers to over 400 Questions Children Ask Most Often.* New York: Grosset & Dunlap.

Lyne, Sandford, ed. 1996. *Ten-Second Rainshowers.* New York: Simon and Schuster.

MacLachlan, Patricia. 1991. *Journey.* New York: Delacorte Press.

———. 1995. *What You Know First.* New York: HarperCollins.

MacLeish, Archibald. 1952. *Collected Poems, 1917–1952.* Boston: Houghton Mifflin.

———. 1985. *Collected Poems, 1917–1982.* Boston: Houghton Mifflin.

MacNeil, Robert. 1989. *Wordstruck.* New York: Viking.

Margolis, Richard. 1984. *Secrets of a Small Brother.* New York: Macmillan.

Merwin, W. S. 1973. *Writings to an Unfinished Accompaniment.* New York: Atheneum.

Milosz, Czeslaw, ed. 1996. *A Book of Luminous Things.* New York: Harcourt Brace.

Moyers, Bill. 1999. *Fooling with Words.* New York: Morrow.

Murray, Donald. 1996. *Crafting a Life in Essay, Story, Poem.* Portsmouth, NH: Heinemann Boynton/Cook.

Nye, Naomi S. 1976. "Little Blanco River." In *Tattooed Feet.* Texas Portfolio Chapbook Series.

———. 1992a. *Lullaby Raft.* New York: Simon and Schuster.

———. 1994. *Sitti's Secrets.* New York: Four Winds Press.

———. 1995. *Words Under the Words.* Portland, OR: Eighth Mountain Press.

———. 1996. *Never in a Hurry: Essays on People and Places.* Columbia: University of South Carolina Press.

———. 1998. *Fuel.* Rochester, NY: BOA Editions.

Nye, Naomi S., ed. 1992. *This Same Sky.* New York: Four Winds Press.

———. 1995. *The Tree Is Older Than You Are.* New York: Simon and Schuster.

———. 1998. *The Space Between Our Footsteps.* New York: Simon and Schuster.

———. 1999a. "My First True Love." *CBC Features* 52, 1: pp. 2–3.

———. 1999b. *What Have You Lost?* New York: Greenwillow Books.

———. 2000. *Salting the Ocean: 100 Poems by Young Poets.* New York: HarperCollins.

O'Hara, Frank. 1974. *The Selected Poems of Frank O'Hara,* ed. Donald Allen. New York: Vintage Books.

Oliver, Mary. 1992. *New and Selected Poems.* Boston: Beacon Press.

———. 1994. *A Poetry Handbook.* New York: Harcourt Brace.

———. 1995. *Blue Pastures.* New York: Harcourt Brace.

———. 1998. *Rules for the Dance: A Handbook for Writing and Reading Metrical Verse.* Boston: Houghton Mifflin.

Orr, Gregory. 1993. "Four Temperaments and the Forms of Poetry." In *Richer Entanglements: Essays and Notes on Poetry and Poems.* Ann Arbor: University of Michigan Press.

Orr, Gregory, and Ellen B. Voight, eds. 1996. *Poets Teaching Poets: Self and the World.* Ann Arbor: University of Michigan Press.

Parini, Jay. 1999. *Robert Frost: A Life.* New York: Henry Holt.

Paterson, Katherine. 1989. *The Spying Heart.* New York: Dutton.

Piaget, Jean. 1969. *The Child's Conception of Time,* trans. A. J. Pomerans. New York: Ballantine.

Piercy, Marge. 1982. *Circles on the Water.* New York: Knopf.

Pinsky, Robert. 1998. *The Sounds of Poetry.* New York: Farrar, Straus, Giroux.

Pollan, Michael. 1997. *A Place of My Own.* New York: Random House.

Ray, Katie. 1999. *Wondrous Words: Writers and Writing in the Elementary Classroom.* Urbana, IL: National Council of Teachers of English.

Rilke, Rainer Maria. 1934. "Letter #4." In *Letters to a Young Poet,* trans. M. D. Herter. New York: W. W. Norton.

Rosen, Michael J., ed. 1992. *Home.* New York: HarperCollins.

Rothenberg, Jerome, ed. 1985. *Technicians of the Sacred: A Range of Poetries from Africa, America, Asia, Europe, and Oceania.* Berkeley: University of California Press.

Rylant, Cynthia. 1982. *When I Was Young in the Mountains.* New York: Dutton.

———. 1984. *Waiting to Waltz: A Childhood.* New York: Simon and Schuster.

———. 1989. *But I'll Be Back Again.* New York: Orchard Books.

———. 1991. *Appalachia: The Voices of Sleeping Birds.* San Diego: Harcourt Brace Jovanovich.

———. 1994. *Something Permanent.* New York: Harcourt Brace.

Simic, Charles. 1986. *Unending Blues.* New York: Harcourt Brace.

———. 1994. *The Unemployed Fortune-Teller: Essays and Memoirs.* Ann Arbor: University of Michigan Press.

Snyder, Gary. 1986. *Left Out in the Rain: New Poems 1947–1985.* New York: Farrar, Straus, Giroux.

———. 1990. *The Practice of the Wild.* New York: Farrar, Straus, Giroux.

Spicer, Jack. 1975. *Collected Books of Jack Spicer.* Santa Rosa, CA: Black Sparrow Press.

Stafford, William. 1986. *You Must Revise Your Life.* Ann Arbor: University of Michigan Press.

———. 1996. *Even in Quiet Places.* Lewiston, ID: Confluence Press.

———. 1998. *The Way It Is: New & Selected Poems.* St. Paul, MN: Graywolf Press.

Steptoe, Javaka, ed. and illus. 1997. *In Daddy's Arms I Am Tall: African Americans Celebrating Fathers.* New York: Lee & Low.

Stevens, Wallace. 1957. "Adagia." In *Opus Posthumous,* ed. S. F. Morse. New York: Knopf. Rev. ed., ed. M. J. Bates. New York: Knopf, 1989.

Strunk, William, and E. B. White. 1959. *The Elements of Style.* New York: Macmillan.

Szymborska, Wislawa. 1993. *View with a Grain of Sand.* New York: Harcourt Brace.

Ward, Geoffrey C. 1994. *Baseball: An Illustrated History.* New York: Knopf.

Williams, William Carlos. 1995. *Paterson,* Rev. ed. Christopher MacGowan. New York: New Directions.

Worth, Valerie. 1994. *all the small poems and fourteen more.* New York: Farrar, Straus, Giroux.

Yolan, Jane. 1987. *Owl Moon.* New York: Philomel Books.

Zinsser, William, ed. 1987. *Inventing the Truth: The Art and Craft of Memoir.* Boston: Houghton Mifflin.

Index of Poem Titles
and First Lines

Index of Published Authors

(Boldface refers to page on which poem appears. Italics refers to prose quotation.)

Credits